PERSONALITY AND CONTROL

WARSAW LECTURES IN PERSONALITY AND SOCIAL PSYCHOLOGY

Published in cooperation with the Institute of Psychology,
Polish Academy of Sciences, Warsaw, Poland

Volume 1
PERSONALITY FROM BIOLOGICAL, COGNITIVE, AND SOCIAL PERSPECTIVES
Edited by Tomasz Maruszewski, Małgorzata Fajkowska, and Michael W. Eysenck

Volume 2
PERSONALITY, COGNITION, AND EMOTION
Edited by Michael W. Eysenck, Małgorzata Fajkowska, and Tomasz Maruszewski

Volume 3
PERSONALITY DYNAMICS: MEANING CONSTRUCTION, THE SOCIAL WORLD, AND THE EMBODIED MIND
Edited by Daniel Cervone, Małgorzata Fajkowska, Michael W. Eysenck, and Tomasz Maruszewski

Volume 4
PERSONALITY AND CONTROL
Edited by Philip J. Corr, Małgorzata Fajkowska, Michael W. Eysenck, and Agata Wytykowska

PERSONALITY AND CONTROL

Edited by

Philip J. Corr
City University London
London, United Kingdom

Małgorzata Fajkowska
Polish Academy of Sciences
Warsaw, Poland

Michael W. Eysenck
Roehampton University, Whitelands College
London, United Kingdom

Agata Wytykowska
University of Social Sciences and Humanities
Warsaw, Poland

ELIOT WERNER PUBLICATIONS, INC.
CLINTON CORNERS, NEW YORK

Library of Congress Cataloging-in-Publication Data

Personality and control / edited by Philip J. Corr, City University London, London, United Kingdom, Malgorzata Fajkowska, Polish Academy of Sciences, Warsaw, Poland, Michael W. Eysenck, Roehampton University, Whitelands College, London, United Kingdom, Agata Wytykowska, Warsaw School of Humanities and Social Sciences, Warsaw, Poland.
pages cm. – (Warsaw lectures in personality and social psychology ; Volume 4)
Includes bibliographical references and index.
ISBN 978-0-9898249-5-8 – ISBN 0-9898249-5-0
1. Personality. 2. Control (Psychology) I. Corr, Philip J., editor. II. Fajkowska, Malgorzata, editor.
BF698.P3583 2015
155.2 – dc23

2015013635

ISBN-10: 0-9898249-5-0
ISBN-13: 978-0-9898249-5-8

PO Box 268, Clinton Corners, New York 12514
http://www.eliotwerner.com

Printed in the United States of America

Contributors

Charles S. Carver • Department of Psychology, University of Miami, Coral Gables, Florida USA

Philip J. Corr • Department of Psychology, City University London, London, United Kingdom

Michael W. Eysenck • Department of Psychology, Roehampton University, Whitelands College, London, United Kingdom

Małgorzata Fajkowska • Institute of Psychology, Polish Academy of Sciences, Warsaw, Poland

Joanna Kantor-Martynuska • Institute of Psychology, Polish Academy of Sciences, Warsaw, Poland

Shulamith Kreitler • Department of Psychology, Tel Aviv University, Tel Aviv, Israel

Ezequiel Morsella • Department of Psychology, San Francisco State University, San Francisco, California USA; Department of Neurology, University of California at San Francisco, San Francisco, California USA

Howard J. Rosen • Department of Neurology, University of California at San Francisco, San Francisco, California USA

Jessica J. Tomory • Department of Psychology, San Francisco State University, San Francisco, California USA

Agata Wytykowska • Faculty of Psychology, University of Social Sciences and Humanities, Warsaw, Poland

Pareezad Zarolia • Department of Psychology, University of Denver, Denver, Colorado USA

Preface

This new volume in the Warsaw Lectures in Personality and Social Psychology comprises chapters on personality and control, and this was the theme of the fourth Biennial Symposium on Personality and Social Psychology (BSPSP) held in Kazimierz Dolny, Poland, in August 2012, on which the book is based. Chapters showcase the importance that must be attached to control processes, varied in their form and manifold in their influence, which lay at the heart of a scientific approach to personality psychology and its extensions to a panoply of psychological phenomena, ranging from the mundane (e.g., anxiety) to the exotic (e.g., consciousness). As the contributors to this volume amply demonstrate, control processes are indeed ubiquitous across the whole psychological landscape; and it is this reality that confronts any attempt to furnish a viable scientific account of both their stability and variability as reflected in traits, cognition, affect, and action.

Both the symposium and this volume underscore the challenges facing not only personality psychology but psychology more generally, where control processes are write large and individual differences in them are a crucial source of variation observed routinely in empirical studies of all kinds—but too often such variation is relegated, and thus neglected, in the statistical "error" term of experimental results. The importance of this systematic variability still needs to be assimilated into mainstream psychology, and it is to be hoped that the current volume goes some way toward enabling this to happen.

On a personal note, Philip Corr is gratified to have been asked to head the 2012 BSPSP Scientific Committee and found serving in this role to have been a pleasure—a task made all the more congenial by the focus and efficiency of the other members of the committee, as well as the members of the Organizing Committee (Ewa Domaradzka, Małgorzata Fajkowska, Joanna Kantor-Martynuska, Dorota Kondiuch, Konrad Maj, Agata Wytykowska, and Anna Zagórska) who organized the meeting. In addition, Eliot Werner, the publisher of this series of volumes, should be properly acknowledged for his commitment to the series; and as all those who have worked with him will know, for his dedication to the highest editorial standards. The conference would not have been possible without financial sponsorship from the Ministry of Science and Higher Education (grant #606/P–DUN/2012) and University of Social Sciences and Humanities (SWPS). Preparation of the book was supported by the National Science Center (formerly the Ministry of Science and Higher Education, grant #106282839 to Agata Wytykowska) and the Institute of Psychology, Polish Academy of Sciences.

The Warsaw Lectures in Personality and Social Psychology continue to provide an important service to the international scientific community. All those who have worked so diligently over the years to secure its success deserve our recognition.

Contents

PART II. COMPLEX MODELS OF CONTROL

PERSONALITY AND CONTROL

INTRODUCTION

Personality and Control

Philip J. Corr
Małgorzata Fajkowska
Michael W. Eysenck
Agata Wytykowska

OVERVIEW

Since 2006 the Biennial Symposia in Personality and Social Psychology have provided an international forum for researchers to come together in a congenial setting in Poland to discuss, in some depth and with wide-ranging implications, specific topics of scientific importance to personality and social psychology. The intellectual stimulation and colleguial enthusiasm engendered by these scientific meetings have resulted in the Warsaw Lectures in Personality and Social Psychology, a series of volumes (Cervone, Fajkowska, Eysenck, & Maruszewski, 2013; Eysenck, Fajkowska, & Maruszewski, 2012; Maruszewski, Fajkowska, & Eysenck, 2010) of which this book is the latest. In 2012 a group of researchers met in Kazimierz Dolny to discuss the specific issue of personality and control. The chapters in this volume showcase the scope of the work presented.

This volume is directed at an audience of academic and research psychologists, and their graduate students, with interests in control mechanisms in personality processes. At the outset we need to acknowledge that the challenge we face is not small. This is, indeed, a large topic and touches on so many fields—including clinical psychology, artistic performance, the influence of incentives on self-regulation,

Personality and Control edited by Philip J. Corr, Małgorzata Fajkowska, Michael W. Eysenck, and Agata Wytykowska. Eliot Werner Publications, Clinton Corners, New York, 2015.

and even the further reaches of the psychological hinterlands of consciousness. As the vast literature on this topic attests, the issue of control is central to any consideration of self-regulative processes (itself a large field of scientific enquiry), and thus its relevance extends far beyond the confines of personality psychology to general psychology and the distant shores of the human sciences more broadly.

The Biennial Symposia in Personality and Social Psychology are not dissimilar to the better-known Nebraska Symposia on Motivation and have attracted a similarly high-quality international cast of speakers who were invited to contribute to the accompanying publications. Experience over the past ten years provides ample testimony to the value of focused attention on a single aspect of personality and social psychology; this approach especially has merit, since it has the potential to yield fresh insights that may be less forthcoming when researchers are either working alone or with groups who have a mixed range of scientific interests.

Inviting researchers with different theoretical perspectives and research interests to focus on a highly specific topic in an informal setting has much to commend it. Science is very much a team sport and the Warsaw Lectures in Personality and Social Psychology have proved fecund in encouraging and enabling open-mindedness and stimulating scientific cross-fertilization and creativity.

LEVELS OF CONTROL

Numerous aspects of control are examined in this volume, but running through them is the issue of the *level* of control. This is more than a mere delineation of systems; it also entails consideration of conscious awareness and processing, and how these still-mysterious forms of control ever manage to orchestrate behavior. The importance of the issue of different levels of control is attested to by the variety and number of applications and theoretical perspectives (for a review see Carver, 2005). The apparent necessity of assuming different levels of control itself suggests that evolution had to face conflicting demands—namely, how to achieve adaptive "quick and dirty" behavioral responses, especially in reflex-like reactions, as well as "slow and clean" behavioral responses that require deliberate and controlled cognitive processes appropriate to immediate environmental contingencies. Somewhere along this evolutionary path, control processes became instantiated in brain-behavioral systems, individual differences in which give rise to heterogeneity in personality states and traits.

This point is highlighted by Carver, Johnson, and Joormann (2008), who note that in studies from cognitive, personality, social, and developmental psychology, there is a convergence to the conclusion that there exist (at least) two modes of information processing and action regulation, which operate simultaneously and often—and not always in coordination. For example, in the field of economics, the rejection of the neoclassical view of the rational economic agent—the elusive and, if such an agent exists, seclusive *homo economicus*—has largely given way, especially in behavioral economics, to the view that different systems of control regulate judgement, decision making, and action (Kahneman, 2012): levels of control *writ large*!

But, as noted by Corr (2010), there remain a number of unresolved theoretical issues that impede the construction of a coherent and viable model of control in personality psychology, as well as the wider psychological sciences. He contends that in order to advance this debate—especially concerning the integration of motivation, emotion, cognition, and conscious experience—several major, and thorny, problems need first to be acknowledged.

As is well known, dual process models of control contain the following features:

- *System 1.* Reflexive: fast, coarse-grained, automatic, ballistic, and preconscious/nonconscious.
- *System 2.* Reflective: slow, fine-grained, deliberative, controlled (explicit/declarative learning), and (as far as we can tell) open to conscious awareness.

The importance of these two systems was highlighted in the introduction to *The Cambridge Handbook of Personality Psychology*, where editors Philip Corr and Gerald Matthews (2009) observed:

> A persistent theme has been the multi-layered nature of personality, expressed in individual differences in neural functioning, in cognition and information-processing, and in social relationships. Abnormal personality too is expressed at multiple levels. Despite the inevitable difficulties, a major task for future research is to develop models of personality that integrate these different processes. (pp. xxxviii–xxxix)

Dual process models are found across the spectrum of psychology and include implicit and explicit memory, procedural and declarative learning, top-down (concept) processing versus bottom-up (data) processing, visual processing "action system" (dorsal stream) and "perception system" (ventral stream), clinical neuropsychology (e.g., "blindsight" and "touchsight"), emotions (e.g., the very well-known Zajonc–Lazarus debate), and personality (impulsivity vs. constraint). Specific theories include Epstein's (1973, 1994) rational-experiential model, Hirsh's (1974) S–R and cognitive systems, Toates's (1998) "on-line" and "off-line," and Carver's (2005) impulsivity versus constraint (see also Evans, 2003). Ortony, Norman, and Revelle's (2005) three-system model does an excellent job of summarizing these systems and their implications specifically for personality psychology.

In support of the relevance of these theories, Velmans (1991) reviewed a large experimental literature from which he concluded that all the following processes are capable of being, and normally are, completed preconsciously: (a) analysis of sensory input; (b) analysis of emotion content and input; (c) phonological and semantic analysis of heard speech; (d) phonological and semantic analysis of one's own spoken words and sentences; (e) learning; (f) formation of memories; and (g) choice and preparation of voluntary acts. Standing somewhat aside from this specific issue is the *lateness* of conscious awareness (Libet, 1985, 2004), which seems to rob it of any causal influence on the immediate processes it represents. This matter is discussed in detail by Corr (2010).

SELF AND SELF-REGULATION

There is also a large literature on the psychology of the self (Robinson & Sedikides, 2009) and conscious awareness of the self, and here too issues of control loom large. Assuming that the self is not merely the hot air of the epiphenomenalist's kettle, self-regulation (e.g., willpower) needs to be taken into theoretical account. Human beings certainly believe and act as if the self is important and has agency, although not always in the precise way it may seem. For example, in relation to the functions of emotion, Baumeister, Vohs, DeWall, and Zhang (2007) contend that the view that emotion has a direct causation on behavior is increasingly untenable. Instead they argue that emotion is part of a feedback system whose influence on behavior is typically indirect. It provides feedback and affords retrospective appraisal of actions such that conscious emotional states facilitate learning and change future behavior. These authors review a large body of empirical evidence to justify their conclusions.

What the arguments of Baumeister et al. (2007) contribute to this literature is to highlight the lateness of higher-order cognitive and emotional processes. As they state:

> The assumption that the purpose of full-blown, conscious emotion is to cause behavior directly appears to be widespread and indeed deeply embedded in psychological theorizing. Yet it appears to be far less true than many researchers (ourselves included) have assumed. (p. 194)

However, this issue often seems abstract and, at times, even a distraction from the real business of psychological science—namely, to get on with identifying and describing mechanisms. There is also the long history of philosophy (often imbued with quasi-religious undertones) with which to contend. Nevertheless, all of the above matters are of fundamental importance when considering the true nature of control processes in personality and beyond.

Along with other issues, these are some of the difficult theoretical questions that attend any serious consideration of the psychological nature of control processes in personality psychology. As readers will see, all these issues rear their heads in the collection of stimulating and thought-provoking essays that comprise this volume.

WHAT'S AHEAD IN THIS BOOK

The chapters in this volume are presented from the general to the specific and are contained in two sections, "Basic Models of Control" and "Complex Models of Control." The chapters illustrate how the issue of control in personality psychology can be examined from a variety of theoretical perspectives and practical applications. This range of uses also documents the scientific potential of tackling this central topic from a number of different angles. Regarding these challenges, the authors rose admirably to the task set for them and they did so with aplomb.

Part I: Basic Models of Control

Starting at the highest level of cognitive control—namely, deliberative control and conscious awareness—Philip Corr and Ezequiel Morsella acknowledge the seminal role that the behavioral inhibition system (BIS; Gray, 1982) has played in personality and examine the implications of this theory for the still-mysterious nature of consciousness. Few people doubt its centrality in behavioral control yet there is little knowledge about *why* or *how* it achieves its ends and, as discussed above, there are difficult theoretical issues surroundings its scientific status.

After summarizing Gray's (1995) comparator model of consciousness, which specifies why only certain stimuli attract conscious processing, Corr and Morsella combine this model with ideomotor theory, which complements it (e.g., it explains how the comparator model helps explain the mechanisms underlying the deliberative control of behavior). Of significance, this chapter tries to explain why both the comparator model and ideomotor theory contend that consciousness is perceptual-like: this is because it renders the contents of consciousness communicable and most capable of being detected and processed by multiple brain systems. Specifically, according to Gray's (2004) formulation, conscious contents are broadcast to various systems via a single perception-like code. Representations need to be in a format that is understood by multiple systems, especially systems involved in behavioral control and perceptual-like representations—which may be the appropriate format because most brain systems evolved to be sensitive to such representations.

This chapter concludes with the observation that although intrapsychic conflict would not be considered by the engineer of a von Neumann computer, this solution may have evolved by natural selection as a clever way for the nervous system to resolve the conflict between competing goals that are inevitable in any complex environment. This view goes a long way to explaining where aberration of consciousness attends many clinical conditions (e.g., depression and schizophrenia).

Continuing the theme of high-level cognition, in a theoretical discussion supported by a new interference task and experimental data, Pareezad Zarolia, Jessica Tomory, Howard Rosen, and Ezequiel Morsella argue that basic mechanisms of control are related to both conscious processings and the skeletal muscle effector system, and that consideration of the dual role of these different processes may provide an important clue as to why only some contents enter concious awareness and attract detailed cognitive processing. In particular, they call attention to the need to include "hot" components of everyday significance (e.g., incentives) in standard "cold" interference tasks (e.g., the flanker task). They advance their empirical case in this important literature by the adaptation of existing paradigms to produce a new subtle one, which includes the kinds of incentive-related and emotion-related phenomena that we may expect to influence control processes across a wide span of everyday life applications.

As Zarolia et al. discuss, this new experimental paradigm might be useful for the examination of stronger manipulations (e.g., involving physiological incentives), as well as in clinical patients who are suffering from a variety of addiction and impulse control disorders. They rightly highlight the need for further studies of the nature of the pushes and pulls of incentive interference that affect control and consciousness; these may be especially instructive in relation to the contents that enter conscious awareness and recruit precious cognitive resources.

Returning to the more specific functions of the BIS, Agata Wytykowska, Philip Corr, and Małgorzata Fajkowska discuss the role played by a BIS-related comparator in many areas of psychology as a central process in the self-regulation of behavior. As these authors note, the notion of a comparator has its origins in a cybernetic view of the mind, which serves the vital function of comparing input states with desired reference states. When a mismatch is detected, control processes are initiated to reduce this disparity; this is accompanied by a range of motoric, memoric, emotional, and behavioral outputs.

Wytykowska et al. make the case that, at the cognitive level, the comparator function of the BIS is concerned with the dissimilarity-oriented attentional mode. This elaboration of the usual functions assigned to the BIS contends that conflict resolution processes aimed at reduction of mismatch entail selective attention to error-generating signals and, by this route, the BIS exercises control over information processing sufficient to resolve the mismatch. More specifically, this proposal extends the notion of the BIS as one that biases processing exclusively toward threatening stimuli; it achieves this by proposing that selective attention is directed (more generally) also toward dissimilarity. The authors present a series of experiments to support their elaborated cognitive model of the BIS.

Part II: Complex Models of Control

Opening this section with a general discussion of the widespread importance of control issues in the human sciences, Shulamith Kreitler highlights the central role that they play in the initiation of an output and its discontinuation, in the rhythm or tempo of execution, and also in processes of inhibition and excitation that accompany the performance of behavior. She notes too that control has a long history in personality psychology and related areas such as mental illness—for example, seen in psychoanalysis in terms of regulating the competing demands of the id, superego, and reality in order to satisfy one's desires with minimal pain and punishment. She also raises the issue that in some respects control may be a limited resource, as suggested by the findings of studies on willpower. Whether there is a limited resource more generally on control is an unanswered question.

Kreitler makes an important observation in relation to rationality of judgment and decision making. The banal fact that *homo sapiens* do not conform to the rational tenets of *homo economicus* is evident to all (see above), at least those not blindly inculcated by neoclassical economics, and it would be a capital mistake to assume—as many models of rationality do—that behavior is regulated fully by deliberate decision making of System 2. Even assuming that people can in principle make deliberate decisions, it does not follow that they always or typically do. Reflecting the importance of dual process models (discussed above), control does not always function on the level of awareness and not necessarily through reasoned decision-making acts. It is quite possible that it often functions outside awareness through automatic-procedural routines or various learned behaviors and strategies.

To further our understanding of control, Kreitler advances a cognitive orientation theory that is a motivational theory of behavior designed to enable understanding, predicting, and changing behavior in different domains. It contains many of the features of standard cognitive models (e.g., the roles played by attitudes and beliefs), eschews allegiance to the notion of rational decision making, and seeks a more psychologically realistic model of control. The features of this cognitive model, and its implications, are laid out in this highly stimulating and informative chapter.

As a specific example of control in the context of a domain of complex performance, Joanna Kantor-Martynuska discusses the literature and its implications as it relates to music making. As this author notes, musical expertise develops with the ability to exercise control over the many processes and functions entailed by the planning, preparation, and execution of practice, as well as monitoring and valuating practice and performance. In particular, control is vital in the ability to resist distraction and inhibit impulsive action, and to undertake and carry out self-initiated activity.

With an adept blending of theory, method, and practice, Kantor-Martynuska illustrates the many control processes inherent in musicianship—which consists of practicing an instrument, mastering a piece of music, and delivering a performance. These are highly demanding of cognitive, emotional, and motivational resources, not to mention physical endurance. There needs to be fine control of basic motor and cognitive levels of auditory processing and music making, higher levels of control comprising emotional and motivational self-regulation, and metacognitive control.

Not only does this chapter provide a performance context to illustrate the integration of many forms and levels of control, its theoretical analysis yields insights that have practical applications. As with music making itself, this chapters offers a powerful blend of theory and practice, presented in a coherent and coordinated fashion.

As one of the leading writers on cognitive psychology and its applications, Michael Eysenck moves the discussion on to the clinical domain, focusing on the cognitive control of anxiety and depression—where problems of control are evident in presenting symptoms. He presents the well-formulated and well-tested model of processing efficiency, which states that anxiety impairs the functioning of the working memory system (which contains three components: an attention-like central executive, a phonological loop, and a visuo-spatial sketchpad for visuo-spatial processing and brief storage). Processing efficiency theory states that anxiety specifically impairs the central executive. In more detail Eysenck outlines the main functions of the central executive: an inhibitory function, which controls the processing of irrelevant stimuli and responses; a shifting function, which controls the switching of attention within and between sets; and an updating function, which is used to update and monitor information currently accessible to working memory.

Once more reflecting the different levels of processing discussed above, Eysenck's attentional theory argues for two attentional systems: one related to goal-directed, top-down processing; and the other to a stimulus-driven system that exerts bottom-up control. In this discussion an important distinction is made in relation to self-regulation. That is, although anxiety impairs processing efficiency, this does not automatically lead to impaired performance effectiveness. Individuals high in anxiety may use additional processing resources to compensate for these deleterious effects on processing efficiency.

Although much less is known about the cognitive processes of depression, Eysenck applies an equally rigorous theoretical perspective to understanding the control problem in this major clinical disorder. But unlike the attentional and future-oriented cognitive failures in anxiety, depression seems more related to problems of interpretation (e.g., attribution) and is past oriented. The importance of cognitive control theory for these clinical conditions is explicated in a way that points to new areas of enquiry and, possibly, application.

Finally, Charles Carver closes the circle of our presentation of control processes in personality psychology by discussing a major issue that underlies all issues of control, starting with a regulatory puzzle in personality psychology—which concerns all aspects of the dimension of reflexive reactivity versus constraint, or impulsive versus deliberative control of action (once more the dual process nature of control rears its head). This chapter begins with a discussion of two accounts of a basis for this dimension of variability in personality psychology.

Critically, this dimension is related to the neurobiological function of serotonin; more specifically, brain regions that are serotonergically innervated may help moderate the expression in behavior of the outputs of more basic systems for approach and avoidance. Elaborating on the clinical theme of Michael Eysenck, Carver argues that deficits in serotonergic function may be related to a range of social and emotional problems, ranging from antisocial behavior to depression.

Many forms of control reflect the distinction between impulsivity and restraint, and for this reason Carver's chapter is important, especially in light of its widespread applications. And this is a well-honed distinction, seen at least since the time of Freud. Variously, the debate has centered around delay of gratification, planfulness, socialization, and id versus ego. Once more there might be an evolutionary balance to be had, and talk of "adaptive" and "maladaptive" may be missing more than one important point. As Carver observes, when manifested as spontaneity, impulsiveness brings a sense of vigor and freedom to the human experience—but when misapplied it can bring misery. Impulsivity is not always a bad thing, and when environmental challenges demand a rapid reaction without the leisurely deliberation of high-level thought (e.g., in a defensive situation), it can be highly adaptive and sometimes even life saving.

The linking of dual process models and the neurobiology of impulsivity and restraint with a wide range of social and clinical behaviors highlights the importance that must be attached to the neuropsychology of control—and in all of this personality processes are central.

SUMMARY

The chapters that comprise this volume represent only a small fraction of all possible chapters, yet they serve the useful function of highlighting the importance of control processes in personality psychology and showing how they relate to a wide variety of psychological outcomes. Dual process models in one form or another dominate this debate, and it is important to remember here that discussion of the formal (descriptive) bases of these systems should not exclude consideration of the experiential aspects that dominate human life. Of overriding significance is the existence of consciousness, aberrations in which are seen in clinical disorder (Gray, 2003).

The psychology of control is distinctive in a number of respects: it demands an integrated view of cognition and behavior, as does personality psychology itself; it shows the complex orchestration of the processes that regulate the competing demands with which people must negotiate; and it highlights the role of personality differences in these control processes that lead to the production of the variety of normal and abnormal behaviors that dominate the study of psychology.

The psychology of control processes raises some daunting challenges, as does the whole field of personality psychology, but it also points in the direction of fertile scientific ground where the further fruits of knowledge may be harvested by the judicious application of theory, method, and scientific passion of the type promoted by the Warsaw Lectures in Personality and Social Psychology.

REFERENCES

Baumeister, R. F., Vohs, K. D., DeWall, C. N., & Zhang, L. (2007). How emotion shapes behavior: Feedback, anticipation, and reflection, rather than direct causation. *Personality and Social Psychology Review*, *11*, 167–203.

Carver, C. S. (2005). Impulse and constraint: Perspectives from personality psychology, convergence with theory in other areas, and potential for integration. *Personality and Social Psychology Review*, *9*, 312–333.

Carver, C. S., Johnson, S. L., & Joormann, J. (2008). Serotonergic function, two-mode models of self-regulation, and vulnerability to depression: What depression has in common with impulsive aggression. *Psychological Bulletin*, *134*, 912–943.

Cervone, D., Fajkowska, M., Eysenck, M. W., & Maruszewski, T. (Eds.). (2013). *Personality dynamics: Meaning construction, the social world, and the embodied mind*. Clinton Corners, NY: Eliot Werner Publications.

Corr, P. J. (2010). Automatic and controlled processes in behavioural control: Implications for personality psychology. *European Journal of Personality*, *24*, 376–403.

Corr, P. J., & Matthews, G. (2009). Editors' general introduction. In P. J. Corr & G. Matthews (Eds), *The Cambridge handbook of personality psychology* (pp. xxii-xlii). Cambridge, UK: Cambridge University Press.

Epstein, S. (1973). The self-concept revisited: Or a theory of a theory. *American Psychologist*, *28*, 404–416.

Epstein, S. (1994). Integration of the cognitive and psychodynamic unconscious. *American Psychologist*, *49*, 709–724.

Evans, J. St. B. T. (2003). In two minds: Dual-process accounts of reasoning. *Trends in Cognitive Sciences*, *7*, 454–459.

Eysenck, M. W., Fajkowska, M., & Maruszewski, T. (Eds.). (2012). *Personality, emotion, and cognition*. Clinton Corners, NY: Eliot Werner Publications.

Gray, J. A. (1982). *The neuropsychology of anxiety: An enquiry into the functions of the septo-hippocampal system*. Oxford, UK: Oxford University Press.

Gray, J. A. (1995). The contents of consciousness: A neuropsychological conjecture. *Behavioral and Brain Sciences, 18,* 659–676.

Gray, J. A. (2003). How are qualia coupled to functions. *Trends in Cognitive Sciences*, 7, 192-194.

Gray, J. A. (2004). *Consciousness: Creeping up on the hard problem*. Oxford, UK: Oxford University Press.

Hirsh, R. (1974). The hippocampus and contextual retrieval of information from memory. *Behavioral Biology*, *12*, 421–444.

Kahneman, D. (2012). *Thinking, fast and slow.* London: Penguin.

Libet, B. (1985). Unconscious cerebral initiative and the role of conscious will in voluntary action. *Behavioral and Brain Sciences*, *8*, 529–566.

Libet, B. (2004). *Mind time: The temporal factor in consciousness*. Cambridge, MA: Harvard University Press.

Maruszewski, T., Fajkowska, M., & Eysenck, M. W. (Eds.). (2010). *Personality from biological, cognitive, and social perspectives*. Clinton Corners, NY: Eliot Werner Publications.

Ortony, A., Norman, D. A., & Revelle, W. (2005). Affect and proto-affect in effective functioning. In J. M. Fellous, & M. A. Arbib (Eds.), *Who needs emotions? The brain meets the machine* (pp. 95–199). New York: Oxford University Press.

Robinson, M. D., & Sedikides, C. (2009). Traits and the self: Toward an integration. In P. J. Corr, & G. Matthews (Eds), *The Cambridge handbook of personality psychology* (pp. 457–472). Cambridge, UK: Cambridge University Press.

Toates, F. (1998). The interaction of cognitive and stimulus-response processes in the control of behaviour. *Neuroscience and Biobehavioral Reviews*, *22*, 59–83.

Velmans, M. (1991). Is human information processing conscious? *Behavioral and Brain Sciences*, *14*, 651–726.

PART I

Basic Models of Control

CHAPTER 1

The Conscious Control of Behavior
Revisiting Gray's Comparator Model

Philip J. Corr
Ezequiel Morsella

INTRODUCTION

This chapter was inspired by the authors' admiration for Jeffrey Gray (1934–2004), a scientist who contributed much to our understanding of the mind/brain—including the study of the elusive relationship between consciousness[1] and behavioral control, which is the focus of this chapter. One of us (PJC) had the good fortune of being a protégé of Gray; the other (EM) had the great pleasure not only of reading and benefiting from Gray's theorizing, but from having once met him in New York to discuss his ideas for several hours—thanks to John Bargh, who generously arranged the meeting.

During this wonderful conversation, which took place more than a decade ago, it became apparent to both the distinguished scientist and the young Ph.D. that Gray's (1995) comparator model of conscious processing (presented in *Behavioral and Brain Sciences*) could explain more about consciousness and behavioral control than even envisioned by its author, which was already quite a bit—including disparate phenomena such as the contents of consciousness (Gray, 1995), the neuropsychology of anxiety (Gray, 1982a, 1982b; Gray & McNaughton, 2000), and the positive symptoms of acute schizophrenia (Gray, 1998; Gray, Feldon, Rawlins, Hemsley, & Smith, 1991). These extensions of Gray's theory of the behavioral inhibition system are the focus of this chapter.

Personality and Control edited by Philip J. Corr, Małgorzata Fajkowska, Michael W. Eysenck, and Agata Wytykowska. Eliot Werner Publications, Clinton Corners, New York, 2015.

GRAY'S COMPARATOR MODEL

To appreciate the insights discussed on that day, now many years ago, it is important to understand Gray's comparator model of consciousness. The model explains, among other things, the lateness of conscious processing (Gray, 2004; Libet, 2004; Velmans, 1991, 2000), error detection in behavioral control, and most importantly how some contents—but not others—are selected to enter consciousness. Perhaps no one explained the model better than Gray (2002) himself.

> The essential computational function discharged by the comparator is to compare, non-consciously and quite generally, information currently received via all thalamocortical sensory pathways (up to the level of neocortical analysis) with a prediction as to what that information should be. The prediction is based jointly upon previous stimulus-stimulus and response-stimulus regularities (stored as memories) under circumstances similar to those operating now; the circumstances "operating now" are themselves defined by the output of the comparator at the preceding comparison process. In addition, the comparator takes account of the subject's ongoing motor program, as what the world will be like in the next moment depends upon what the subject is doing in this one. These processes occur on a time base of the order of 100 ms from the termination of one process of comparison to termination of the next. The output from the comparison process selects a series of items in the neocortical description of the sensory world in the light of their novelty/familiarity and predictedness/unpredictedness (these concepts are not identical to one another). . . . The selection is biased towards items which are novel, either because they occur despite not being expected or because they fail to occur despite being expected; and towards items which are goals or sub-goals for an ongoing motor program. The selected items are reactivated by feedback from the comparator system to those areas of the sensory neocortex (visual, auditory, somatosensory, etc.) in which they have just been non-consciously analysed. It is this reactivation by feedback from the comparator that selects these items for entry into consciousness. (pp. 4–5)

As Gray noted, similar ideas had been proposed before (e.g., by Jackendoff, 1987; Miller, Galanter, & Pribram, 1960; Neisser, 1967). However, until Gray's own model, no "nuts and bolts" theory existed that contained as much specificity regarding both the component processes of consciousness (e.g., detecting, com-

---

[1] Here we are speaking of the most basic kind of consciousness. This kind of consciousness, also referred to as "sentience" (Pinker, 1997), "phenomenal state" (Tye, 1999), "qualia" (Gray, 2004), and subjective experience, has perhaps been best defined by the philosopher Thomas Nagel (1974), who proposed that an organism possesses subjective experiences if there is *something it is like* to be that organism—something it is like, for example, to be human and experience pain, love, or breathlessness. Similarly, Block (1995) claimed, "[T]he phenomenally conscious aspect of a state is what it is like to be in that state" (p. 227).

paring, and matching) and its neuranatomical substrates (see Gray, 1995, for hypotheses about the hippocampus and neocortex in conscious processing).

According to the model, unconscious motor programs (discussed below) lead to expressed action, which then leads to action effects—which are perceptual in nature—that are then compared with the anticipated action effects, which themselves are perceptual-like memories based on previous experience (Gray, 1995). The stages of processing in situations in which the comparator detects a mismatch could be conceptualized as follows.

> *Unconscious motor programs* [Stage 1] → *perceptual-like action effects* [Stage 2] → *comparator process* [Stage 3] → *mismatch detection* [Stage 4] → *entry into consciousness of mismatched, perceptual-like information and error signals (along with other goal-relevant information)* [Stage 5].

As is clear in this sequence, consciousness occurs late, as when one withdraws one's hand reflexively from a hot pot. In this case consciousness regarding the action is experienced only *after* the pain withdrawal action is already mediated successfully, albeit unconsciously, by the nervous system (Gray, 2004). According to Gray (2002), the pain (the quale that is a consequence of late error detection) influences not so much the nature of ongoing action at the moment (for the appropriate action to the situation already took place in an unconsciously mediated manner), but future actions transpiring in a similar context. In this way entry into consciousness influences future behavior in a manner that is not well understood (see treatment in Corr, 2011).

In this comparator framework, when outcomes from actions do not match expected outcomes, representations of the salient features about these unexpected outcomes enter consciousness—as, for example, when we learn that the pot was hotter than expected. This representation occurs also for actions that do not involve pain: any outcome mismatch has the potential to have its salient features represented in the contents of conscious awareness. For example, imagine the case in which a child intended to say something but then, unexpectedly and for the first time in its life, found itself coughing. The child becomes very much aware of this cough experience, long after the motor plans engendering the cough behavior transpires.

It was while discussing mechanisms such as these, during our conversation more than a decade ago, that something became clear. When the sequence of the comparator is reversed, such that the stages flow from 5 to 1 rather than from 1 to 5, the model resembles ideomotor theory (Greenwald, 1970; Harleß, 1861; Hommel, 2009; Hommel, Müsseler, Aschersleben, & Prinz, 2001; James, 1890/1950; Lotze, 1852), a historic approach illuminating how behavior can be controlled voluntarily. Interestingly, the ideomotor approach developed independently of comparator frameworks, but the two have much in common—as we will now discuss.

IDEOMOTOR APPROACHES TO BEHAVIORAL CONTROL

In ideomotor approaches one's conscious knowledge regarding action production and control is limited to the perceptual consequences of expressed action (or action effects). From this standpoint motor control—which specifies the muscles that should be activated at a given time in order to express an action (e.g., flexing a finger)—is largely unconscious (see evidence in Fecteau, Chua, Franks, & Enns, 2001; Goodale & Milner, 2004; Grossberg, 1999; Heath, Neely, Yakimishyn, & Binsted, 2008; Jeannerod, 2006; Liu, Chua, & Enns, 2008; Rosenbaum, 2002; Rossetti, 2001). In this way, before an act the mind is occupied with perception-like representations of what that act is to be. As William James stated, "In perfectly simple voluntary acts there is nothing else in the mind but the kinesthetic idea . . . of what the act is to be" (James, 1890/1950, p. 771). These action-generated perceptual effects include bodily states (e.g., a flexed finger) or remote effects in the external world, such as the change in position of a lever (Hommel, 1998; Hommel & Elsner, 2009; Jordan, 2009). Harleß (1861) referred to these perceptual consequences of a given action as the *Effektbild* (i.e., the picture of the effect).

Motor Programming as an Unconscious Process

From the perspective of ideomotor theory, one is unconscious of efference generation to the muscles. According to a minority of theorists, one is conscious of the efference to the muscles (what Wundt called the feeling of innervation; see James, 1890/1950). Although this efference was believed to be responsible for action outcomes (see a review in Sheerer, 1984), Wundt himself later abandoned the feeling-of-innervation hypothesis (Klein, 1970). Following the controversy James (1890/1950) concluded, "There is no introspective evidence of the feeling of innervation" (p. 775).

In everyday acts such as grasping a handle, one is unconscious of the efference that is sent to the muscles. This efference dictates which fibers should be activated at which time. Highly flexible and "online" adjustments are made unconsciously during an act such as grasping a fruit (Rosenbaum, 2002). Because the spatial relationship between the objects of the world and one's body is seldom fixed (e.g., a fruit is sometimes at left or right), each time an action is performed, new motor programs must be generated unconsciously to deal with the peculiarities of each setting (Rosenbaum, 2002). One is unconscious of these complicated programs (see compelling evidence in Johnson and Haggard, 2005) but—as noted by James—is often aware of their proprioceptive and perceptual consequences (e.g., perceiving the hand grasping; Gottlieb & Mazzoni, 2004; Gray, 2004).[2]

An influential case study revealing the unconscious nature of motor control was reported by Milner and Goodale (1995). In this case study Patient D. F., following a brain lesion, displayed a striking dissociation between action control and

[2] See Berti and Pia (2006) for a review of motor awareness and its disorders.

conscious perception. Patient D. F. suffered from a kind of visual form agnosia and was incapable of, for example, reporting the orientation of a tilted slot. However, this patient could nonetheless insert an object into the slot, much as one deposits a letter into a mailbox. This is not an isolated case. Other patients with lesions in the perception pathway (the ventral-visual system; Goodale & Milner, 2004) cannot identify (recognize) objects but are still able to reach for them and manipulate them when prompted to do so.

From such observations Milner and Goodale (1995) propose that conscious perception and action control are dissociable systems in the brain. In support of this conclusion, it is documented that there are patients who—because of a brain lesion—may be able to correctly identify an object (e.g., an object held up to them by an experimenter), but may be unable to reach for it correctly based on its spatial orientation (e.g., whether the orientation is horizontal or vertical). Thus one group exhibits appropriate action tendencies toward an object in the absence of consciousness about that object (i.e., action without perception), while the other group is conscious of the object but cannot act appropriately toward it (i.e., perception without action).

Dissociations between action control and consciousness are found not only in neurological populations, but also in neurologically intact populations. First, such a dissociation is observed in how neurologically intact subjects respond to visual illusions (Wraga, Creem, & Proffitt, 2000). When responding motorically to such illusions, although subjects' conscious self-reports reflect the illusion that one circle appears larger than another in the Ebbinghaus/Titchener illusion, the manual behavior of subjects toward the visual objects responsible for the illusion is accurate and does not reflect what subjects report.[3] In support of these conclusions stemming from research on illusions, there are many findings revealing that one can be unconscious of the adjustments that are made "online" as one performs a motor act (Fecteau et al., 2001; Fourneret & Jeannerod, 1998; Heath et al., 2008; Liu, Chua, & Enns, 2008; Rossetti, 2001).

Second, the dissociation is supported by research demonstrating not only the unconscious guidance of motor control, but the unconscious learning of motor sequences. In these experiments (see review in Taylor & Ivry, 2013), subjects are trained to perform a series of key presses with their fingers, much as piano players play a sequence of keys to perform a song. Unbeknownst to subjects, some sequences are repeated more times than other sequences. The subjects demonstrate a performance benefit for these repeated sequences, even though they are unaware that these sequences were repeated. This type of effect has been construed as a case of implicit procedural learning. Implicit motor learning is also evidenced in

[3] For arguments against the notion of perception-action dissociations, see Cooper, Sterling, Bacon, and Bridgeman (2012), Franz, Gegenfurtner, Bülthoff, and Fahle (2000), and Jeannerod (2003). Stottinger and Perner (2006) conclusively demonstrated the dissociation using an illusion (the diagonal illusion) that is free of the kinds of limitations found in previous experiments.

certain forms of amnesia in which a patient, such as the famous Patient H. M. (Milner, 1966), shows a performance benefit from extensive rehearsal even though the patient cannot remember—and is thus unconscious of—the rehearsal episodes that led to the performance benefit.

Perceptual Representations of Action Consequences Can Direct Future Action

Ideomotor theory also proposes that when these perceptual-like representations are activated in the future, they automatically activate the unconscious motor programs responsible for enacting the action that led to them. For example, when holding the image in mind of flexing one's finger, the image of the action activates the motor programs that would give rise to the action. In short, activation of the (perceptual-like) representation of action effects leads to the automatic expression of the associated action.

According to James (1890/1950), this form of ideomotor action must always take place—unless, that is, one simultaneously has activated in mind the perceptual consequences of an incompatible action. From this standpoint mere thoughts of action effects produce impulses that, if not curbed or controlled by "acts of express fiat" (i.e., the representation of incompatible action effects), result in the performance of those actions). Thus James emphasized that the image of the sensorial effects of an action leads to the corresponding action. Of importance in this framework is that there is no central homunculus, preferring to realize one action effect over another: the process is effortless, automatic, and without any knowledge of the motor programs involved. Rather, activation of the representations of action effects lead to those actions, unless there is also the activation of representations of incompatible action effects. To take one example, when one imagines one's finger moving but decides not to move the finger, it is only because—when imagining the former—one also had activated the idea of not moving the finger, which is an incompatible idea.

In this way voluntary action can be guided by the activation of the perceptual-like representations of action effects. In some situations this guidance is intentional and is accompanied by the sense of agency (Moore, Wegner, & Haggard, 2009), especially when action outcomes match one's action goals. According to ideomotor theory, voluntary action control requires memory of previous action effects. The process unfolds as follows.

> *Activation of conscious, perceptual-like representations of action effects* [Stage 1] → *activation of unconscious motor programs* [Stage 2] → *perceptual action effects* [Stage 3] → *comparator process* [Stage 4] → *entry into consciousness of, say, mismatching perceptual consequences* [Stage 5].

One can appreciate that this resembles the reversed sequence of Gray's comparator model, which begins not with the conscious action effects, but with the unconscious motor program. (For treatments of how these ideas are related to social cognition, see Johnson & Shiffrar, 2013; Jordan, 2009.) It was implicit in Gray's model that (always automatic) actions were elicited, or afforded, by stimuli; however, it was never made explicit how such stimuli trigger these actions. Ideomotor theory provides an account of this process and highlights the recursive interplay of automatic processes and controlled (often conscious) processes. Neither process is in exclusive control of behavior; rather, they are joint causal partners in an experience-action system of coordination.

Ideomotor Theory and Mirror Neuron Approaches

In line with ideomotor accounts, contemporary research on mirror neurons (see review in Rizzolatti, Sinigaglia, & Anderson, 2008) suggests that there is overlap in the neural networks involved in (a) the perception of actions (e.g., the perception of actions by others) and (b) the execution of one's own actions. It is through such overlap that one can learn to perform actions based on imitation (Rizzolatti et al., 2008). From the perspective of research on mirror neurons, perceptual processing is an inextricable part of action control (Iacoboni, 2005; Jordan, 2009; Miall, 2003).[4]

From this standpoint voluntary action can be guided by the perceptual representations not only of the behaviors performed by one, but by the observed behaviors of others. Consistent with both ideomotor and mirror neuron accounts, Desmurget et al. (2009) concluded in their brain stimulation study (on awake patients undergoing brain surgery for the treatment of epilepsy) that action intentions in perceptual regions may be processed in terms of the perceptual consequences of the intended action (see review of convergent evidence in Jordan, 2009; Miall, 2003). Complementing these findings is research on the role of reafference in action control, which reveals that reafference to perceptual areas of the brain, such as the parietal cortex (Berti & Pia, 2006; Chambon, Wenke, Fleming, Prinz, & Haggard, 2013; Iacoboni, 2005; Miall, 2003), is essential to the control of intentional action.

In summary, theorizing falling under the rubrics of ideomotor, common code, or mirror neuron research supports the counterintuitive hypothesis that the perceptual representations about the external world—including those about the behaviors of others—can be a major influence on behavioral control (see discussion in Jordan, 2009). As such, mirror neuron research supplies theoretically important empirical support for the ideomotor theories advanced by William James and others. It is intriguing to see how they can easily be incorporated into Gray's neuropsychological model of behavioral control and consciousness.

---

[4] It is worth mentioning that this is consistent with contemporary ideomotor models, which propose that perceptual action effects and action codes share the same representational format—hence the description of these accounts as "common code" theories of perception-and-action (Hommel, 2009).

SUBJECTIVE ASPECTS OF SKINNER'S THREE-TERM CONTINGENCY

Ideomotor theory, Gray's neuropsychological work, and more recent insights from mirror neuron research highlight the importance of the stimulus-response processes favored by Skinner and other radical behaviorists; their work can now be extended to understanding the machinery hidden in their black boxes. Neglected in traditional ideomotor accounts is the mechanism by which currently experienced favorable outcomes from action production increase the likelihood that only some behaviors are expressed in the future.

As far as we know, and in accordance with Loewenstein (1996),[5] operant conditioning remains the best mechanistic model to explain this phenomenon—especially when considering Skinner's (1953) three-term contingency description of operant learning. From this point of view, the traditional circumstance under which operant conditioning takes place involves three different terms. The first term involves the discriminative stimulus (S_D), which is the stimulus that signifies the appropriate context for expressing the operant. In a standard operant conditioning experiment, a lever may be the discriminative stimulus. In everyday life a traffic light signaling green may be a discriminative stimulus. The S_D is considered the first term of the three-term contingency.

Faced with this S_D the organism issues the operant behavior, or response (*R*). It is important to note in this framework that the operant is not a simple response. When a rat depresses a lever, the action can be accomplished by the leg or the snout. Similarly, the operant may be getting the soccer ball into the goal, one way or another, as in a game of soccer. This can be accomplished through several means (e.g., pushing the ball in the goal with the left leg, the right leg, or instead by a header). That the same action goal (which Gray referred to simply as "goals") can be accomplished through several motoric means is called motor equivalence (Lashley, 1942). The operant (*R*), learned through trial and error, is the second term of the three-term contingency.

The third and last term of the three-term contingency is the most relevant to our question regarding how behavioral outcomes could reinforce (i.e., increase the likelihood of) some behaviors over others in a specific context (i.e., when faced with a particular S_D). This is the outcome variable, or *O*. The outcome is either a

---

[5] Why one choice of action over another is selected in the future remains mysterious. It seems that, regardless of mentalistic or decision-making dynamics, past behavior is still the most reliable predictor of future behavior. Speaking of decision-making approaches following the cognitive revolution, Loewenstein (1996) concludes, "Another area in which the decision making perspective falls short is its treatment of motivation and effort. In the decision paradigm there is no qualitative distinction between choosing, say one car over another, or 'deciding' to pick up one's pace in the last mile of a marathon; both are simply decisions. Years after the decline of behaviorism, behaviorists still offer the most coherent theoretical perspective on motivation and the most sophisticated and comprehensive program of research" (p. 287).

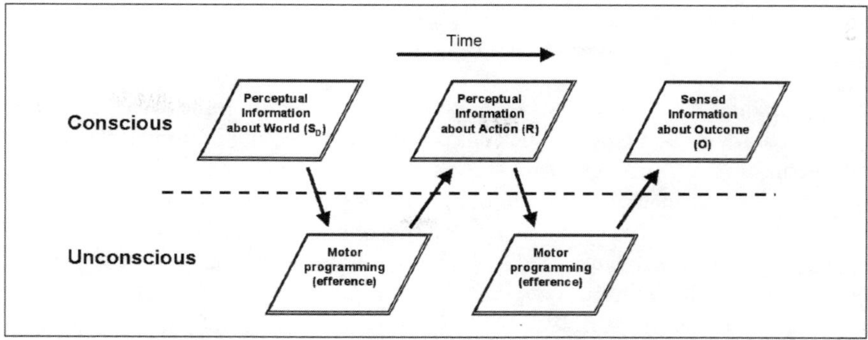

Figure 1. Conscious and unconscious aspects of Skinner's three-term contingency.

reinforcer, which increases the likelihood of a certain operant in the presence of a given S_D (e.g., the presentation of something positive or removal of something negative) or a punisher, which decreases the likelihood of a certain operant in the presence of a given S_D (e.g., the presentation of something negative or removal of something positive). Skinner (1953) explains that, in the three-term contingency ($S_D \rightarrow R \rightarrow O$), it is the outcome term (O) that determines the strength of the association between S_D and R. If the outcome is a reinforcer, then the association is strengthened, making R more likely in the presence of S_D. If the outcome is a punisher, then the association between S_D and R is weakened, such that R is now less likely to occur when S_D is presented.

According to Gray, because S_D is part of the perceptual world, it is a conscious representation—as is, importantly, the action effect and outcome term (O). However, the motor aspects of R are unconscious. This is consistent with both Gray (1995, 2004) and ideomotor theory. Figure 1 diagrams schematically that which is conscious and unconscious in the three-term contingency and reveals that what falls within consciousness can be described, in terms of its neural processing, as afference or reafference (Sherrington, 1906).

Neural Correlates of the Subjective Aspects of the Three-Term Contingency

Gray (1995, 2004) was more concerned with the nature of the different component processes of the comparator model than with the actual neural substrates of these processes. Speaking of alternative models, Gray (2002) concludes:

> Where I stress the hippocampal system, more recent views tend to emphasise the prefrontal, anterior cingulate and/or parietal cortex. The precise anatomical localisation of the computations, however, does not bear upon the issues raised. . . . What does bear upon these issues is the emphasis in all these mod-

els upon the interaction of top-down (contextual) and bottom-up (perceptual) processing as giving rise to the contents of consciousness. (p. 6)

Regarding the conscious aspects of behavioral control in the three-term contingency, it seems that much of the control-related processing in frontal cortex may be unconscious. Consistent with this view and with ideomotor frameworks, it seems—as mentioned above—that one does not have direct, conscious access to motor programs or other kinds of efference generators (Grossberg, 1999; Morsella & Bargh, 2010; Rosenbaum, 2002), including those for language (Levelt, 1989), emotional systems (e.g., the amygdala; Anderson, & Phelps, 2002; Öhman, Carlsson, Lundqvist, & Ingvar, 2007), or executive control (Crick, 1995; Suhler & Churchland, 2009). The notion that efference generation is largely unconscious illuminates why, when speaking, one does not always know exactly which words one will utter next (Levelt, 1989; Slevc & Ferreira, 2006).

Neural Correlates of the Perceptual Dimensions of the Control of Action

Regarding conscious awareness of action effects, there is evidence implicating posterior perceptual regions (e.g., parietal areas), rather than frontal areas, as being the key regions responsible for conscious states (see review in Godwin, Gazzaley, & Morsella, 2013).[6] In addition, in a study with seven patients undergoing awake brain surgery, direct electrical stimulation of parietal areas of the brain gave rise to the subjectively experienced will (an "urge") to perform an action. Interestingly, increased activation made subjects believe that they actually executed the corresponding action (e.g., flexing a finger), even though no action was performed (Desmurget et al., 2009; Desmurget & Sirigu, 2010). Activating frontal motor areas (e.g., in premotor areas) resulted in the performance of the actual action, but surprisingly subjects believed that they did not perform any action (see also Fried et al., 1991). "Stimulation of the premotor region triggered overt mouth and contralateral limb movements. Yet, patients firmly denied that they had moved" (Desmurget et al., 2009, p. 811).

These observations are consistent with the age-old Sensorium Hypothesis first proposed by the great Johannes Müller and then advocated, in one fashion or another, by others (Godwin et al., 2013; Gray, 2004; James, 1890/1950; Müller, 1843). The Sensorium Hypothesis is that action/motor processes are largely unconscious (Goodale & Milner, 2004; Gray, 2004; Grossberg, 1999) and that the contents of consciousness are influenced primarily by perceptual-based (as opposed to action-based) events and processes, which is in direct agreement with Gray (1995) and ideomotor theory. Consistent with these perspectives,

---

[6] Relevant to this hypothesis is research on the phenomenon of sensory neglect (cf. Graziano, 2001; Heilman, Watson, & Valenstein, 2003).

Desmurget et al. (2009) concluded in their brain stimulation study that action intentions in perceptual regions may be processed in terms of the perceptual consequences of the intended action (see reviews of convergent evidence in Jordan, 2009; Miall, 2003).

Complementing these findings is research on the role of reafference in action control. This research reveals that a key component of the control of intentional action is reafference to perceptual areas of the brain, such as parietal cortex (Berti & Pia, 2006; Chambon et al., 2013; Iacoboni, 2005; Miall, 2003). Accordingly, it has been proposed that what characterizes conscious content in neural processing is the notion of perceptual afference (information arising from the world that affects sensory-perceptual systems) or perceptual reafference, such as the proprioceptive information generated during action production.[7]

Finally, consistent with Gray (1995), the conscious contents (e.g., urges and perceptual representations) of behavioral control are similar to—or perhaps one and the same as—the contents occupying the "buffers" in working memory (WM), a large-scale mechanism that is used to sustain the activation of content-based representations in mind (e.g., for information manipulation) and is intimately related to both consciousness and action production (Baddeley, 2007; Fuster, 2003). Recent developments reveal that WM is intimately related to both action control and consciousness (LeDoux, 2008), as is evident in the title and contents of a treatise on WM—*Working Memory, Thought, and Action* (Baddeley, 2007).

Indeed, perhaps no mental operation is as reliably coupled with conscious processing as WM (LeDoux, 2008). When trying to hold in mind action-related information, a person's consciousness is consumed by this goal (James, 1890/1950). For instance, when holding a to-be-dialed telephone number in mind (or when gargling with mouthwash for thirty seconds), action-related mental imagery occupies one's consciousness during the delayed action phase. Similarly, before making an important toast (or, more dramatically, making the toast in an unmastered language), a person has conscious imagery regarding the words to be uttered—much as when an actor rehearses lines for an upcoming scene. In this way, before an act the mind is occupied with perception-like representations of what that act is to be—again, as James (1890/1950) stated, "In perfectly simple voluntary acts there is nothing else in the mind but the kinesthetic idea . . . of what the act is to be" (p. 771). Thus voluntary action control often occupies both WM and perceptual consciousness.

In conclusion, it is clear that there are several contemporary accounts that are consistent with Gray (1995) and with the age-old hypothesis that the urges associ-

---

[7] Sherrington (1906) aptly referred to these two, similar kinds of information as exafference, when the source of information stems from the external world, and reafference, when the source is feedback from overt actions. There is also similar feedback from the activation of internal action plans (e.g., information arising from "corollary discharges" or "efference copies" of our own action plans; Chambon et al., 2013; Christensen et al., 2007; Jordan, 2009; Miall, 2003; Obhi, Planetta, & Scantlebury, 2009).

ated with intentional action should involve regions of the brain that have historically been associated with perceptual processing. Faced with these insights, one may ask the question "What is it about the sensorium?"

Proposals have been made regarding why consciousness is associated with Müller's sensorium but not with his motorium. For example, according to one framework about the microarchitecture of cognition (Grossberg, 1999), motor programming involves a neural process called inhibitory matching, which is unconscious and does not involve resonant states (according to Grossberg, 1999, all conscious states are resonant states, but not all resonant states are conscious states), whereas perceptual detection often involves excitatory matching, which can be conscious (see Grossberg, 1999).

THE PRIMARY ROLE OF CONSCIOUS PROCESSING

According to several frameworks, the primary function of conscious processing is to integrate processes that would be unintegrated otherwise (Baars, 1988, 2002; Boly et al., 2011; Clark, 2002; Damasio, 1989; Dehaene & Naccache, 2001; Del Cul, Baillet, & Dehaene, 2007; Doesburg, Green, McDonald, & Ward, 2009; Freeman, 1991; Koch, 2004; Llinás & Ribary, 2001; Ortinski & Meador, 2004; Sergent & Dehaene, 2004; Tononi & Edelman, 1988; Ulhaas et al., 2009; Varela, Lachaux, Rodriguez, & Martinerie, 2001; Zeki & Bartels, 1999). These accounts have fallen under the integration consensus (Morsella, 2005). Evidence for the integration consensus stems from both perception-based and action-based research. Regarding the former, it has been demonstrated that the neural correlates of conscious perceptual representations involve a wider network of brain regions than the neural correlates of unconscious representations (Dehaene & Naccache, 2001; Del Cul et al., 2007). Regarding the latter, the neural correlates of consciously mediated actions involve a more extensive network of regions than the neural correlates of unconsciously mediated actions (Kern, Jaradeh, Arndorfer, & Shaker, 2001; McKay, Evans, Frackowiak, & Corfield, 2003; Ortinski & Meador, 2004).[8]

The "Broadcasting" of Conscious Contents

Germane to Gray (1995), according to the integration consensus, conscious contents are available to various systems, as if the contents were somehow "broadcast." It has been proposed that for contents to have such communicability, the contents of consciousness must be communicable (Fodor, 1983). For communica-

---

[8] It has been proposed that it might be more parsimonious to hypothesize that consciousness is not for this form of integration, but instead for suppression or for the mappings of arbitrary stimulus-response mapping, but there are problems with these accounts (see Poehlman, Jantz, & Morsella, 2012).

bility to occur successfully, representations must be in a format that is understood by multiple systems, especially systems involved in behavioral control. Some theorists have proposed that this format must be perceptual in nature, since most brain systems evolved to be sensitive to perceptual-like representations (Morsella, Lanska, Berger, & Gazzaley, 2009). These representations provide information about what Gestalt psychologists described as the "distal" object (Koffka, 1922).[9] In terms of neural processing, the representations rely on afference from the external world as well as on perceptuo-semantic knowledge (Most, Scholl, Clifford, & Simons, 2005).

Regarding these perceptual-like representations, one must consider that multiple systems in the brain respond in various ways to the same perceptual stimulus. In the processing of emotion-related stimuli, for example, LeDoux (1996) proposes that the same perceptual afference is processed by a "quick and dirty" subcortical pathway and by a slower, more accurate cortical pathway. In either case it is perceptual afference that is capable of activating analysis by systems that, most likely, evolved at different times and follow distinct operating principles. Independent of these considerations, Fodor (1983) proposed that the most communicable kind of representation in the brain is that of the perceptual kind. Figuratively speaking, the perceptual-like information is the common currency or lingua franca of the brain.

The Simulacrum of the World in Consciousness

The idea that consciousness represents a model of the external world, and one's place and inclinations within that world, is not new and has become uncontroversial (Hesslow, 2002; Merker, 2007; Yates, 1985). However, it should be noted that the representations making up this simulacrum represent a small subset of what is really "out there." This subset includes objects and other physical information that are of concern (Frijda, 1986) to the organism. We humans, for example, do not represent in our conscious simulacrum ultraviolet radiation. This is of little consequence because such energies are not of terrible concern to human welfare, though detection of such energies is essential for other species. It is also important to add that this simulacrum serves to afford adaptive action (Morsella, Montemayor, Hubbard, & Zarolia, 2010) and is not in the business of accurately representing the external world.

Such an evolutionary-based perspective on the nature of the conscious simulacrum begins with the assumption that most mental phenomena are primarily concerned with how the organism should behave at one moment in time. (This was the functionalist approach adopted by William James and others.) As beautifully explained in Gray (2004), the nature of the isomorphism to the world remains unclear

[9] See research on how perceptual analysis reaches the stage of processing known as "objecthood" in Goodhew, Dux, Lipp, & Visser (2012).

with respect to many representational processes. What of the outside world is represented by a "mood"? What does the aversive feeling of holding one's breath represent? What does the pungent flavor of hydrogen peroxide represent? This nasty chemical differs molecularly from water only by the addition of a single oxygen atom, but few would perceive it as "water with a little too much oxygen." Instead the toxic chemical is perceived (or represented) as something that "tastes bad" and should be violently expelled from the body. Similarly, in the real (physical) world out there, the color blue and red are just the same thing (electromagnetic frequencies) occurring at different speeds, but no one perceives the color red as a slower version of the color blue. Rather, color perception is intimately associated with action (and not the way the world is): it evolved for selecting fruits and detecting camouflaged prey (Morsella et al., 2010).

Some representations in vision (e.g., the spatial layout of a garden) do seem isomorphic to what is out there in the real world. In such cases it happens that representing space as accurately as possible does lead to the most adaptive response. But representing how things are is not the primary goal of the conscious simulacrum. Thus representational accuracy is secondary to the adaptive guidance of a response.

CONSCIOUSNESS AND ENCAPSULATION

To summarize the foregoing conclusions, there are several independent accounts—based on different considerations—proposing that conscious representations should be of a perceptual-like nature, which is in complete accord with Gray (1995, 2004). These representations possess an interesting property: encapsulation. Visual illusions such as the Ebbinghaus/Titchener illusion reveal how conscious percepts can be encapsulated (Fodor, 1983), which means that the representations cannot be affected by beliefs or other conscious contents (e.g., motivation). Even though one knows that the two circles in the Ebbinghaus/Titchener illusion are of exactly the same size, one cannot help but perceive them as having different diameters. It has been argued that such encapsulation is adaptive (Firestone & Scholl, 2014). One argument is that if perception could be "corrupted" by beliefs and desires, it would lose its value as a system for negotiating a real, external world. That perceptual processes are encapsulated and independent of voluntary processing is also evident in the phenomenon of earworms (e.g., when one cannot "get a song out of one's head") and in certain forms of psychopathology (e.g., when a patient knows that a percept is a hallucination but the abnormal percept persists in consciousness).

Such encapsulation occurs not only for perceptual processing, but also in action control—as in the case of action-related urges, which are triggered in a predictable and insuppressible manner by certain stimuli. For example, when one holds one's breath while underwater or runs barefoot across hot sand, one cannot help but consciously experience the inclinations to inhale or to avoid touching the hot sand, respectively (Morsella, 2005). These urges arise despite one's beliefs (e.g., holding one's breath underwater is a good thing) and desires. The conscious strife triggered by the external stimuli cannot be turned off voluntarily (Morsella, 2005; Öhman & Mineka, 2001). In these cases the externally activated action-related urges are encapsulated from voluntary control. In this way, although inclinations triggered by external stimuli can be behaviorally suppressed, they often cannot be mentally suppressed (Bargh & Morsella, 2008). One can think of many examples in which externally triggered conscious contents are more difficult to control than is overt behavior (cf. Bargh & Morsella, 2010).

Higher-Level Processes Stemming from Encapsulation

Because of encapsulation, suppressed actions and their resultant inclinations can function like internalized reflexes (Vygotsky, 1962), which is consistent with Sherrington's (1941) definition of pain as "the psychical adjunct of an imperative protective reflex" (p. 286). These internalized reflexes can be co-opted to play an essential, evaluative role in the high-level mental operation of mental simulation. As known by strategists and engineers, short of performing an action, the best way of knowing the consequences of a course of action is by simulating it. Simulators train novice pilots and laser scopes on a rifle simulate the destination of a rifle shot. One obvious value of simulation is that knowledge of an action outcome is learned without the risks of performing the action (Barsalou, 1999).[10]

Importantly, the outcome of simulation must be evaluated. Because of encapsulation, most knowledge regarding what is favorable or not is already built into the organism: It is possessed by the very processes that, in the absence of suppression, control behavior directly (Bargh & Morsella, 2008). The encapsulated inclinations respond to simulacra as if they were responding to real, external stimuli. Changes in consciousness, in response to the simulacra constructed voluntarily within our minds, lead to statements such as "I would rather not do or even imagine doing that."

From this point one immediately has a sense of whether a simulated bodily action outcome (e.g., an approach-approach situation) is desirable, although such a judgment must take many considerations into account. Accordingly, research has shown that faced with options, people can experience inexplicable "gut feelings" (or somatic markers; Tranel & Damasio, 1985) reflecting the inclinations of agents whose inner workings and learning histories are opaque to awareness (Öhman & Mineka, 2001).

The Three-Term Contingency Redux

Returning to our three-term contingency, that which enters consciousness (the S_D and outcome) is not the kind of nervous event that is directly associated with ef-

---

[10] Indeed, some theories propose that the function of explicit, conscious memory is to simulate potential future actions (Schacter & Addis, 2007).

ference generation; instead it is the kind of event that resembles perceptual processing. Gray (1995, 2004) argues that conscious awareness comprises what, in everyday life, we refer to as perception. Regarding why this kind of processing can be associated with consciousness, whereas so many other kinds of processes cannot, Gray (2002) states, "I have no serious idea how such an 'entry into consciousness' actually occurs, but then neither does anyone else; this is the nub of the Hard Problem" (p. 5). Here Gray is referring to the so-called "hard problem of consciousness": How does consciousness arise from physical, brain processes?

It remains a mystery why this form of perception-related processing in the brain can bring with it subjectivity. Explaining why this is so is one of the greatest puzzles in science, one that has been tackled by the some of the greatest scientific minds—including Nobel Laureates Leon Cooper, Francis Crick, Gerald Edelman, Eric Kandel, and Charles Sherrington. At this stage of understanding, the field possesses not even an inkling regarding how physical events in the brain (or anywhere else) can give rise to a subjectivity of any kind (Godwin et al., 2013). As philosophers such as Karl Popper long ago noted, physical-objective systems are closed, neither needing nor able to accommodate the subjective material of the mind, especially the contents of the conscious mind that is so central to psychology.

The type of approach epitomized by Gray (2004), as well as the other theorists noted above, of creeping up on this hard problem may be starting to bear fruit. There does seem a convergence of theory and data, of which the mirror neuron work is one recent example, that can trace its origins at least back to the ideomotor theory of William James. More creeping will be needed, but our prey—the understanding of the function and form of the conscious sensorium—may well be within albeit indistinct sight, if not immediate grasp. This is especially the case regarding the outcome term of the three-term contingency, to which we now turn.

Although behaviorism avoided mention of mentalistic variables, consciousness is inevitably encountered when examining the three-term contingency. The outcome term, for example, is said to be a reinforcer if it increases the future likelihood of a behavior. This definition was criticized for being circular. That which renders something a reinforcer is that it increases the likelihood of a behavior. When one asks, "Why does a reinforcer increase the likelihood of behavior?" The answer is "Because it is a reinforcer." When one then asks, "Why is it a reinforcer?" the answer is "Because it increases the likelihood of a behavior."

As is clear, this line of reasoning is circular and it seems that there must be something else at play for something to be a reinforcer. In everyday life one would argue that this extra something may be pleasure, joy, relief, or some other kind of positive feeling. It is this kind of mentalistic variable that may play a role in operant conditioning and even in decision making (Loewenstein, 1996). Consider, for example, Hull's (1943) law of least work (or law of least effort), which states that given two means to reach some end, an organism tends to select the means associated with the least effort/aversiveness (see recent treatments in Botvinick, 2007). In this case the negative affect associated with effort (Morsella, Feinberg, Cigarchi,

Newton, & Williams, 2011) is one of the variables in the calculation regarding which course of action to take, as Loewenstein (2007) states.

> Humans have the capacity, perhaps uniquely, to deliberate about their own behavior and to make trade-offs between near-term and long-term rewards. Such deliberations require consciousness, but consciousness is not enough. To make trade-offs between rewards at different points in time, there has to be *something* to trade off. The subjective sensations of affective states provide that thing; they allow us to make conscious trade-offs between, for example, the immediate pleasure of indulging in dessert and being thin, or between smoking a cigarette and enjoying better health. We may not make such trade-offs optimally, but were it not for the subjective feelings associated with affective states, we would have no basis for making them at all. (p. 409)

As Loewenstein (2007) further notes, it is an undeniable aspect of conscious life that some states are preferred over others. The pleasure of drinking when thirsty is more positive than enduring pain. As quotidian as these examples are, they remain mysterious. Indeed, this is the very basis of the reinforcement-based theory of personality for which Gray is perhaps most famous (for reviews of this literature, see Corr, 2008; Corr & McNaughton, 2012). But how can a physical system *prefer* some states over others? That is, how can something be an affinity-based system in which the system prefers—and strives to be in—some states over others?

One may say that the northern pole of magnet A prefers to be adjacent to the southern pole of another magnet, but few would propose that magnet A prefers subjectively such a situation. That some physical systems, such as the nervous system, have inclinations of this kind remains outside of our current explanatory scope (Shallice, 1972). Chomsky (1988) adds that unlike machines, which are compelled to act in one way or another, we humans can also be *inclined* to act in a certain way. It is this peculiar state of being inclined to act one way, but to not act overtly, that currently remains unexplained from a mechanistic point of view. Gray (2005; Gray, Williams, Nunn, & Baron-Cohen, 1997) astutely points out that because of such undeniable mentalistic variables (positive and negative subjective states), a strict functionalistic account of nervous function in which understanding is based solely on the association between objective variables (e.g., neural activity and behavior), without invoking the physical processes underlying consciousness (e.g., Dennett, 1991), does not provide a complete picture of nervous function.

Gray's Insights About Consciousness from Synesthesia

To make this argument, Gray (2005) entertains the phenomenon of synesthesia. In this phenomenon sensory qualities from one modality (e.g., color) are experienced when perceiving stimuli from another modality (sound). For example, a synesthete may reliably experience the color red when hearing a high-pitched sound or when seeing the letter *A* (Gray et al., 1997). In synesthesia two people may experience different quale toward the same object, even though the overt behavior of both people may be the same toward the object. For example, when perceiving an apple, John may have the experience of Rachel's *blue*, and Rachel may experience what John experiences as *red*. Yet both Rachel and John refer to the apple as *red*. According to Gray et al. (1997), this provides evidence against a strict interpretation of functionalism (e.g., Dennett, 1991) in which consciousness is directly tied to overt behavior.

Regarding the mystery of consciousness, one may argue that the real mystery is not so much the existence of an affinity-based system, but rather the subjectivity that is associated with the inclinations of such a system. From this standpoint subjectivity is the unsolved puzzle regarding not only inclinations, but all brain processing—including color perception, music perception, and other conscious states (the very states that make human life worthwhile). As mentioned in note 1, an organism possesses subjectivity (or basic consciousness) if there is *something it is like* to be that organism. One may argue that the real puzzle is not how a physical thing could prefer to be in one state versus another, but how such a preference could be experienced subjectively, which is part of a larger question: how could anything ever have a subjective experience of any kind?

Nevertheless, it seems that the three-term contingency—our best conceptual account explaining how favorable outcomes can increase the likelihood of a given R in the presence of a given S_D—requires mention of mentalistic states in order to explain everyday operant conditioning in humans. Why should there be any central states in operant conditioning when all that needs to occur for instrumental learning is for the connection between S_D and R to be strengthened?

Function of Central States

The case for central states was made long ago by Neal Miller (1959), who claimed that central states render the nervous system more efficient in terms of its many connectivities. This proposal is obvious in the following scenario.

Imagine a simplified nervous system that only experiences two inclinations: to approach and to avoid. Now consider that in the simplified environment of this organism, there are eight discriminative stimuli, four of which (such as food) should be approached and four of which (such as noxious stimuli) should be avoided (Figure 2, top left). In addition to these eight discriminative stimuli, there are several different potential motor responses, some for approach and some for avoidance (Figure 2, top right).

Miller reasoned that it would be inefficient in terms of processing speed and wiring for there to be direct connections between all S_Ds and all potential Rs. Instead Miller proposed that it would be more efficient for the inputs and outputs to be connected to a central state (Figure 2, bottom), one for the state of "approach" and one for the state of "avoid." These two states obviously resemble positive and negative affect, respectively (Frijda, 1986). This would be even more true in an actual nervous system, in which there is a larger set of discriminative stimuli and potential responses. Which particular *R* is selected may depend on contextual details (e.g., a rat freezing, fleeing, or attacking, depending on the context). Once the central states are established, then, depending on context, the appropriate action can be selected. In some contexts an organism should freeze when under threat; in other circumstances an organism should flee (Corr, 2011, 2013).

The view that central states may serve such a functional role in the nervous system, and that these states may involve consciousness, whose contents are often "projected" on to an apparently external world (Merker, 2007), is consistent with the aforementioned integration consensus about the function of consciousness. According to the consensus, conscious states integrate information processes that would otherwise be independent. The consensus is consistent with evidence from neurology, neuroscience, and psychology (see Zarolia, Tomory, Rosen, & Morsella, this volume) showing that (a) consciously mediated actions involve more information integration than unconsciously mediated actions; (b) conscious states involve a wider network of brain activations than unconscious states; and (c) conscious perceptual information processing involves the integrating, or binding, of more kinds of information than unconscious perceptual processing (see a review in Godwin et al., 2013). The information involved in the conscious state is available to multiple systems, much as information broadcast on television is available to many viewers who can act toward the information as they like, depending on their interests. In other words, the systems that have access to the information must evaluate the information and re-

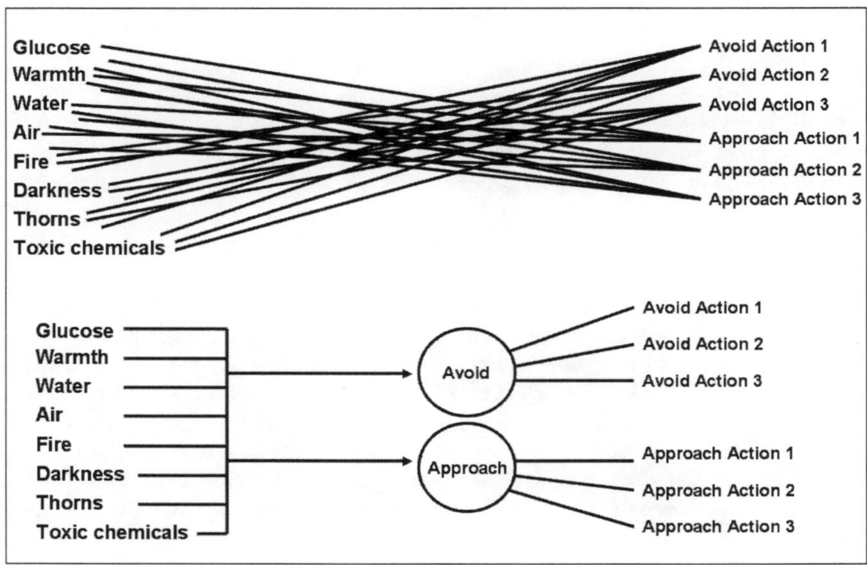

Figure 2. Schematic of Neal Miller's theorizing that direct connections between discriminative stimuli and responses (top) yield a framework that is less efficient than one invoking central states (bottom).

spond to it according to their concerns (Frijda, 1986; Morsella, 2005). Sometimes conscious content can cause systems to provide additional content (which can then too become conscious) or to generate action plans, which can influence behavior directly or indirectly—as in consciously experienced inclinations.

It has been proposed that the integration involving consciousness is intimately related to the skeletal muscle effector system (Morsella, 2005), which, by no accident, has been called voluntary muscle. Interestingly, this effector has been associated with operant conditioning more than any other effector system.[11]

With all this in mind, we will attempt to synthesize the various frameworks that we have discussed—Gray's comparator model, ideomotor theory, the three-term contingency, Miller's central states, and the integration consensus about conscious processing. In doing so, it is clear that these frameworks have much in common.

A New Synthesis

It is a fairly straightforward process to integrate all frameworks into one overarching framework. Let us begin by revisiting the sequence of stages outlined in the comparator model. As mentioned above, in some ways the sequence is the mirror image of that of ideomotor models. In this framework the sequence is as follows.

> *Unconscious motor programs* [Stage 1] → *conscious action effects* [Stage 2], *which are perceptual-like and can include both afference and re-afference* → *comparator process* [Stage 3] → *entry into consciousness of, say, mismatching perceptual consequences or an error signal, as seen in the experience of pain* [Stage 4].

We will present the sequence again but combine it with the sequence of ideomotor models, such that the actor can willfully repeat an expressed action intentionally. This would occur, for example, if, while dancing or playing the drums, one exhibited a strange and unintentional move that led to a favorable outcome, an outcome that should be repeated. In addition, we will add elements

---

[11] Many kinds of information in the nervous system can be integrated unconsciously. Unconscious integrations can involve smooth muscle, such as in the pupillary reflex (see evidence in Morsella, Gray, Krieger, & Bargh, 2009), and intersensory processing. For example, the McGurk effect (McGurk & MacDonald, 1976) involves unconscious interactions between visual and auditory processes: An observer views a speaker mouthing *ba* while presented with the sound *ga*. Surprisingly, the observer is unaware of any intersensory interaction, perceiving only *da*. Similar consciously impenetrable interactions are exemplified in countless other intersensory phenomena (see Morsella, 2005, Appendix A), including the popular ventriloquism effect, in which visual and auditory inputs regarding the source of a sound interact unconsciously (cf. Vroomen & de Gelder, 2003). It appears that the information that requires conscious integration is intimately related to skeletal muscle action, or skeletomotor control (Morsella, Gray et al., 2009; Morsella, Wilson et al., 2009).

of the three-term contingency—specifically, the outcome variable. The resultant sequence is as follows.

> *Unconscious motor programs* [Stage 1] → *conscious action effects* [Stage 2] → *comparator process* [Stage 3] → *entry into consciousness of, say, positive affect (outcome)* [Stage 4] → *activation of representation of conscious action effects* [Stage 5] → *unconscious motor programs* [Stage 6] → *conscious action effects* [Stage 7] → *comparator process* [Stage 8] → *entry into consciousness of, say, positive affect (outcome) from repeating action successfully* [Stage 9].

There are several features in the model that are worthy of some reflection. First, it is no accident that Stages 2, 4, 5, 7, and 9—stages in which information must be evaluated by diverse systems in the brain—involve consciousness, which is consistent with the integration consensus. Second, the conscious states of these stages resemble the central states to which Miller (1959) alluded, especially the outcome variables (e.g., positive or negative affect). Third, consistent with Morsella (2005), the action-related conscious states in Stages 5–9 influence behavior only through skeletal muscle. Fourth, one can appreciate that efference generation is unconscious and that the actor only has conscious access to the representations of action effects, which are perceptual-like (Gray, 2004) and are experienced after action production (as in the comparator model) and can be experienced before action production (as in ideomotor control).

Regarding the limited information to which the actor has access, James (1890/1950) proposes that—in behavioral control—all *the will* can do is pay attention to the representation of one action effect versus another. It is by this allotment of attention that the actor can, through ideomotor mechanisms, influence behavior intentionally: activation (through attention) to the representation of a given action effect will lead to the expression of that action through unconscious motor control. This, of course, fails to occur if there is simultaneously the activation of a representation of an incompatible action effect (James, 1890/1950; Lotze, 1852). In this way behavioral control is only through mental control, involving perceptual-like representations (Gray, 1995). As a pleasing by-product of this analysis, our model assigns a causal role to attention—viz., to recruit processing resources toward salient areas of the phenomenal field and by so doing appropriate affording automatic actions. It is perhaps no surprise that we "pay attention" to what we consider to be important.

CONCLUSION

In this chapter we revisited Gray's (1995) pioneering comparator model of consciousness, which focuses on the control of behavior and the contents of consciousness. We then combined this model with that of ideomotor theory, which complements the comparator model in several respects. For instance, it explains how the architecture of something like the comparator model could illuminate the mechanisms underlying the intentional control of behavior. We also revisited the integration consensus and approaches in operant conditioning, which explain the function of consciousness and how outcomes can influence future behaviors, respectively. Both the comparator model and ideomotor theory posit that it is perceptual-like content that is conscious. The integration consensus explains why this is so: it is because this is the content that is the most communicable, the most capable of being detected and processed by multiple systems (Bargh & Morsella, 2010; Fodor, 1983).

What no account to date has been able to explain is why subjectivity must be part of this process. At this stage of understanding, we propose that more knowledge about the limitations of the hardware of the nervous function may reveal why something as strange as consciousness was selected in evolution to perform an integrative—albeit circumscribed—role. From this viewpoint, just as intrapsychic conflict is not something that an engineer would ever program into a von Neumann computer, but in the course of evolution natural selection may have selected it as a solution for biological systems having slow processing units (i.e., neurons; Livnat & Pippenger, 2006), perhaps—given the constraints and limits of biological function—consciousness is actually a clever solution for the challenges faced by the nervous system.

REFERENCES

Anderson, A. K., & Phelps, E. A. (2002). Is the human amygdala critical for the subjective experience of emotion? Evidence of intact dispositional affect in patients with amygdala lesions. *Journal of Cognitive Neuroscience, 14*, 709–720.

Baars, B. J. (1988). *A cognitive theory of consciousness*. Cambridge, UK: Cambridge University Press.

Baars, B. J. (2002). The conscious access hypothesis: Origins and recent evidence. *Trends in Cognitive Sciences, 6*, 47–52.

Baddeley, A. D. (2007). *Working memory, thought, and action*. Oxford, UK: Oxford University Press.

Bargh, J. A., & Morsella, E. (2008). The unconscious mind. *Perspectives on Psychological Science, 3*, 73–79.

Bargh, J. A., & Morsella, E. (2010). Unconscious behavioral guidance systems. In C. R. Agnew, D. E. Carlston, W. G. Graziano, & J. R. Kelly, (Eds.), *Then a miracle occurs: Focusing on behavior in social psychological theory and research* (pp. 89–118). New York: Oxford University Press.

Barsalou, L. W. (1999). Perceptual symbol systems. *Behavioral and Brain Sciences, 22*, 577–609.

Berti, A., & Pia, L. (2006). Understanding motor awareness through normal and pathological behavior. *Current Directions in Psychological Science, 15*, 245–250.

Block, N. (1995). On a confusion about a function of consciousness. *Behavioral and Brain Sciences, 18*, 227–287.

Boly, M., Garrido, M. I., Gosseries, O., Bruno, M-A., Boveroux, P., Schnakers, C., et al. (2011). Preserved feedforward but impaired top-down processes in the vegetative state. *Science, 332*, 858–862.

Botvinick, M. (2007). Conflict monitoring and decision making: Reconciling two perspectives on anterior cingulate function. *Cognitive, Affective, and Behavioral Neuroscience, 7*, 356–366.

Chambon, V., Wenke, D., Fleming, S. M., Prinz, W., & Haggard, P. (2013). An online neural substrate for sense of agency. *Cerebral Cortex, 23*, 1031–1037.

Chomsky, N. (1988). *Language and problems of knowledge: The Managua lectures*. Cambridge, MA: MIT Press.

Christensen, M. S., Lundbye-Jensen, J., Geertsen, S. S., Petersen, T. H., Paulson, O. B., & Nielsen, J. B. (2007). Premotor cortex modulates somatosensory cortex during voluntary movements without proprioceptive feedback. *Nature Neuroscience, 10*, 417–419.

Clark, A. (2002). Is seeing all it seems? Action, reason and the grand illusion. *Journal of Consciousness Studies, 9*, 181–202.

Cooper, A. D., Sterling, C. P., Bacon, M. P., & Bridgeman, B. (2012). Does action affect perception or memory? *Vision Research, 62*, 235–240.

Corr, P. J. (2008). The reinforcement sensitivity theory (RST): Introduction. In P. J. Corr (Ed.), *The reinforcement sensitivity theory of personality* (pp. 1–43). Cambridge, UK: Cambridge University Press.

Corr, P. J. (2011). Anxiety: Splitting the phenomenological atom. *Personality and Individual Differences, 50*, 889–897.

Corr, P. J. (2013). Approach and avoidance behavior: Multiple systems and their interactions. *Emotion Review, 5*, 285–290.

Corr, P. J., & McNaughton, N. (2012). Neuroscience and approach/avoidance personality traits: A two stage (valuation–motivation) approach. *Neuroscience and Biobehavioral Reviews, 36*, 2339–2354.

Crick, F. (1995). *The astonishing hypothesis: The scientific search for the soul*. New York: Touchstone.

Damasio, A. R. (1989). Time-locked multiregional retroactivation: A systems-level proposal for the neural substrates of recall and recognition. *Cognition, 33*, 25–62.

Dehaene, S., & Naccache, L. (2001). Towards a cognitive neuroscience of consciousness: Basic evidence and a workspace framework. *Cognition, 79*, 1–37.

Del Cul, A., Baillet, S., & Dehaene, S. (2007). Brain dynamics underlying the nonlinear threshold for access to consciousness. *PLoS Biology, 5*, e260.

Dennett, D. C. (1991). *Consciousness explained*. Boston: Little, Brown.

Desmurget, M., Reilly, K. T., Richard, N., Szathmari, A., Mottolese, C., & Sirigu, A. (2009). Movement intention after parietal cortex stimulation in humans. *Science, 324*, 811–813.

Desmurget, M., & Sirigu, A. (2010). A parietal-premotor network for movement intention and motor awareness. *Trends in Cognitive Sciences, 13*, 411–419.

Doesburg, S. M., Green, J. L., McDonald, J. J., & Ward, L. M. (2009). Rhythms of consciousness: Binocular rivalry reveals large-scale oscillatory network dynamics mediating visual perception. *PLoS, 4*, 1–14.

Fecteau, J. H., Chua, R., Franks, I., & Enns, J. T. (2001). Visual awareness and the online modification of action. *Canadian Journal of Experimental Psychology, 55*, 104–110.

Firestone, C., & Scholl, B. J. (2014). "Top-down" effects where none should be found: The El Greco fallacy in perception research. *Psychological Science, 25*, 38–46.

Fodor, J. A. (1983). *Modularity of mind: An essay on faculty psychology*. Cambridge, MA: MIT Press.

Fourneret, P., & Jeannerod, M. (1998). Limited conscious monitoring of motor performance in normal subjects. *Neuropsychologia, 36*, 1133–1140.

Franz, V. H., Gegenfurtner, K. R., Bülthoff, H. H., & Fahle, M. (2000). Grasping visual illusions: No evidence for a dissociation between perception and action. *Psychological Science, 11*, 20–25.

Freeman, W. J. (1991). The physiology of perception. *Scientific American,* February, 78–85.

Fried, I., Katz, A., McCarthy, G., Sass, K. J., Williamson, P., Spencer, S. S., & Spencer, D. D. (1991). Functional organization of human supplementary motor cortex studied by electrical stimulation. *Journal of Neuroscience, 11*, 3656–3666.

Frijda, N. H. (1986). *The emotions*. Cambridge, UK: Cambridge University Press.

Fuster, J. M. (2003). *Cortex and mind: Unifying cognition.* New York: Oxford University Press.

Godwin, C. A., Gazzaley, A., & Morsella, E. (2013). Homing in on the brain mechanisms linked to consciousness: Buffer of the perception-and-action interface. In A. Pereira and D. Lehmann (Eds.), *The unity of mind, brain and world: Current perspectives on a science of consciousness* (pp. 43–76). Cambridge, UK: Cambridge University Press.

Goodale, M., & Milner, D. (2004). *Sight unseen: An exploration of conscious and unconscious vision*. New York: Oxford University Press.

Goodhew, S. C., Dux, P. E., Lipp, O. V., & Visser, T. A. W. (2012). Understanding recovery from object substitution masking. *Cognition, 122*, 405–415.

Gottlieb, J., & Mazzoni, P. (2004). Neuroscience: Action, illusion, and perception. *Science, 303*, 317–318.

Gray, J. A. (1982a). *The neuropsychology of anxiety: An enquiry into the functions of the septo-hippocampal system*. Oxford, UK: Oxford University Press.

Gray, J. A. (1982b). Précis of *The Neuropsychology of Anxiety: An Enquiry into the Functions of the Septo-Hippocampal System*. *Behavioral and Brain Sciences, 5*, 469–484.

Gray, J. A. (1995). The contents of consciousness: A neuropsychological conjecture. *Behavioral and Brain Sciences, 18,* 659–676.

Gray, J. A. (1998). Integrating schizophrenia. *Schizophrenia Bulletin, 24,* 249–266.

Gray, J. A. (2002). The sound of one hand clapping. *Psyche, 8*, 8–11. http://psyche.cs.monash.edu.au/v8/psyche-8-11-gray.html.

Gray, J. A. (2004). *Consciousness: Creeping up on the hard problem.* New York: Oxford University Press.

Gray, J. A. (2005). Synesthesia: A window on the hard problem of consciousness. In L. C. Robertson & N. Sagiv (Eds.), *Synesthesia: Perspectives from cognitive neuroscience* (pp. 127–146). New York: Oxford University Press.

Gray, J. A., Feldon, J., Rawlins, J. N. P., Hemsley, D. R., & Smith, A. D. (1991). The neuropsychology of schizophrenia. *Behavioral and Brain Sciences, 14*, 1–20.

Gray, J. A., & McNaughton, N. (2000). *The neuropsychology of anxiety: An enquiry into the functions of the septo-hippocampal system* (2nd ed.). Oxford, UK: Oxford University Press.

Gray, J. A., Williams, S. C. R., Nunn, J., & Baron-Cohen, S. (1997). Possible implications of synaesthesia for the hard question of consciousness. In S. Baron-Cohen & J. E. Harrison (Eds.), *Synaesthesia: Classic and contemporary readings* (pp. 173–181). Oxford, UK: Blackwell.

Graziano, M. S. A. (2001). Awareness of space. *Nature, 411*, 903–904.

Greenwald, A. G. (1970). Sensory feedback mechanisms in performance control: With special reference to the ideomotor mechanism. *Psychological Review, 77*, 73–99.

Grossberg, S. (1999). The link between brain learning, attention, and consciousness. *Consciousness and Cognition, 8*, 1–44.

Harleß, E. (1861). Der apparat des willens [The apparatus of the will]. *Zeitshrift für Philosophie und Philosophische Kritik, 38,* 499–507.

Heath, M., Neely, K. A., Yakimishyn, J., & Binsted, G. (2008). Visuomotor memory is independent of conscious awareness of target features. *Experimental Brain Research, 188*, 517–527.

Heilman, K. M., Watson, R. T., & Valenstein, E. (2003). Neglect: Clinical and anatomic issues. In T. E. Feinberg & M. J. Farah (Eds.), *Behavioral neurology and neuropsychology* (2nd ed., pp. 303–311). New York: McGraw-Hill.

Hesslow, G. (2002). Conscious thought as simulation of behavior and perception. *Trends in Cognitive Sciences, 6,* 242–247.

Hommel, B. (1998). Perceiving one's own actions—and what it leads to. In J. S. Jordan (Ed.), *Systems theories and a priori aspects of perception* (pp. 143–179). Amsterdam: Elsevier/North-Holland.

Hommel, B. (2009). Action control according to TEC (theory of event coding). *Psychological Research, 73*, 512–526.

Hommel, B., & Elsner, B. (2009). Acquisition, representation, and control of action. In E. Morsella, J. A. Bargh, & P. M. Gollwitzer (Eds.), *Oxford handbook of human action* (pp. 371–398). New York: Oxford University Press.

Hommel, B., Müsseler, J., Aschersleben, G., & Prinz, W. (2001). The theory of event coding: A framework for perception and action planning. *Behavioral and Brain Sciences, 24*, 849–937.

Hull, C. L. (1943). *Principles of behavior*. New York: Appleton-Century-Crofts.

Iacoboni, M. (2005). Understanding others: Imitation, language, and empathy. In S. Hurley & N. Chater (Eds.), *Perspectives on imitation: From mirror neurons to memes* (pp. 77–99). Cambridge, MA: MIT Press.

James, W. (1950). *The principles of psychology*. New York: Dover. (Original work published in 1890)

Jackendoff, R. (1987). *Consciousness and the computational mind.* Cambridge, MA: MIT Press.

Jeannerod, M. (2003). Simulation of action as a unifying concept for motor cognition. In S. H. Johnson-Frey (Ed.), *Taking action: Cognitive neuroscience perspectives on intentional acts.* Cambridge, MA: MIT Press.

Jeannerod, M. (2006). *Motor cognition: What action tells the self.* New York: Oxford University Press.

Johnson, H., & Haggard P. (2005). Motor awareness without perceptual awareness. *Neuropsychologia, 43*, 227–237.

Johnson, K. L., & Shiffrar, M. (2013). *People watching: Social, perceptual, and neurophysiological studies of body perception*. New York: Oxford University Press.

Jordan, J. S. (2009). Forward-looking aspects of perception-action coupling as a basis for embodied communication. *Discourse Processes, 46*, 127–144.

Kern, M. K., Jaradeh, S., Arndorfer, R. C., & Shaker, R. (2001). Cerebral cortical representation of reflexive and volitional swallowing in humans. *American Journal of Physiology: Gastrointestinal and Liver Physiology, 280*, G354–G360.

Klein, D. B. (1970). *A history of scientific psychology: Its origins and philosophical backgrounds*. New York: Basic Books.

Koch, C. (2004). *The quest for consciousness: A neurobiological approach*. Englewood, CO: Roberts & Company.

Koffka, K. (1922). Perception: An introduction to the *Gestalt-Theorie*. *Psychological Bulletin, 19*, 531–585.

Lashley, K. S. (1942). The problem of cerebral organization in vision. In H. Kluver (Ed.), *Visual mechanisms* (Biological Symposia, Vol. 7, pp. 301–322). Lancaster, PA: Cattell Press.

LeDoux, J. E. (1996). *The emotional brain: The mysterious underpinnings of emotional life*. New York: Simon & Schuster.

LeDoux, J. E. (2008). Emotional colouration of consciousness: How feelings come about. In L. W. Weiskrantz & M. Davies (Eds.), *Frontiers of* consciousness (pp. 69–130). Oxford, UK: Oxford University Press.

Levelt, W. J. M. (1989). *Speaking: From intention to articulation*. Cambridge, MA: MIT Press.

Libet, B. (2004). *Mind time: The temporal factor in consciousness*. Cambridge, MA: Harvard University Press.

Liu, G., Chua, R., & Enns, J. T. (2008). Attention for perception and action: Task interference for action planning, but not for online control. *Experimental Brain Research, 185*, 709–717.

Livnat, A., & Pippenger, N. (2006). An optimal brain can be composed of conflicting agents. *Proceedings of the National Academy of Sciences, 103*, 3198–3202.

Llinás, R. R., & Ribary, U. (2001). Consciousness and the brain: The thalamocortical dialogue in health and disease. *Annals of the New York Academy of Sciences, 929*, 166–175.

Loewenstein, G. (1996). Out of control: Visceral influences on behavior. *Organizational Behavior and Human Decision Processes, 65*, 272–292.

Loewenstein, G. (2007). Defining affect. *Social Science Information, 46*, 405–410.

Lotze, R. H. (1852). *Medizinische Psychologie oder Physiologie der Seele* [Medical psychology or physiology of the soul]. Leipzig, Germany: Weidmann'sche Buchhandlung.

McGurk, H., & MacDonald, J. (1976). Hearing lips and seeing voices. *Nature, 264*, 746–748.

McKay, L. C., Evans, K. C., Frackowiak, R. S. J., & Corfield, D. R. (2003). Neural correlates of voluntary breathing in humans determined using functional magnetic resonance imaging. *Journal of Applied Physiology, 95*, 1170–1178.

Merker, B. (2007). Consciousness without a cerebral cortex: A challenge for neuroscience and medicine. *Behavioral and Brain Sciences, 30*, 63–134.

Miall, R. C. (2003). Connecting mirror neuron and forward models. *NeuroReport, 14*, 1–3.

Miller, G. A., Galanter, E., & Pribram, K. H. (1960). *Plans and the structure of behavior*. New York: Henry Holt.

Miller, N. E. (1959). Liberalization of basic S-R concepts: Extensions to conflict behavior, motivation and social learning. In S. Koch (Ed.), *Psychology: A study of a science, Vol. 2* (pp. 196–292). New York: McGraw-Hill.

Milner, B. (1966). Amnesia following operation on the temporal lobes. In C. W. M. Whitty & O. L. Zangwill (Eds.), *Amnesia* (pp. 109–133). London: Butterworths.

Milner, A. D., & Goodale, M. (1995). *The visual brain in action*. New York: Oxford University Press.

Moore, J. W., Wegner, D. M., & Haggard, P. (2009). Modulating the sense of agency with external cues. *Consciousness and Cognition, 18*, 1056–1064.

Morsella, E. (2005). The function of phenomenal states: Supramodular interaction theory. *Psychological Review, 112*, 1000–1021.

Morsella, E., & Bargh, J. A. (2010). What is an output? *Psychological Inquiry, 21*, 354–370.

Morsella, E., Feinberg, G. H., Cigarchi, S., Newton, J. W., & Williams, L. E. (2011). Sources of avoidance motivation: Valence effects from physical effort and mental rotation. *Motivation and Emotion, 35*, 296–305.

Morsella, E., Gray, J. R., Krieger, S. C., & Bargh, J. A. (2009). The essence of conscious conflict: Subjective effects of sustaining incompatible intentions. *Emotion, 9*, 717–728.

Morsella, E., Lanska, M., Berger, C. C., & Gazzaley, A. (2009). Indirect cognitive control through top-down activation of perceptual symbols. *European Journal of Social Psychology, 39*, 1173–1177.

Morsella, E., Montemayor, C., Hubbard, J., & Zarolia, P. (2010). Conceptual knowledge: Grounded in sensorimotor states, or a disembodied deus ex machina? *Behavioral and Brain Sciences, 33*, 455–456.

Morsella, E., Wilson, L. E., Berger, C. C., Honhongva, M., Gazzaley, A., & Bargh, J. A. (2009). Subjective aspects of cognitive control at different stages of processing. *Attention, Perception, and Psychophysics, 71*, 1807– 824.

Most, S. B., Scholl, B. J., Clifford, E., & Simons, D. J. (2005). What you see is what you set: Sustained inattentional blindness and the capture of awareness. *Psychological Review, 112*, 217–242.

Müller, J. (1843). *Elements of physiology*. Philadelphia: Lea & Blanchard.

Nagel, T. (1974). What is it like to be a bat? *Philosophical Review, 83*, 435–450.

Neisser, U. (1967). *Cognitive psychology*. New York: Appleton-Century-Crofts.

Obhi, S., Planetta, P., & Scantlebury, J. (2009). On the signals underlying conscious awareness of action. *Cognition, 110*, 65–73.

Öhman, A., Carlsson, K., Lundqvist, D., & Ingvar, M. (2007). On the unconscious subcortical origin of human fear. *Physiology and Behavior, 92*, 180–185.

Öhman, A., & Mineka, S. (2001). Fears, phobias, and preparedness: Toward an evolved module of fear and fear learning. *Psychological Review, 108*, 483–522.

Ortinski, P., & Meador, K. J. (2004). Neuronal mechanisms of conscious awareness. *Neurological Review, 61*, 1017–1020.

Pinker, S. (1997). *How the mind works*. New York: Norton.

Poehlman, T. A., Jantz, T. K., & Morsella, E. (2012). Adaptive skeletal muscle action requires anticipation and "conscious broadcasting." *Frontiers in Psychology, 3*, 369.

Rizzolatti, G., Sinigaglia, C., & Anderson, F. (2008). *Mirrors in the brain: How our minds share actions, emotions, and experience*. New York: Oxford University Press.

Rosenbaum, D. A. (2002). Motor control. In H. Pashler (Series Ed.) & S. Yantis (Vol. Ed.), *Stevens' handbook of experimental psychology: Vol. 1. Sensation and perception* (3rd ed., pp. 315–339). New York: Wiley.

Rossetti, Y. (2001). Implicit perception in action: Short-lived motor representation of space. In P. G. Grossenbacher (Ed.), *Finding consciousness in the brain: A neurocognitive approach* (pp. 133–181). Amsterdam: Benjamins.

Schacter, D. L., & Addis, D. R. (2007). The cognitive neuroscience of constructive memory: Remembering the past and imagining the future. *Philosophical Transactions of the Royal Society of London, Series B: Biological Sciences, 362*, 773–786.

Sergent, C., & Dahaene, S. (2004). Is consciousness a gradual phenomenon? Evidence for an all-or-none bifurcation during the attentional blink. *Psychological Science, 15*, 720–728.

Shallice, T. (1972). Dual functions of consciousness. *Psychological Review, 79*, 383–393.

Sheerer, E. (1984). Motor theories of cognitive structure: A historical review. In W. Prinz & A. F. Sanders (Eds.), *Cognition and motor processes*. Berlin: Springer-Verlag.

Sherrington, C. S. (1906). *The integrative action of the nervous system*. New Haven, CT: Yale University Press.

Sherrington, C. S. (1941). *Man on his nature*. New York: Macmillan.

Skinner, B. F. (1953). *Science and human behavior*. New York: Macmillan.

Slevc, L. R., & Ferreira, V. S. (2006). Halting in single word production: A test of the perceptual loop theory of speech monitoring. *Journal of Memory and Language, 54*, 515–540.

Stottinger, E., & Perner, J. (2006). Dissociating size representation for action and for conscious judgment: Grasping visual illusions without apparent obstacles. *Consciousness and Cognition, 15*, 269–284.

Suhler, C. L., & Churchland, P. S. (2009). Control: Conscious and otherwise. *Trends in Cognitive Sciences, 13*, 341–347.

Taylor, J. A., & Ivry, R. B. (2013). Implicit and explicit processes in motor learning. In W. Prinz, M. Beisert, & A. Herwig (Eds.), *Action science* (p. 63–87). Cambridge, MA: MIT Press.

Tononi, G., & Edelman, G. M. (1988). Consciousness and complexity. *Science, 282*, 1846–1851.

Tranel, D., & Damasio, A. R. (1985). Knowledge without awareness: An autonomic index of facial recognition by prosopagnosics. *Science, 228*, 1453–1454.

Tye, M. (1999). Phenomenal consciousness: The explanatory gap as cognitive illusion. *Mind, 108*, 705–725.

Ulhaas, P. J., Pipa, G., Lima, B., Melloni, L., Neuenschwander, S., Nikolic, D., et al. (2009). Neural synchrony in cortical networks: History, concept and current status. *Frontiers in Integrative Neuroscience, 3*, 17.

Varela, F., Lachaux, J. P., Rodriguez, E., & Martinerie, J. (2001). The brainweb: Phase synchronization and large-scale integration. *National Review of Neuroscience, 2*, 229–239.

Velmans, M. (1991). Is human information processing conscious? *Behavioral and Brain Sciences, 14*, 651–669.

Velmans, M. (2000). *Understanding consciousness*. London: Routledge.

Vroomen, J., & de Gelder, B. (2003). Visual motion influences the contingent auditory motion aftereffect. *Psychological Science, 14*, 357–361.

Vygotsky, L. S. (1962). *Thought and language* (E. Hanfmann & G. Vakar, Trans.). Cambridge, MA: MIT Press.

Wraga, M., Creem, S. H., & Proffitt, D. R. (2000). Perception-action dissociations of a walkable Müller–Lyer configuration. *Psychological Science, 11*, 239–243.

Yates, J. (1985). The content of awareness is a model of the world. *Psychological Review, 92*, 249–284.

Zeki, S., & Bartels, A. (1999). Toward a theory of visual consciousness. *Consciousness and Cognition, 8*, 225–259.

CHAPTER 2

The Subjective Aspects of Self-Control

Theory and Experimental Paradigms

Pareezad Zarolia
Jessica J. Tomory
Howard J. Rosen
Ezequiel Morsella

INTRODUCTION

Recent empirical and theoretical advances have begun to shed light on the basic mechanisms underlying control, as in cognitive control and self-control. These advances reveal it is no accident that in the history of neuroscience, neurology, and psychology, control has been associated with both conscious processing and voluntary muscle (i.e., skeletal muscle). Much of this progress has stemmed from response interference paradigms (e.g., the classic Stroop task; Stroop, 1935), in which cognitive control is challenged systematically by experimental manipulations. In this chapter we review a subset of these empirical and theoretical advances and introduce some initial data from an experimental project that extends current interference paradigms. First, however, it is essential to discuss the nature of the most complicated phenomenon at hand—conscious processing.

Personality and Control edited by Philip J. Corr, Małgorzata Fajkowska, Michael W. Eysenck, and Agata Wytykowska. Eliot Werner Publications, Clinton Corners, New York, 2015.

CONSCIOUS PROCESSING

At this stage of scientific understanding, conscious processing is easier to identify than define (see definition of consciousness in note 1, Corr & Morsella, this volume). Regarding its identification, it is obvious that consciousness is associated with some nervous events (e.g., pain, yellow afterimages, and the urge to perform an action) but not others (e.g., the pupillary reflex, peristalsis). Not all physical processes in the body are associated with consciousness.

How such consciousness emerges from nervous events remains one of the most daunting challenges in science (Roach, 2005) but some progress has been made. Contemporary research has reached the consensus that conscious processing is associated with only a subset of all brain processes (see review in Godwin, Gazzaley, & Morsella, 2013). Much of brain function, including complicated motor and perceptual processing, occurs unconsciously (Bargh & Morsella, 2008; see a review of the evidence in Morsella & Bargh, 2011).

CONSCIOUSNESS AND ACTION CONTROL

Investigations into the links between consciousness and control have revealed that one is usually unconscious of the complicated motor programs that, in action production, calculate which muscles should be activated at a given time (James, 1890; Johnson & Haggard, 2005; Rosenbaum, 2002; for a discussion of unconscious motor control, see Corr & Morsella, this volume).

Although much of action control is unconscious, some aspects of action control do perturb consciousness reliably—as when action-related mental imagery and urges (and other subjective inclinations) arise under conditions of action conflict. Regarding the latter, it has been demonstrated that the simultaneous activation of incompatible action plans, as when holding one's breath while underwater (where one is inclined to both inhale and not inhale) or performing the Stroop task (described below), reliably influence changes in consciousness (see quantitative review of evidence in Morsella, Berger, & Krieger, 2011). Such incompatible intentions lead to conscious conflicts (Morsella, 2005).

Conscious and Unconscious Conflicts

This stands in contrast to the conflicts involving smooth muscle (e.g., the pupillary reflex; cf., Morsella, Gray, Krieger, & Bargh, 2009) and perceptual processing, as in the case of ventriloquism and the McGurk effects (McGurk & MacDonald, 1976; see explanation of the McGurk effect in note 11, Corr & Morsella, this volume). The conflicts can be mediated unconsciously. However, in everyday life it is obvious that exerting self-control yields changes in conscious experience. There is a subjective cost to such control (Morsella, 2005), whereas no such subjectivity accompanies many other kinds of conflict in the nervous system (Morsella, Gray et al., 2009). For example, one is not fatigued (subjectively) when experiencing ventriloquism or the McGurk effect, but such is not the case when the conflict involves incompatible skeletal muscle plans (skeletomotor plans, for short).

The notion that incompatible skeletomotor plans must affect subjective experience is predicted by an action-based theoretical framework on the function of consciousness. The theoretical approach, supramodular interaction theory (SIT; Morsella, 2005), is based on the integration consensus (Sergent & Dehaene, 2004; Tononi, 2012; Tononi & Edelman, 1988; see discussion in Corr & Morsella, this volume). The consensus proposes that consciousness integrates neural activities and information-processing structures that would otherwise be independent. This consensus is supported by findings from diverse areas of research, including research on perceptual processing (Dehaene & Naccache, 2001; Del Cul, Baillet, & Dehaene, 2007), action (Kern et al., 2001; Ortinski & Meador, 2004), and anesthesia (Alkire, Hudetz, & Tononi, 2008; Boveroux et. al., 2010; Långsjö et al., 2012; Lee, Kim et al., 2009; Lewis et al., 2012; Schroter et al., 2012; Schrouff et al., 2011). In each of these fields, it has been demonstrated that conscious processing (e.g., of a perceptual representation) involves a wider network of brain regions than do comparable processes that are unconscious. (For further discussion of the integration consensus, see Corr & Morsella, this volume.)

One limitation of the integration consensus is that it does not distinguish conscious from unconscious integrations, which is the contribution of the SIT. Based on diverse kinds of evidence (see Morsella, 2005), the SIT specifies which kinds of integration require consciousness and which kinds do not. (The SIT is based on an unconventional perspective: instead of examining the processes giving rise to conscious perceptual representations, the approach works backward from overt action to the underlying, central processes.) Specifically, the SIT proposes that the primary function of conscious states is to permit a form of integration involving crosstalk and interaction among skeletomotor actional systems. Hence the activation of incompatible skeletomotor plans (e.g., to look both left *and* right) must trigger detectable changes in subjective experience. Although the SIT was intended to explain the subjective aspects of conflicts involving basic needs (e.g., the suppression of inhaling, eating, or micturating) and to contrast these conscious conflicts with unconscious conflicts (e.g., smooth muscle or intersensory conflicts), additional evidence for this framework is found in the innocuous and "cooler" (cf., Metcalfe & Mischel, 1999) conflicts that are instantiated by standard laboratory response interference paradigms.

From the standpoint of the SIT, in the nervous system there are three distinct kinds of integrations or "bindings" (Morsella & Bargh, 2011). Afference binding is the binding of perceptual processes and representations. This form of unconscious binding takes place in feature binding (e.g., the binding of shape to color; Zeki & Bartels, 1999) and intersensory binding, as in the McGurk effect mentioned above. Another form of binding, linking perceptual processing to action/motor processing, is known as efference binding (Haggard, Aschersleben, Gehrke, & Prinz, 2002). This kind of stimulus-response binding allows one to press a button when presented with a cue. Observation of reflexes and many laboratory experiments have shown that responding on the basis of efference binding can occur unconsciously (Morsella & Bargh, 2011). For example, Taylor and McCloskey (1990, 1996) demonstrated in several experiments that participants in a choice response time (RT) task could select the correct motor response (one of two button presses) when confronted with subliminal stimuli (Hallett, 2007). In many cases the stimuli are rendered subliminal through the technique of backward masking. The third kind of binding, efference-efference binding, occurs when two streams of efference binding are trying to influence skeletomotor action simultaneously (Morsella & Bargh, 2011). This occurs when one holds one's breath, suppresses uttering something, or voluntarily breathes faster for some reward.

Integrated and Unintegrated Actions

According to the SIT, it is the instantiation of conflicting efference-efference binding that requires consciousness. Consciousness is the "crosstalk" medium that allows conflicting actional processes to influence action collectively, leading to integrated actions (Morsella & Bargh, 2011) such as holding one's breath. Absent consciousness, behavior can be influenced by only one of the efference streams, leading to *un-integrated actions* such as unconsciously inhaling while underwater or reflexively removing one's hand from a hot object. One fruit of the SIT is an explanation of why skeletal muscle has been historically construed as voluntary muscle. From the standpoint of SIT, this effector is voluntary because its actions are directed by brain processes that—in order to be integrated and influence action collectively—must involve the conscious field, as described by the principle of parallel processes into skeletal muscle (PRISM; Morsella, 2005). Just as a prism can integrate various colors into one single, white light, the conscious field can integrate multiple inclinations (e.g., to inhale *and* not inhale) into one integrated action (e.g., holding one's breath). Without the conscious field, such integration breaks down and only one action inclination can influence overt action. PRISM correctly predicts that control involving emotional behaviors, sexual behaviors, parental behaviors, and addiction-related behaviors should perturb the conscious field since this form of control involves skeletomotor control. In synthesis, the SIT is unique in its ability to explain subjective data from (a) intersensory conflicts, (b) smooth muscle conflicts, and (c) conflicts from skeletomotor conflicts (e.g., holding one's breath and Stroop-like interference). The SIT also explains why skeletal muscle is voluntary muscle.

At this stage of understanding the thorny topic of consciousness and the brain, we focus only on the integrative role of consciousness within the context of immediate, simple actions (e.g., holding one's breath). However, one can appreciate that the integrative role of conscious processing, in which perceptual systems can interact with the incentive systems associated with various needs, may also benefit the evaluation of potential actions to be expressed in the future (see discussion in Corr & Morsella, this volume). In line with this view, it has been proposed that the function of conscious memory is not only to "travel down memory lane," but to simulate future potential courses of action (Schacter & Addis, 2007). Such simulations require an evaluative component that determines whether a potential outcome is favorable or not. Such an evaluation may require the crosstalk between systems that consciousness affords (Bargh & Morsella, 2008).

EVIDENCE FROM RESPONSE INTERFERENCE PARADIGMS

Additional support for the SIT is found in response interference paradigms, where it has been shown that incompatible action plans reliably produced theoretically predictable changes in consciousness. For example, evidence is found in the classic Stroop (Stroop, 1935) and flanker tasks (Eriksen & Eriksen, 1974), which will be described in tandem. In the Stroop task, one must name the color in which a word is written. When the word and color are incongruous (e.g., *red* in blue), response conflict leads to interference—such as increased response times, error rates, and participants' reported urges to make a mistake (a subjective measure of cognitive activity; Morsella, Berger et al., 2011; Morsella, Gray et al. 2009). This subjective measure reflects in part the changes in consciousness from the activation of incompatible action plans (Morsella, Gray et al., 2009). To record these subjective effects, after each trial participants are asked a question (e.g., "How strong was your urge to make a mistake?") and respond using a Likert scale, as explained below.

By contrast, when the color matches the word (e.g., *red* in red) or is presented on a neutral stimulus (e.g., an array of five X's), there is little or no such behavioral interference (Eidels, Townsend, & Algom, 2010; Roelofs, 2010) or subjective effects. As explained below, one limitation of the level of experimental control in Stroop-like paradigms is that the distractor effects are based on learning that occurred outside of the laboratory, sometimes over the course of a lifetime; in addition, Stroop-like tasks usually cannot discern the effects of different kinds of interference (e.g., perceptuo-semantic interference or interference at the level of response selection; Eriksen & Schultz, 1979).

The Flanker Task

These limitations are absent in variants of the classic flanker task (Eriksen & Eriksen, 1974). In this task one must respond to a visual target and disregard flanking distractors (flankers, for short). In one version of the task (Eriksen & Schultz, 1979), during flanker training participants are first trained to press one button with one finger (the index finger) when presented with the letter *S* or *M* and to press another button with another finger (the middle finger) when presented with the letter *P* or *H*. Participants are then instructed to respond to the stimulus presented in the center of an array and to disregard the flanking distractors. Interference (e.g., increased error rates, RTs, and urges to err) is strongest when distractors and targets are associated with different actions (response interference; RI), as in the case of *SSPSS*. Interference is substantially less when distractors and targets look different but are associated with the same response (perceptual interference; PI; Eriksen, 1995; Morsella, Wilson et al., 2009; van Veen, Cohen, Botvinick, Stenger, & Carter, 2001), as in the case of *SSMSS*. Shortest RTs occur in the *Identical* condition (e.g., *SSSSS*).

Unlike with the Stroop task, with the flanker task one can discern the consequences of different kinds of interference—as in the case of the contrast between PI and RI. For example, consistent with the patterns of results found by Eriksen and Schultz (1979) and Morsella, Wilson et al. (2009), van Veen et al. (2001) found that RI led to a mean RT of 624 ms ($SD = 79$) and PI led to a mean of 565 ms ($SD = 74$), with the difference between RI and PI being 59 ms. Similarly, in Morsella, Wilson et al. (2009) RI led to a mean RT of 734.01 ms ($SEM = 31.78$) and PI led to mean of 672.51 ms ($SEM = 33.52$), with the difference between RI and PI being 61.5 ms.

Evidence suggests that RI stems from the automatic, stimulus-triggered activation of action plans by distractors (DeSoto, Fabiani, Geary, & Gratton, 2001). Accordingly, psychophysiological research shows that competition in RI involves simultaneous activation of the brain areas associated with the target-related and distractor-related responses (DeSoto et al., 2001; Mattler, 2005). In addition, functional brain imaging research has shown that RI and PI have different neural signatures, with RI involving more activations in frontal cortex and regions associated with motor processes (van Veen & Carter, 2006; van Veen et al., 2001). In this way these subjective variants of the classic interference paradigms have revealed aspects of processing that could not be learned from RT or error rates alone (see review in Morsella, Berger et al., 2011).

One interesting example is the Stroop congruent condition. That urges to err are low for this condition is interesting because it is known that participants often do read the stimulus word inadvertently in that condition. "The experimenter (perhaps the participant as well) cannot discriminate which dimension gave rise to the response on a given congruent trial" (MacLeod & MacDonald, 2000, p. 386).[1] Urges to err for the congruent condition are comparable to those of the neutral condition of the Stroop task, in which the color is presented on an illegible letter string (Morsella, Wilson et al., 2009). In a within-subjects Stroop manipulation, urges to err by reading the word were greater when words were presented in standard black font than when the same words were presented in a congruent color (Molapour, Berger, & Morsella, 2011), suggesting that the act of color naming masks introspection of the reading process that may be occurring automatically. This finding has been explained as an instance of synchrony blindness, in which one is unaware that two distinct cognitive operations are activated when the operations lead to the same action plan (Molapour et al., 2011). This notion is consistent with the view that one is conscious only of the "outputs" of processes, not of

[1] See treatments of the Stroop congruent condition in Eidels et al. (2010) and Roelofs (2010).

the processes themselves (Lashley, 1951; for a review of this notion, see Morsella & Bargh, 2010.)

LIMITATIONS OF CONTEMPORARY "COOL" RESPONSE INTERFERENCE PARADIGMS

Laboratory paradigms featuring high levels of experimental control have shown that the mere presence of incidental stimuli can automatically activate action-related processes that interfere with one's intended response to a target stimulus (e.g., Ellis, 2009; Eriksen & Eriksen, 1974; Levine, Morsella, & Bargh, 2007; Morsella & Miozzo, 2002). A basic form of this effect has been demonstrated for decades in the classic Stroop task (Stroop, 1935).

However, one limitation of both the standard and subjective variants of the flanker task is that unlike in everyday life, in which conflicts are often "hot" (to use the term by Metcalfe & Mischel, 1999), involving emotional processes and constituted by incentivized stimuli, the conflicts induced by laboratory tasks usually involve only "cool" processes. For example, little research has examined the subjective and behavioral interference effects of incentivized distractors—that is, distractors that have come to be associated with incentive stimuli.

INCENTIVE INTERFERENCE

Perhaps nothing is more distracting than the mere presence of objects in one's environment that have come to be associated with incentivized stimuli (Maner et al., 2003; Rupp & Wallen, 2007). When one is driving home after a long day at work and should be keeping one's eyes on the road, for instance, the mere presence of a billboard displaying a logo associated with tasty food (e.g., a single letter presented in yellow) can often pull one's attention and eyes away from the road. Thus it is obvious that in everyday experience incentivized stimuli can trigger attentional and motor responses (e.g., the visual grasp reflex; Sumner & Husain, 2008), processes that can interfere with the task at hand.[2]

It should be mentioned that some Stroop-like paradigms have been used to examine the interference resulting from the color-naming response to emotional words (e.g., *joy* presented in red; Algom, Chajut, & Lev, 2005) versus unemotional, control words (e.g., *pen* in red); and some flanker-like tasks have examined the interference effects of, say, the incongruent image of a happy face flanked by the word *sad* (cf. Ochsner, Hughes, Robertson, Cooper, & Gabrieli, 2009). In addi-

---

[2] For the role of frontal cortex in such processes, and for the implications of such processes in neurological disorders such as frontotemporal dementia, see Piquard, Lacomblez, Derouesné, and Siéroff (2009).

tion, the influence of incentivized stimuli on mental processes has been examined with the dot-probe paradigm. Decades of research utilizing this paradigm provide substantial evidence that incentivized stimuli modulate attention and subsequent action (for a review see Bar-Haim, Lamy, Pergamin, Bakermans-Kranenburg & van IJzendoorn, 2007). In the paradigm participants are told that they will be presented with two images, one of which is typically neutral and the other incentivized or affectively laden (e.g., threat-related words). After the images are removed from the screen, they are presented with a dot that cues participants to respond by pressing a button. Importantly, the dot probe is presented in the vicinity of either the neutral or incentivized image. Reaction times are faster when the dot probe is presented in the vicinity of where the incentivized image had been presented. This demonstrates an attentional bias toward the incentive stimulus (MacLeod, Mathews, & Tata, 1986).

This effect has been demonstrated primarily in individuals who are socially anxious, revealing that those who suffer from social anxiety display an attentional bias toward threat-based stimuli. By contrast, individuals suffering from depression and control participants reveal results suggesting that they avoid threat-based stimuli (Bar-Haim, et al., 2007; MacLeod, et al., 1986; Smith, Most, Newsome, & Zald, 2006). Subsequent research has extended these findings beyond the domain of affective disorders to pathologies such as opiate dependence and nicotine addiction (Lubman, Peters, Mogg, Bradley & Deakin, 2000; Ehrman et al., 2002; see below for a treatment of other relevant paradigms).

Incentive-Based Conflict in a Flanker Task

However, although paradigms such as the Stroop and dot-probe tasks certainly do tap into affect/emotional processing (and perhaps, in some cases, semantic conflict), the conflicts instantiated by them are different from the kind of incentive-based conflict in which we are interested. Rather, our aim is to develop a flanker-like paradigm that (a) features the level of experimental control and subtlety of the 1979 flanker, (b) lacks the shortcomings of the Stroop task (mentioned above), and (c) can assess different kinds of interference, including a very subtle form incentive interference.

Can stimuli that are associated with incentives yield interference in a subtle flanker-like task? Moreover, can the pairing between the distractors and incentive be learned only in the laboratory, as stimulus-response flanker associations are learned in the laboratory? Can incentive interference arise even when no actual incentive stimuli are presented during the critical (e.g., flanker) trials?

To answer these questions, our first goal was to produce an incentivized version of the flanker PI condition, one in which the incentivized flankers interfere with responding to targets because the distractors are associated with an enticing, incentivized object/experience. We selected the flanker task because it is the most reliable and informative paradigm for assessing different forms of interference (e.g., PI versus RI; cf. Eriksen, 1995). Our second goal pertained to when and where this association was learned. In traditional flanker-like interference, what renders the flankers as distracting is based on learning that occurred not in the outside world, but in the laboratory (e.g., Eriksen & Schultz, 1979). For this reason our second goal was to have the associations between flankers and incentive stimuli occur only in the laboratory, under the kinds of controlled conditions under which flanker training occurs. Our third goal was to obtain an effect with the weakest manipulation possible and with no actual incentive stimuli being presented during test.

Regarding the future of the paradigm, our first long-term goal is for this paradigm to be used with stronger forms of incentive interference. Such interference could involve incentive stimuli associated with drives/basic needs (e.g., food or sexual stimuli). Our second long-term goal is for this paradigm to be used to study incentive interference in clinical populations, including those suffering from addictions or disorders of action control (e.g., frontotemporal dementia).

THE INCENTIVE INTERFERENCE FLANKER PARADIGM

Building on the 1979 flanker task described above (Eriksen & Schultz, 1979; van Veen et al., 2001), we developed a new kind of flanker task that has, in addition to the PI and RI conditions, an incentive interference condition and trial-by-trial subjective measures of performance. Thus the task yielded error rates, RT effects, and subjective effects (e.g., urges to make a mistake). To mirror the high level of control and subtlety of the flanker, what rendered distractors as incentivized stimuli was learned only in the laboratory, under highly controlled conditions. Specifically, along with the stimulus-response mapping that the participants must learn for the 1979 flanker (e.g., S = index finger; P = middle finger), participants also learned a contingency during training in which button pressing to a target letter led to a pleasant and mildly engaging event.

We deliberated at length about the nature of the incentive stimulus (i.e., the mildly engaging event). One of our aims was to avoid using incentive stimuli (e.g., a tasty food stimulus) that some participants would like but toward which others would hold ambiguous attitudes. The goal was to find a stimulus that would be found to be "pleasant and engaging," and not disliked, by most participants. Because we wanted the stimulus to be engaging, we decided to have a visual stimulus that involved motion, which would be more engaging than a still image; we also wanted the motions of the pleasant stimulus to be unpredictable, so that participants did not become habituated to the stimuli during flanker training.

The Experimental Manipulation

With these considerations in mind, we developed the following manipulation. For a specific stimulus-response mapping learned during flanker training, when the participant pressed a specified button after being presented with a letter, he or she saw a stick figure pleasantly move about the screen, accompanied by the presentation of pleasant images of natural scenery. In short, the participant was presented with a movie in which a stick figure—positioned next to a still image of natural scenery—moved around on the screen unpredictably (Figure 1). After considering using the presentation of written jokes, still pictures associated with positive affect, or images of tasty foods as the incentive stimulus during training, on the basis of piloting ($n = 6$) and many deliberations, we concluded that this stick figure movie was the most effective, animate, and fun stimulus that, importantly, no participant was likely to dislike or find offensive. In addition, the manipulation was as subtle as that of most flanker manipulations. According to piloting ($n = 6$), the final actions of the stick figures chosen were "very pleasant." Again, by design the actions performed by the stick figure were always novel (the stick figure never performed the same action twice), so that participants would not habituate to them and would always be somewhat interested in what the character would do next. Notably, such novelty is believed to be rewarding (Guitart-Masip, Bunzeck, Stephan, Dolan, & Düzel, 2011).

Importantly, the incentive-related experience occurred only during training and—as in the manipulations of the 1979 flanker—the manipulation was as subtle as possible. Because our paradigm was intended to be an incentive version of the flanker task, it was very important that our paradigm resemble the classic flanker as much as possible. Hence, as in the flanker, only letter stimuli and no incentive stimuli were presented during the test (i.e., during the critical trials). The letter stimuli learned through training were presented only as targets and flanker stimuli. As mentioned above, future versions of the paradigm could easily incorporate stronger incentive stimuli during training. As in other flanker tasks, the test session involved only the presentation of letter stimuli and participants' button pressing. Hence the test session could easily be coupled with neuroimaging technology, where an experimenter is constrained regarding the nature of the stimuli presented and the actions of the subject.

We took the opportunity to gather trial-by-trial subjective data because such data reveal theoretically important aspects of processing that are not always evident in behavioral data (Morsella, Berger et al., 2011), and because the explicit (self-report) and implicit (e.g., RT effects) pattern of results are often inconsistent—suggesting that distinct systems are affected differentially by cognitive dynamics such as response conflict (Etkin, Prater, Hoeft, Menon, & Schatzberg, 2010; Morsella, Berger et al., 2011; Morsella, Gray et al., 2009; Morsella, Wilson et al. 2009). For example, though post-error corrections in interference paradigms involve improved performance (e.g., faster RTs) on trials following a trial involving response interference (e.g., an incongruent trial), reported urges to err actually increase in such a trial. This has been explained as a dissociation between implicit measures of performance (e.g., RT) and explicit measures (Etkin et al., 2010; Gyurak, Gross, & Etkin, 2011).

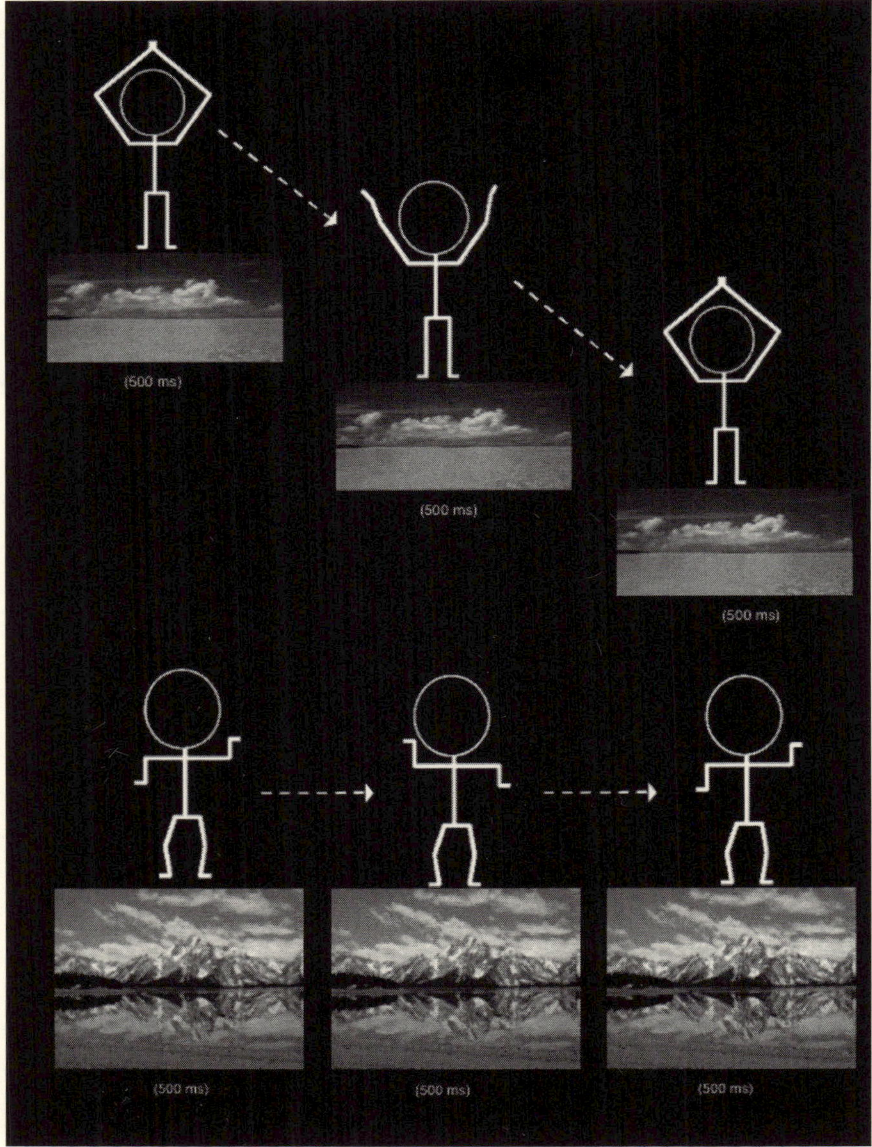

Figure 1. Two sample incentivized movie sequences experienced by participants during flanker training. Still images of pleasant scenery would be accompanied by the pleasant motions of an unpredictable humanoid stick figure.

PREDICTIONS

Based on the strong approach tendencies (e.g., involving attentional capture and potential eye movements; Sumner & Husain, 2008) associated with incidental incentive stimuli (Maner et al., 2003; Rupp & Wallen, 2007), we predicted that whenever targets are flanked by incentive-related distractors (incentive distractors, for short), interference should arise—even though the distractor is just a letter and is not itself the incentive stimulus, and even though the flankers and targets are associated with the same response. Interference from *very* incidental, attention-grabbing stimuli was already found in Morsella, Larson, Zarolia, and Bargh (2011).

Specifically, for the present study we predicted that even though in the incentive interference condition targets and distractors are associated with the same response, the incentive interference condition will lead to greater RTs than the PI condition. We also predicted that because RI is the strongest form of interference (leading to the strongest behavioral and subjective interference effects found in the literature; cf. Morsella, Berger et al., 2011), and because there is less variability for RI than there would be from interference from incentive stimuli, RI will lead to more interference than the incentive interference condition. In short, our prediction was that the RT results would fall in a specific pattern: PI < Incentive Interference < RI.

One advantage of this paradigm over previous "cool" paradigms is that it involves processes that are more "hot"; however, such hot processes are more likely to be more variable across participants. In our experience studies involving the liking or disliking of objects (e.g., Morsella, Feinberg, Cigarchi, Newton, & Williams, 2011), or involving any other kind of valence measure, are more likely to engender interindividual variability than the kinds of cool processes that are necessary to carry out the classic Stroop or flanker tasks. Hence we predicted that, unlike as often happens in the cooler paradigms, systematic interference effects would not be found in every single participant. Also, we anticipated that the link between the incentive experience obtained during training and the arbitrary letter stimulus would decay over time as a function of the trial number of the critical trials. For this reason the critical block of trials was short in duration and included a small number of trials. Regarding the subjective data (i.e., responses to the question "How strong was the urge to make a mistake?"), frameworks about the role of conscious processes in action production (e.g., Morsella, 2005) predict that RI should always lead to the strongest urges.

We would like to emphasize that the primary contribution of our project was intended to be the development of a laboratory paradigm for comparing incentive interference with other kinds of interference (e.g., PI and RI). Our second, related goal was to demonstrate that such a paradigm can capture the kind of incentive interference that occurs in everyday life.

Method

Forty-one undergraduate San Francisco State University students participated for class credit.

Stimuli and Apparatus

Stimuli were presented on a 50.8 cm Apple iMac computer with a viewing distance of approximately 48 cm. Stimulus presentation was controlled by PsyScope software (Cohen, MacWhinney, Flatt, & Provost, 1993). Participants pressed buttons on a PsyScope button box (Response Box; ioLab Systems, UK). Incentive stimuli were composed of two-dimensional humanoid figures that appeared to move in a rhythmic manner, along with a still image of natural scenery (Figure 1). Fifteen unique humanoid-scene pairings were used; no pairing was presented more than once. The figures never moved in the same manner twice. Stimuli were generated by the experimenters and were subjectively matched for pleasantness: stimuli were selected only after independent judges ($n = 6$) concluded that the stimuli were "very pleasant."

When designing the study, we kept in mind that the influence of the newly acquired pairings between letters and incentive stimuli would decay quickly over time and that participants would habituate to the distractors as a function of trial number and of practice at responding (Berlyne, 1960, 1970, 1972; Stroop, 1935). For this reason we presented the critical trials immediately after the training session and kept the length of the critical test session short (only fourteen trials). Any effects from incentivized distractors would be most noticeable during the first presentation of the incentive distractors, when participants are unlikely to be habituated to the distractor stimuli. Thus our initial goal was to present the incentive distractors only once, as occurs in many studies in which effects rely on one critical trial. Such one-trial studies are found in studies on perceptual adaptation, in which there are many training trials and one test trial. However, such a scenario would not provide enough trials to obtain a representative mean. Hence we decided to present the incentive interference condition twice and the other critical conditions (PI and RI) the same number of times. Importantly, this number of trials was sufficient to yield the traditional RI–PI contrast, leading us to believe that we had sufficient trials of the incentive interference condition per participant.

As in Morsella and Miozzo (2002), to diminish the kinds of strategic and demand characteristics artifacts that arise when participants discern the underlying purpose of a study, each critical condition constituted only 14.3% (two of fourteen) of all the test trials. For this kind of experiment, the number of trials per critical condition influences the nature of the effect for that condition (MacLeod, 1991; MacLeod & MacDonald, 2000). Thus the critical conditions needed to be equal in number. As in Morsella and Miozzo (2002), the rest of the trials were "filler" trials.

For the filler trials, we initially considered having nonsense flankers or targets presented with no flankers (i.e., with the target presented alone), but both kinds of situations lead to peculiar effects (cf. Morsella, Wilson et al., 2009). For this reason we selected as our filler trials stimuli in which the target and distractors are identical. This satisfied the concern that, on every trial, the same number of stimuli be presented on the screen (i.e., no trials in which targets are presented alone), which diminishes random error. Importantly, because increasing the proportion of identical trials increases the interference effects found with incongruous trials (MacLeod, 1991), having identical distractors and targets in the filler trials increased the likelihood of finding interference from our subtle manipulation. Thus filler trials constituted 57% of the trials. Our aim was to directly compare incentive interference trials with PI and RI trials.

Procedure

Participants were first trained in sixty trials to press specified buttons when presented with certain letters in the center of a computer screen. For example, when presented with an *S* or *M*, they pressed the green button on the button box with their right index finger; when presented with a *P* or *H*, they pressed the adjacent yellow button with their right middle finger. Each letter was practiced fifteen times and was underlined. For both training and during the critical trials, stimuli were always presented in random order.

The training session included the incentive-association trials, which was the only part of the experiment in which the incentive letter was associated with the incentive stimulus. Each time a participant responded to the incentive letter, he or she was presented with an incentive stimulus. An incentive-association training trial proceeded as follows. A crosshair appeared in the center of the screen (1 second), followed by the incentive letter (i.e., *S*, *M*, *P*, or *H*), the participant's button press, and finally a unique incentive stimulus (lasting 1.5 seconds). Importantly, pairing between letters and incentive stimuli was fully counterbalanced across participants and each incentive stimulus was presented a single time. The three other types of training trials were identical to the incentive-association training trials, except that following the button press participants were presented only with the crosshair (1 second) that preceded the next trial.

Following training, participants were told to continue to respond to the underlined letter in the center of the screen (the target) and to disregard any distractors (the flankers). For the filler trials, the target letter was presented with letters identical to it (e.g., *HHHHH*; eight trials; two replications of each possible combination). In the PI condition, targets and distractors were associated with the same response but different letters (e.g., *SSMSS*; two trials; only two of the four possible combinations). In the incentive interference condition, targets and distractors were associated with the same response but the target or the distractor was the incentive letter (e.g., *SSHSS*, where *S* or *H* was associated with the incentive stimulus during training; two trials; only two of the two possible combinations). In the RI condition, targets and distractors were associated with different responses and different letters (e.g., *SSPSS*; two trials; two of the four possible combinations).

To obtain the subjective measure, participants were asked after each trial "How strong was your urge to make a mistake?" and rated their responses on an eight-point scale, in which 1 signified "not strong at all" and 8 signified "extremely strong." Participants completed a total of fourteen critical trials. The conclusion of the experiment was followed by funneled debriefing (following the procedures detailed in Bargh & Chartrand, 2000) to assess participants' knowledge about the hypothesis at hand. Participants were asked:

- "What do you think was the purpose of this experiment?"
- "What do you think this experiment was trying to study?"
- "Did you think that any of the tasks you did were related in any way? (Circle Yes or No)."
- "If you circled Yes, in what way were they related?"
- "Did anything you did or saw during the study affect your ability to respond to the stimulus presented during a given trial?"
- "Did you have any goal or strategy while responding to the stimulus?"
- "Did you base your urge rating on the urges you felt toward the stimulus? (Circle Yes or No)."
- "If you circled No, what did you base your urge ratings on?"

Careful analysis of the funneled debriefing data revealed that no participants discerned the hypothesis at hand.

Based on Woodworth and Schlosberg (1954), in Morsella, Wilson et al. (2009) flanker RT data below 200 ms and above 2000 ms were excluded from analysis. We based the current RT analysis on this window but added 1500 ms to the upper limit (making the window from 200 to 3500 ms), because—as predicted—this task produced more variability than the standard flanker task, and previously used trimming methods would have resulted in the loss of too much data. Our goal was to include as much data as possible without including flawed trials. Importantly, as explained below, the same general pattern of RT findings is obtained with the raw data (though significance then trends at $p = 0.13$) or when one removes from analysis responses that exceed ±3 standard deviations from the participants' mean ($p < 0.01$). The data from two participants were excluded from analysis because the participants did not follow instructions.

RT Analysis

After removing the thirty trials in which participants erred (5.3%) and the seven trials involving data trimming (1.3%), the general mean RT per participant was 994.27 ms (*SEM* = 53.99). (The total number of trials excluded was 37, or 6.6% of 560 trials.) Table 1 displays the descriptive statistics for each of the critical conditions, including information about subjective effects, RTs, and error rates. As predicted, there was a main effect of condition, $F(2, 76) = 7.304$, $p = 0.0013$ ($\eta_p^2 = 0.16$), in which incentive interference produced an RT effect between PI and RI planned contrasts *ps* < 0.05.[3] The same general pattern of results is obtained when, from these data, RTs exceeding ±3 standard deviations from the participant's mean RT are removed, $F(2, 76) = 4.923$, $p = 0.0098$. Importantly, the same general pattern of results is obtained with the raw, untrimmed data (but excluding erroneous trials); in this case, however, the main effect approaches significance but is nonsignificant, $F(2, 76) = 2.077$, $p = 0.13$. In short, in all analyses the pattern is that PI < incentive interference < RI. It is worth noting that these results are substantially more variable than what is found with the traditional flanker. For example, in our sample 23 participants showed greater mean RTs for incentive interference than for PI; 23 showed greater mean RTs for RI than for incentive interference; and 29 showed greater mean RTs for RI than for PI.

Error Analysis

Mean error rate (Table 1) did not vary significantly as a function of condition, $F(2, 78) = 1.187$, $p = 0.31$ ($\eta_p^2 = 0.03$), and the proportions of total data removal, through the removal of errors and from the trimming procedure, also did not vary by condition, $F(2, 76) < 1$.

Subjective Effects

Interestingly, as found previously (e.g., Morsella, Wilson et al., 2009; Morsella, Berger et al., 2011), the pattern of results found with the urge data (Table 1) did not mirror exactly that found with the RT data. Condition had a main effect on urges to err, $F(2, 78) = 6.197$, $p = 0.0032$ ($\eta_p^2 = 0.14$). The planned contrasts between the conditions were significant (*ps* < 0.05) except for that between PI and incentive interference, $t(39) = 0.744$, $p = 0.46$. Participants' typographical errors, or lack of providing a rating, resulted in the loss of only one rating. The mean Pearson product moment correlation coefficient between a participant's urge ratings and RT was 0.44, which is nonsignificant ($p > 0.10$) when there are only fourteen observations per participant.

Discussion

Examination of the nature of the basic mechanisms and dynamics involved in self-control reveals that controlled behavior is often challenged by the enticing nature of incentive stimuli (Metcalfe & Mischel, 1999). These challenges are often accompanied by action-related urges. When attempting to capture in the laboratory the everyday situation in which objects that have come to be associated with incentivized stimuli (e.g., the one-letter logo of a fast food chain) engender interference with the task at hand (e.g., driving), we decided to demonstrate such incentive

---

[3] Because of error-based data removal, one participant had no data representing the RI condition, which of course affected the degrees of freedom of our statistical analysis. Because of this, the actual means used in the ANOVA were $M_{PI} = 895.85$ ms ($SEM = 46.79$), $M_{Incentive} = 1004.23$ ms ($SEM = 75.36$), and $M_{RI} = 1116.28$ ms ($SEM = 79.00$).

TABLE 1. Mean Response Times (ms), Urges to Err, and Error Rates as a Function of Distractor Environment

Distractor environment	Response times (mean SEM)	Urges to err (mean SEM)	Error rates (mean SEM)
Perceptual interference	910.52 (47.91)	2.19 (0.28)	0.05 (0.02)
Incentive interference	1029.10 (77.55)	2.01 (0.19)	0.04 (0.02)
Response interference	1116.28 (79.00)	2.92 (0.29)	0.09 (0.04)

interference in a laboratory paradigm that is considered to be the best task for assessing and comparing different kinds of interference on action production—namely, the Eriksen flanker task (Eriksen, 1995).

To resemble the classic flanker, our manipulation was as subtle as possible, with the incentive experience not involving strong physiological needs and with no incentive stimuli presented during the critical trials. Nevertheless, we supported our hypotheses, and beyond that we successfully replicated the PI and RI response time effects of previous studies (Eriksen & Schultz, 1979; Morsella, Wilson et al., 2009; van Veen et al., 2001), corroborating that our paradigm and training manipulation were effective. Although the main aim of this project was to show that such a flanker-like paradigm is useful and feasible, we also yielded data consistent with the hypothesis that incentive interference effects reside somewhere between PI and RI, as one would anticipate. Incentive interference arose even though targets and distractors in the incentive interference condition were associated with the same response, which usually leads to interference on the scale of that produced by the PI condition. Our paradigm inherits many of the benefits of the 1979 flanker task. Importantly, the pairings between arbitrary stimuli (letters) and the incentivized experience were learned not in the real world, but in the laboratory, moments before the critical trials ensued.

Variability in Our Dependent Measure

Because our manipulation involves incentive-related dispositions that are known to vary from individual to individual, we anticipated that any effect obtained would be less reliable than effects stemming from a "cool" process, such as RI. Indeed, not every participant displayed the predicted pattern of RT effects. To increase the sensitivity of our paradigm, the majority of the trials were filler trials and a small subset of trials involved interference of some kind. Future versions of the paradigm may use stronger incentive stimuli and thus may not require such measures. Nevertheless, despite the variability that must exist between individuals toward an incentive stimulus of a particular kind, such as the image of food (incentive stimuli that are physiologically relevant) or just of a pleasant scene (as in our controlled experiment), we found the exact incentive interference pattern of RT effects that we predicted PI < incentive interference < RI.

Importantly, the experiment also provided subjective measures of performance (urges to err), which corroborates theories (e.g., the SIT; Morsella, 2005) proposing that RI—which requires efference-efference binding—should always be associated with the strongest subjective effects. It is interesting to note that, as in previous studies (e.g., Etkin et al., 2010; Morsella, Berger et al., 2011; Morsella, Gray et al., 2009), the subjective effects (urges to err) did not mirror exactly the behavioral findings.

Comparison with Other Paradigms

Previous paradigms have examined interference resulting from the color-naming response to emotional words (e.g., *happy* presented in red; Algom et al., 2004) versus unemotional control words (e.g., *pen* in red), and flanker-like tasks have examined the interference effects of, say, the incongruent image of a happy face flanked by the word *sad* (cf. Ochsner et al., 2009), but ours is the first study to capture in a laboratory paradigm the kinds of pushes and pulls that occur in everyday life—when the mere presence of an incentive-related stimulus interferes with intended action production.

In addition, our paradigm is unique because no actual incentive stimuli were presented during the critical trials; the manipulation was as weak as that of the traditional flanker; and the pairing of incentives to letter stimuli was learned only in the laboratory. Examining strong, emotional interference effects is imperative to understanding attentional biases in clinical and nonclinical populations (Kelly & Forsyth, 2007), but by utilizing a far less potent incentive stimulus, our paradigm reveals how susceptible action tendencies are to the smallest of incentives. While previous research has paired affectively laden, unconditioned stimuli with benign conditioned stimuli in order to increase interference effects (Kelly & Forsyth, 2007; Krebs, Boehler, & Woldoroff, 2010; Lee, Lim, Lee, Kim & Choi, 2009; Richards & Blanchette, 2004), our procedure attempts to induce such effects with a subtle, simply amusing, unconditioned stimulus—similar to the subtle way in which the symbol for a fast food company nudges one toward choosing its brand over another.

Again, the aim is for this new paradigm to be used eventually with stronger incentives. In this initial version of the incentive interference task, the distractors were stimuli associated with a positive incentive. We focused only on positive incentives for several reasons, including an ethical issue: to demonstrate the feasibility of the paradigm, it was unnecessary to have participants experience negative states or perceive stimuli associated with such states. However, to advance the understanding of the psychological mechanisms in clinical populations, it might be informative to include stimuli that have a negative valence. Stimuli associated with strong incentive stimuli may trigger an orienting response (Sechenov, 1965), which influences the skeletal muscle system and interferes with responses to the target, thereby engendering conflict-related urges in consciousness.

In addition, future investigations could examine how personality characteristics known to be associated with motivational processing and attentional control (e.g., neuroticism) might moderate the interference effect of this paradigm. Moreover, just as the dot-probe task has been applied to various populations, the current paradigm could be extended to investigate psychological processing in various clinical populations. For example, one can imagine how future research could provide additional insights by focusing on incentives that are of interest to not the general population, but only a subset of the population (e.g., cigarette smokers). For instance, in the case of smokers, the distractors could be cigarette cues (e.g., an ashtray). Such a variant of the paradigm could be used for other populations suffering from addictions (e.g., gambling and alcohol).

Although we met our primary goal of developing a paradigm that can compare incentive interference with other kinds of interference, this initial study is limited in several ways. First, as an initial finding, the effect demands conceptual replication. Second, the study brings with it the limitations inherent in all introspection paradigms—that one cannot rule out that judgments were based on self-observations involving RT performance, accuracy, or folk beliefs regarding how one should behave oneself in an experiment about response interference (see treatment of this issue in Morsella, Wilson et al., 2009).

Despite all the shortcomings, it is worth noting that the finding was embedded in a paradigm (the flanker task) that has stood the test of time and has come to be one of the most reliable paradigms in the study of cognitive control and interference. We should mention that it is unlikely that our effects are merely artifacts of the particular letter stimuli or motor responses involved, because the pairings of letters to effectors were fully counterbalanced across participants. In addition, it is unlikely that effects were simply due to the order of presentation in which the flanker trials were presented, because flanker trials were presented in random order. Although the purpose of the present study was to assess the kinds of interference that arise from incentivized distractors in a flanker-like paradigm, one can speculate that the interference arose from participants' approach orientations (e.g., attentional grasp or even eye movements) to the distractors, which hindered responding to targets (cf. Morsella, Larson et al., 2011). Future investigations may home in on the exact mechanism responsible for incentive interference arising from a flanker paradigm.

Conclusion

Our review of the theoretical and empirical advances regarding the basic mechanisms involved in control (along with our treatment of traditional and new interference paradigms) supports a conceptualization of control in which control is intimately related to both conscious processing and to the skeletal muscle effector system. One goal of this chapter was not only to focus attention on the data from extant interference paradigms, but to begin to highlight possible ways to also examine incentive interference, which is the kind of interference that in everyday life challenges control.

Our new paradigm demonstrates that by adapting existing paradigms, the kinds of incentive-related and emotion-related phenomena observed in everyday life can be studied experimentally, with the incentive learning occurring only in the laboratory and with the most subtle manipulation possible. The paradigm we developed is innocuous, minimally influenced by the participant's pre-experiment history, and amenable to neuroimaging technologies that may begin to examine the neural processes that are uniquely associated with incentive interference.

As discussed above, one could envision that the paradigm could be used to examine stronger manipulations (e.g., involving physiological incentives) and the nature of incentive interference in clinical populations suffering from symptoms involving addiction or impulse control (e.g., frontotemporal dementia; Piquard et al., 2009). We hope that this treatise spurs further investigation into the nature of the pushes and pulls of incentive interference—inclinations that influence consciousness and challenge control.

REFERENCES

Algom, D., Chajut, E., & Lev, S. (2004). A rational look at the emotional Stroop phenomenon: A generic slowdown, not a Stroop effect. *Journal of Experimental Psychology: General, 133*, 323–338.

Alkire, M. T., Hudetz, A. G., & Tononi, G. (2008). Consciousness and anesthesia. *Science, 322*, 876–880.

Bar-Haim, Y., Lamy, D., Pergamin, L., Bakermans-Kranenburg, M. J., & van IJzendoorn, M. H. (2007). Threat-related attentional bias in anxious and nonanxious individuals: A meta-analytic study. *Psychological Bulletin*, *133*, 1–24.

Bargh, J. A., & Chartrand, T. L. (2000). The mind in the middle: A practical guide to priming and automaticity research. In H. T. Reis & C. M. Judd (Eds.), *Handbook of research methods in social and personality psychology* (pp. 253–285). New York: Cambridge University Press.

Bargh, J. A., & Morsella, E. (2008). The unconscious mind. *Perspectives on Psychological Science, 3*, 73–79.

Berlyne, D. E. (1960). *Conflict, arousal, and curiosity*. New York: McGraw-Hill.

Berlyne, D. E. (1970). Novelty, complexity, and hedonic value. *Perception and Psychophysics, 8*, 279–286.

Berlyne, D. E. (1972). Reinforcement values of visual patterns compared through concurrent performances. *Journal of the Experimental Analysis of Behavior, 18*, 281–285.

Boly, M., Garrido, M. I., Gosseries, O., Bruno, M-A., Boveroux, P., Schnakers, C., et al. (2011). Preserved feedforward but impaired top-down processes in the vegetative state. *Science, 332*, 858–862.

Boveroux, P., Vanhaudenhuyse, A., Bruno, M. A., Noirhomme, Q., Lauwick, S., Luxen, A., et al. (2010). Breakdown of within- and between-network resting state functional magnetic resonance imaging connectivity during propofol-induced loss of consciousness. *Anesthesiology, 113*, 1038–1053.

Cohen, J. D., MacWhinney, B., Flatt, M., & Provost, J. (1993). PsyScope: A new graphic interactive environment for designing psychology experiments. *Behavior Research Methods, Instruments, and Computers, 25*, 257–271.

Dehaene, S., & Naccache, L. (2001). Towards a cognitive neuroscience of consciousness: Basic evidence and a workspace framework. *Cognition, 79*, 1–37.

Del Cul, A., Baillet, S., & Dehaene, S. (2007). Brain dynamics underlying the nonlinear threshold for access to consciousness. *PLoS Biology, 5*, e260.

DeSoto, M. C., Fabiani, M., Geary, D. C., & Gratton, G. (2001). When in doubt, do it both ways: Brain evidence of the simultaneous activation of conflicting responses in a spatial Stroop task. *Journal of Cognitive Neuroscience 13,* 523–536.

Ehrman, R. N., Robbins, S. J., Bromwell, M. A., Lankford, M. E., Monterosso, J. R., & O'Brien, C. P. (2002). Comparing attentional bias to smoking cues in current smokers, former smokers, and non-smokers using a dot-probe task. *Drug and Alcohol Dependence, 67*, 185–191.

Eidels, A., Townsend, J. T., & Algom, D. (2010). Comparing perception of Stroop stimuli in focused versus divided attention paradigms: Evidence for dramatic processing differences. *Cognition, 114*, 129–150.

Ellis, R. (2009). Interactions between action and visual objects. In E. Morsella, J. A. Bargh, & P. M. Gollwitzer (Eds.), *Oxford handbook of human action* (pp. 214–224). New York: Oxford University Press.

Eriksen, B. A., & Eriksen, C. W. (1974). Effects of noise letters upon the identification of a target letter in a nonsearch task. *Perception and Psychophysics, 16*, 143–149.

Eriksen, C. W. (1995). The flankers task and response competition: A useful tool for investigating a variety of cognitive problems. *Visual Cognition, 2*, 101–118.

Eriksen, C. W., & Schultz, D. W. (1979). Information processing in visual search: A continuous flow conception and experimental results. *Perception and Psychophysics, 25*, 249–263.

Etkin, A., Prater, K., Hoeft, F., Menon, V., & Schatzberg, A. (2010). Failure of anterior cingulate activation and connectivity with the amygdala during implicit regulation of emotional processing in generalized anxiety disorder. *American Journal of Psychiatry, 167*, 545–554.

Godwin, C. A., Gazzaley, A., & Morsella, E. (2013). Homing in on the brain mechanisms linked to consciousness: Buffer of the perception-and-action interface. In A. Pereira and D. Lehmann (Eds.), *The unity of mind, brain and world: Current perspectives on a science of consciousness* (pp. 43–76). Cambridge, UK: Cambridge University Press.

Guitart-Masip, M., Bunzeck, N., Stephan, K. E., Dolan, R. J., & Düzel, E. (2011). Contextual novelty modulates the neural dynamics of reward anticipation. *Journal of Neuroscience, 31*, 12816–12822.

Gyurak, A., Gross, J. J., & Etkin, A (2011). Explicit and implicit emotion regulation: A dual-process framework. *Cognition and Emotion, 3*, 400–412.

Haggard, P., Aschersleben, G., Gehrke, J., & Prinz, W. (2002). Action, binding and awareness. In B. Hommel & W. Prinz (Eds.), *Attention and performance: Vol. 19. Common mechanisms in perception and action* (pp. 266–285). Oxford, UK: Oxford University Press.

Hallett, M. (2007). Volitional control of movement: The physiology of free will. *Clinical Neurophysiology, 117*, 1179–1192.

James, W. (1890). *The principles of psychology* (2 vols.). New York: Henry Holt.

Johnson, H., & Haggard P. (2005). Motor awareness without perceptual awareness. *Neuropsychologia, 43*, 227–237.

Kelly, M. M., & Forsyth, J. P. (2007). Observational fear conditioning in the acquisition and extinction of attentional bias for threat: An experimental evaluation. *Emotion, 7*, 324–335.

Kern, M. K., Jaradeh, S., Arndorfer, R. C., & Shaker, R. (2001). Cerebral cortical representation of reflexive and volitional swallowing in humans. *American Journal of Physiology: Gastrointestinal and Liver Physiology, 280*, G354–G360.

Krebs, R. M., Boehler, C. N., & Woldorff, M. G. (2010). The influence of reward associations on conflict processing in the Stroop task. *Cognition, 117*, 341–347.

Långsjö, J. W., Alkire, M. T., Kaskinoro, K., Hayama, H., Maksimow, A., Kaisti, K. K., et al. (2012). Returning from oblivion: Imaging the neural core of consciousness. *Journal of Neuroscience, 32*, 4935–4943.

Lashley, K. S. (1951). The problem of serial order in behavior. In L. A. Jeffress (Ed.), *Cerebral mechanisms in behavior: The Hixon symposium* (pp. 112–146). New York: Wiley.

Lee, T. H., Lim, S. L., Lee, K., Kim, H. T., & Choi, J. S. (2009). Conditioning-induced attentional bias for face stimuli measured with the emotional Stroop task. *Emotion, 9*, 134–139.

Lee, U., Kim, S., Noh, G. J., Choi, B. M., Hwang, E., & Mashour, G. (2009). The directionality and functional organization of frontoparietal connectivity during consciousness and anesthesia in humans. *Consciousness and Cognition, 18*, 1069–1078.

Levine, L. R., Morsella, E., & Bargh, J. A. (2007). The perversity of inanimate objects: Stimulus control by incidental musical notation. *Social Cognition, 25*, 265–280.

Lewis, L., Weiner, V., Mukamel, E., Donaghue, J., Eskandar, E., Madsen, J., et al. (2012). Rapid fragmentation of neural networks at the onset of propofol-induced unconsciousness. *PNAS, 109*, E3377–E3386.

Lubman, D. I., Peters, L. A., Mogg, K. K., Bradley, B. P., & Deakin, J. W. (2000). Attentional bias for drug cues in opiate dependence. *Psychological Medicine, 30*, 169–175.

MacLeod, C. M. (1991). Half a century of research on the Stroop effect: An integrative review. *Psychological Bulletin, 109*, 163–203.

MacLeod, C., Mathews, A., & Tata, P. (1986). Attentional bias in emotional disorders. *Journal of Abnormal Psychology, 95*, 15.

MacLeod, C. M., & MacDonald, P. A. (2000). Interdimensional interference in the Stroop effect: Uncovering the cognitive and neural anatomy of attention. *Trends in Cognitive Sciences, 4*, 383–391.

Maner, J. K., Kenrick, D.T., Becker, D.V., Delton, A.W., Hofer, B., Wilbur, C. J., et al. (2003). Sexually selective cognition: Beauty captures the mind of the beholder. *Journal of Personality and Social Psychology, 85*, 1107–1120.

Mattler, U. (2005). Flanker effects on motor output and the late-level response activation hypothesis. *Quarterly Journal of Experimental Psychology, 58A*, 577–601.

McGurk, H., & MacDonald, J. (1976). Hearing lips and seeing voices. *Nature, 264*, 746–748.

Metcalfe, J., & Mischel, W. (1999). A hot/cool-system analysis of delay of gratification: Dynamics of willpower. *Psychological Review, 106*, 3–19.

Molapour, T., Berger, C. C., & Morsella, E. (2011). Did I read or did I name? Diminished awareness of processes yielding identical "outputs." *Consciousness and Cognition, 20*, 1776–1780.

Morsella, E. (2005). The function of phenomenal states: Supramodular interaction theory. *Psychological Review, 112*, 1000–1021.

Morsella, E., & Bargh, J. A. (2010). What is an output? *Psychological Inquiry, 21,* 354–370.

Morsella, E., & Bargh, J. A. (2011). Unconscious action tendencies: Sources of "un-integrated" action. In J. Decety & J. T. Cacioppo (Eds.), *The Oxford handbook of social neuroscience* (pp. 335–347). New York: Oxford University Press.

Morsella, E., Berger, C. C., & Krieger, S. C. (2011). Cognitive and neural components of the phenomenology of agency. *Neurocase, 17,* 209–230.

Morsella, E., Feinberg, G. H., Cigarchi, S., Newton, J. W., & Williams, L. E. (2011). Sources of avoidance motivation: Valence effects from physical effort and mental rotation. *Motivation and Emotion, 35,* 296–305.

Morsella, E., Gray, J. R., Krieger, S. C., & Bargh, J. A. (2009). The essence of conscious conflict: Subjective effects of sustaining incompatible intentions. *Emotion, 9,* 717–728.

Morsella, E., Larson, L. R. L., Zarolia, P., & Bargh, J. A. (2011). Stimulus control: The sought or unsought influence of the objects we tend to. *Psicológica: International Journal of Methodology and Experimental Psychology, 32,* 145–170.

Morsella, E., & Miozzo, M. (2002). Evidence for a cascade model of lexical access in speech production. *Journal of Experimental Psychology: Learning, Memory, and Cognition, 28,* 555–563.

Morsella, E., Wilson, L. E., Berger, C. C., Honhongva, M., Gazzaley, A., & Bargh, J. A. (2009). Subjective aspects of cognitive control at different stages of processing. *Attention, Perception, and Psychophysics, 71,* 1807–1824.

Ochsner, K. N., Hughes, B. L., Robertson, E., Cooper, J. C., & Gabrieli, J. (2009). Neural systems supporting the control of cognitive and affective conflict. *Journal of Cognitive Neuroscience, 21,* 1841–1854.

Ortinski, P., & Meador, K. J. (2004). Neuronal mechanisms of conscious awareness. *Archives of Neurology, 61,* 1017–1020.

Piquard, A., Lacomblez, L., Derouesné, C., & Siéroff, E. (2009). Problems in inhibiting attentional capture by irrelevant stimuli in patients with frontotemporal dementia. *Brain and Cognition, 70,* 62–66.

Richards, A., & Blanchette, I. (2004). Independent manipulation of emotion in an emotional Stroop task using classical conditioning. *Emotion, 4,* 275–281.

Roach, J. (2005, June 30). Journal ranks top 25 unanswered science questions. *National Geographic News.* Retrieved July 11, 2010 from news.nationalgeographic.com.

Roelofs, A. (2010). Attention and facilitation: Converging information versus inadvertent reading in Stroop task performance. *Journal of Experimental Psychology: Learning, Memory, and Cognition, 36,* 411–422.

Rosenbaum, D. A. (2002). Motor control. In H. Pashler (Series Ed.) & S. Yantis (Vol. Ed.), *Stevens' handbook of experimental psychology: Vol. 1. Sensation and perception* (3rd ed., pp. 315–339). New York: Wiley.

Rupp, H. A., & Wallen, K. (2007). Sex differences in viewing sexual stimuli: An eye tracking study in men and women. *Hormones and Behavior, 51,* 524–533.

Schacter, D. L., & Addis, D. R. (2007). The cognitive neuroscience of constructive memory: Remembering the past and imagining the future. *Philosophical Transactions of the Royal Society of London, Series B: Biological Sciences, 362,* 773–786.

Schroter, M., Spoormaker, V., Schorer, A., Wohlschlager, A., Czish, M., Kochs, E., et al. (2012). Spatiotemporal reconfiguration of large-scale brain functional networks during propofol-induced loss of consciousness. *Journal of Neuroscience, 32,* 12832–12840.

Schrouff, J., Perlbarg, V., Boly, M., Guillaume, M., Boveroux, P., Vanhaudenhuyse, A., et al. (2011). Brain functional integration decreases during propofol-induced loss of consciousness. *NeuroImage, 57*, 198–205.

Sechenov, I. (1965). *Reflexes of the brain* (S. Belsky, Trans.). Cambridge, MA: MIT Press.

Sergent, C., & Dahaene, S. (2004). Is consciousness a gradual phenomenon? Evidence for an all-or-none bifurcation during the attentional blink. *Psychological Science, 15*, 720–728.

Smith, S. D., Most, S. B., Newsome, L. A., & Zald, D. H. (2006). An emotion-induced attentional blink elicited by aversively conditioned stimuli. *Emotion, 6*, 523–527.

Stroop, J. R. (1935). Studies of interference in serial verbal reactions. *Journal of Experimental Psychology, 18,* 643–662.

Sumner, P., & Husain, M. (2008). At the edge of consciousness: Automatic motor activation and voluntary control. *Neuroscientist, 14*, 474–486.

Taylor, J. L., & McCloskey, D. I. (1990). Triggering of preprogrammed movements as reactions to masked stimuli. *Journal of Neurophysiology, 63*, 439–446.

Taylor, J. L., & McCloskey, D. I. (1996). Selection of motor responses on the basis of unperceived stimuli. *Experimental Brain Research, 110*, 62–66.

Tononi, G. (2012). *Phi: A voyage from brain to the soul.* New York: Pantheon.

Tononi, G., & Edelman, G. M. (1988). Consciousness and complexity. *Science, 282*, 1846–1851.

Ulhaas, P. J., Pipa, G., Lima, B., Melloni, L., Neuenschwander, S., Nikolic, D., & Singer, W. (2009). Neural synchrony in cortical networks: History, concept and current status. *Frontiers in Integrative Neuroscience, 3*, 17.

van Veen, V., & Carter, C. S. (2006). Conflict and cognitive control in the brain. *Current Directions in Psychological Science, 5*, 237–240.

van Veen, V., Cohen, J. D., Botvinick, M. M., Stenger, V. A., & Carter, C. C. (2001). Anterior cingulate cortex, conflict monitoring, and levels of processing. *NeuroImage, 14*, 1302–1308.

Woodworth, R. S., & Schlosberg, H. (1954). *Experimental psychology* (2nd ed.). New York: Holt, Rinehart & Winston.

Zeki, S., & Bartels, A. (1999). Toward a theory of visual consciousness. *Consciousness and Cognition, 8*, 225–259.

CHAPTER 3

Dissimilarity Focus as an Attentional Mode of BIS-Related Comparator Function

Agata Wytykowska
Philip J. Corr
Małgorzata Fajkowska

INTRODUCTION

The notion of a comparator has been popular in behavioral psychology, especially in accounts couched in terms of a cybernetic system. The function of a comparator is to control processes related to the regulation of behavior. This takes the form of comparing input states with desired reference states, and when a discrepancy is detected the system switches to control mode and activates cognitive processes designed to reduce disparity (Carver & Scheier, 1998; Corr, 2010).

This chapter is concerned with the comparator function of the behavioral inhibition system (BIS). To date the postulated comparator function of the BIS (i.e., conflict detection and resolution) has been largely dedicated to theoretical speculation rather than empirical validation (a few exceptions are Amodio, Master, Yee, & Taylor, 2008; Leue, Lange, & Beauducel, 2012; Moore, Mills, Marshman, & Corr, 2012). Moreover, sufficient empirical validation—especially of those parts of the model that postulate the cognitive processes and mechanisms underlying the BIS comparator function—is lacking.

Personality and Control edited by Philip J. Corr, Małgorzata Fajkowska, Michael W. Eysenck, and Agata Wytykowska. Eliot Werner Publications, Clinton Corners, New York, 2015.

In this chapter we offer proposals to advance understanding of BIS theory in these various respects. More precisely, we suggest that the comparator function of the BIS at the cognitive level is associated with the dissimilarity-oriented attentional mode. The theoretical arguments stem from the analysis of the regulative function of the BIS as a comparator, which is based on the negative feedback loop (Carver & Scheier, 1998) and governed by the detected discrepancy to the no-conflict standard (Corr, 2010). It is assumed that if conflict resolution processes are aimed at reduction of discrepancy, then selective attention to signals that are divergent from the standard should be expected to exert control over information processing and facilitate conflict monitoring and ultimately resolution. Additionally, the theoretical advances presented in this chapter are supported by empirical data.

The Behavioral Inhibition System: New Approach or Revised Approach?

The theory of the BIS has been elaborated (Corr, 2010; Corr & McNaughton, 2008) and new theoretical considerations are offered by this revision. Revised reinforcement sensitivity theory, of which the BIS is the most reformulated part, highlights the importance of a greater variety of cognitive processes (e.g., Hoffmann, 2010; Matthews, 2008; Revelle & Wilt, 2008). These elaborated processes are especially important since the BIS as a comparator is engaged in detection of conflict and discrepancy and its activation is aimed at conflict resolution (Corr, 2008). Conflict detection and conflict resolution processes are the parts of cognitive control theory (Botvinick, Cohen, & Carter, 2004) or executive system of attention (Rueda, Posner, & Rothbart, 2004) that are viewed by some researchers as meta-cognition (executive system) or related to the generation and contents of consciousness (Corr, 2010; Fernandez-Duque, Barid, & Posner, 2000). Dealing with conflict is exerted under cognitive control supervision, where some higher-order cognitive processes (e.g., cognitive inhibition, top-down selective attention, planning, resource allocation) are activated to monitor and resolve the conflict.

In the revised approach to the BIS (see Figure 1), the only cognitive characteristic that is considered is the biased processing of threatening stimuli (stimuli based as well as memory based) governed by the mechanisms of selective attention and selective retrieval. Such a bias controls the level of the perception of threat in incoming stimulation and is used in risk assessment. It is believed that these processes are a crucial part of conflict resolution processes. In this chapter we propose that selective attention toward dissimilarity might be another important mechanism that facilitates control processes of conflict monitoring and resolution.

The chapter is organized into four parts. The first part describes the BIS and biological basis of its comparator function. The second and most important part presents the idea that the effective operation of the BIS as a comparator requires specific organization of cognitive processes: information processing (atten-

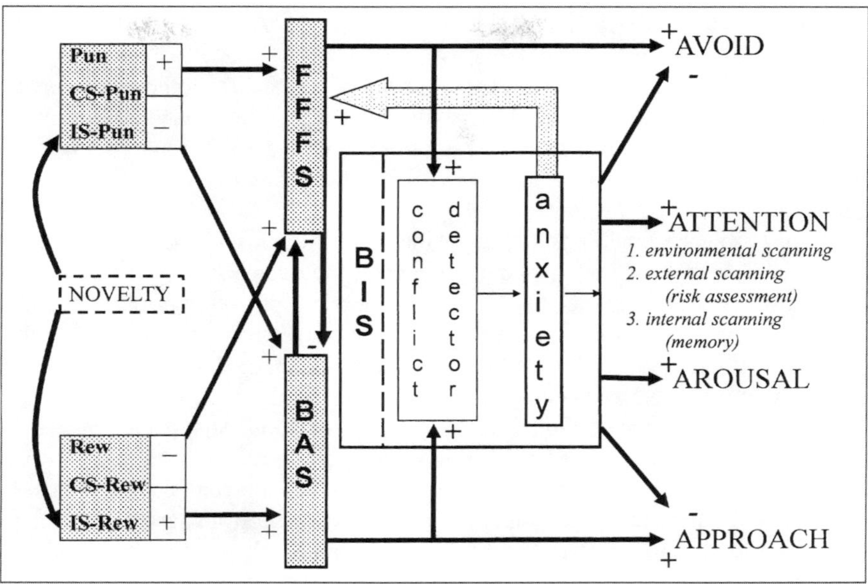

Figure 1. Relations of the behavioral inhibition system (BIS), fight-flight-freeze system (FFFS), and behavioral approach system (BAS). The simplest way to activate the BIS is concurrently to activate the FFFS and BAS (i.e., face the animal with an approach-avoidance conflict). In this case both simple approach and simple avoidance are inhibited and replaced with environmental scanning (in the form of altered attention), external scanning (risk assessment behavior), and internal scanning of memory. All these scanning operations are aimed at detecting affectively negative information and involve an increase in the salience of such information. As a result, a secondary consequence of activation of the BIS is normally a shift of the balance between approach and avoidance tendencies in the direction of avoidance. The inputs to the system are classified in terms of the delivery (+) or omission (−) of primary rewards (Rew) or punishments (Pun) or conditional stimuli (CS) or innate stimuli (IS) that predict such primary events. (Adapted from Corr & McNaughton, 2012; Gray & McNaughton, 2000.)

tion/perception) oriented toward dissimilarity. The third part demonstrates the empirical evidence on the relation between the BIS and dissimilarity focus. The fourth part comprises a discussion of the necessity of further empirical validation of the location and role of the orientation to dissimilarity within the whole model of the BIS, and on the specificity of the behavioral regulation under BIS control. Finally, we discuss the limitations of the studies presented.

THE BEHAVIORAL INHIBITION SYSTEM AS A COMPARATOR

The BIS in the reinforcement sensitivity theory of personality is thought to operate as a comparator (e.g., Corr, 2008, 2010; McNaughton & Gray, 2000), examining incoming sensory information in relation to expectation. This comparison function yields one of two outputs: either the values being compared are demonstrably different from one another or they are not (Carver & Scheier, 1998). When the comparison process indicates that the incoming stimulus matches the expected value, the system does not change anything and the comparator works in a relatively passive, "just checking" mode. The current behavior runs unchanged, mainly under automatic regulation. However, when a discrepancy is registered between the actual and expected state of the environment, the comparator changes into an active control mode to detect and resolve the source of error (Corr, 2010). Therefore the BIS operates actively when a mismatch between expectation and input is detected—at a more general level, when goal conflict (which implies that there are opposing forces that cannot be readily resolved by mere approach or avoidance) is detected.

This error-triggering mechanism results in switching from automatic to controlled information processing and is likely to engage the awareness of salient features of the conflicting stimuli (cf. Corr, 2010). However, the processing of mismatch, errors, or goal conflict itself is an automatic, pre-attentive process (detection of conflict information during reasoning is an implicit and effortless process; Franssens & de Neys, 2009). According to the BIS model (see Figure 1 above), detection of discrepancy between the actual and reference values generates specific outputs at the cognitive, emotional, and behavioral levels—all of which are directed at reducing the discrepancy and potential negative consequences, as well as restoring the state of conformity (no-discrepancy state; Corr, 2010).

The BIS is thought to resolve conflict elicited by simultaneous incompatible goals by (a) suppressing ongoing approach or avoidance behaviors; (b) increasing cognitive processing of and attention toward potential sources of threat; and (c) increasing the negative affective valence of stimulus encoding. In addition, arousal is increased that serves to strengthen any resulting defensive fight, flight, or freeze response. It also serves to potentiate behaviors related to the behavioral approach system (BAS) if the outcome of BIS conflict resolution is a return to approach behavior, which can lead to a seemingly paradoxical effect of conflict detection—namely, strengthened BAS behavior (Corr, 2010).

Therefore, at the cognitive level information processing (attentional and memory processes) is pressed into the service of the control of any negative consequences resulting from the possible means of goal conflict resolution (Corr, 2010; McNaughton & Corr, 2008; McNaughton & Gray, 2000). Such emotionally biased cognitive processing related to the BIS (trait anxiety) is well documented (see, e.g., Bar-Haim, Lamy, Pergamin, Bakermans-Kranenburg & van IJzendoorn, 2007; Gomez & Gomez, 2002; Rutherford, MacLeod, & Campbell, 2004) and is not discussed further in this chapter.

Since the main focus of this chapter is on the cognitive aspects of BIS activation, we propose that in addition to the emotionally biased cognition noted above, there is another specific organization of attentional processing—namely, dissimilarity focus that may be the mechanism that facilitates fulfilling the control function of the BIS as a comparator.

Standard BIS theory refers to anxiety as the result of conflict detection and to the behavioral, emotional, and cognitive consequences of anxiety. The standard version, however, does not point to any specific cognitive processes or mechanisms that would be directly related to the comparator function of the BIS. Therefore what seems to be missing in standard BIS theory is the cognitive process that would reflect more directly the comparator function of the BIS. We propose that the early attentional mechanism related to sensitivity to discrepancies results in controlled attentional processing reflected in orientation to dissimilarity. We believe that studying the proposed attentional mechanism could help fill this gap.

We want to highlight the biological basis as well as the cognitive and affective mechanisms and processes as especially important in developing the BIS-dependent orientation to dissimilarity.

CONFLICT DETECTION RELATED TO THE BIS AS A COMPARATOR: BIOLOGICAL PROCESSES AND MECHANISMS

According to Corr (2004) and Gray and McNaughton (2000), the neurobiological basis of the BIS is related to hierarchically linked neural structures involving the periaqueductal gray, septo-hippocampal system, amygdala, anterior cingulate cortex (ACC), and dorsal prefrontal cortex. The simple comparison of the sensory input with the expected one is fulfilled by the septo-hippocampal system, whereas the amygdala system is associated with the increased arousal output of the BIS (Gray & McNaughton, 2000). In the revised theory, the ACC involved in conflict processing in the form of error detection (Corr, 2010) and the dorsolateral prefrontal cortex as a part engaged in conflict resolution (Corr, 2010) start to play an important role (Krug & Carter, 2010).

Neurocognitive studies confirm that neurobiological structures associated with the BIS are also engaged in mismatch detection. For example, Kumaran and Maguire (2006) demonstrated that detection of associative mismatches between expectations that are based on retrieval of past experience and current sensory input engages the hippocampus. They investigated brain responses to novel sequences of objects using functional magnetic resonance imaging while subjects performed an incidental target detection task. The results showed that hippocampal activation was maximal when predictions concerning which objects would appear next in a sequence were violated by sensory reality. These authors suggested that the hippocampus might generate predictions about how future events would unfold and critically detect when these expectancies are violated, even when the task did not require it (Kumaran & Maguire, 2006).

These findings are in line with the postulated function of the BIS as a comparator, which is engaged in "what if" simulations of future behavior (Corr, 2008, 2010). When the process of error detection is involved in more cognitively demanding tasks, such as monitoring of ongoing performance errors or response conflicts that demand cognitive control, then the dorsal ACC is engaged (e.g., Ridderinkhof, Ullsperger, Crone, & Nieuwenhuis, 2004; Spunt, Lieberman, Cohen, & Eisenberger, 2012). This error processing is reflected in error-related negativity (ERN), registered as a sharp negative deflection in the event-related potential that peaks approximately 50 ms after an unintended response (Falkenstein, Hoormann, Christ, & Hohnsbein, 2000) and is generated in the ACC. Thus the ACC generates ERN immediately after the commission of an error or whenever the outcomes are worse than expected (Holroyd & Coles, 2002).

However, ACC activity was also registered during correct responses in the course of a Go/NoGo task, where the participant had to respond to the letter *X* after an *A* was presented and ignore all other letter combinations. The results showed that the more competitive stimuli were presented (producing conflict between response tendencies), the more the ACC was activated (Carter et al., 1998). Conflict that induces the dorsal part of ACC activation conveys competing response tendencies or semantic or conceptual representations (Badre & Wagner, 2004; van Veen & Carter, 2005; Weissman, Giesbrecht, Song, Mangun, & Woldorff, 2003). In the literature the error detection function of the ACC (reinforcement learning approach) is closely related to ACC conflict theory (Carter & van Veen, 2007; for a review see Krug & Carter, 2010). However, the ACC is also associated with experiencing negative emotional states.

Affective Consequences of Conflict Detection

It is proposed that the rostral areas of the ACC are involved in emotional processing, including emotional aspects of error monitoring (through its strong connections to other structures related to emotional processing, like the amygdala), while the dorsal areas of the ACC are related to cognitive processes linked to error or conflict detection (Bush, Luu, & Posner, 2000). Indeed, recently collected neurocognitive data show that conflict detection produced a state of negative affect (NA; Compton et al., 2007; Dreisbach & Fischer, 2012; Hajcak & Foti, 2008; Wiswede, Munte, Goschke, & Rüsseler, 2009). The ERN reflected affective response to errors detected (Hajcak and Foti, 2008; Luu, Collins, & Tucker, 2000) or motivational value of ongoing events (Bush et al., 2000; Hajcak, Moser, Yeung, & Simons, 2005). If ERN response indicates increased negative affect as a reaction to error detection, then we should expect that BIS sensitivity should increase ERN amplitude in response to errors. Compared with subjects with low BIS scores, Boksem, Tops, Wester, Meijman, and Lorist (2006) confirmed that high-scoring BIS subjects (measured by the BIS/BAS scale of Carver & White, 1994) showed larger ERN amplitudes in response to error trials in the flanker task.

Since the number of studies directly examining the relation between the BIS and ERN amplitude are limited, we will refer further to the anxiety-related analysis. Anxiety and rumination were examined by Hajcak, McDonald, and Simons (2003). They confirmed that worry and anxiety enhance the ERN in response to errors and the same relation was replicated for generalized anxiety disorder (Weinberg, Olvet, & Hajcak, 2010). Moser, Moran, Schroeder, Donnellan, and Yeung (2013) recently conducted a meta-analysis of studies on anxiety and error-related negativity amplitude, which showed that anxious apprehension/worry—rather than anxious arousal—is the dimension of anxiety closely associated with error monitoring. These authors argued that a content analysis of the BIS scale (Carver & White, 1994) suggests its strong relation to the apprehension type of anxiety, which supports linking the BIS with the ACC function of error monitoring and emotional reaction to error or conflict detection.

Etkin, Enger, and Kalisch (2011) showed that both regions of the ACC and medial prefrontal cortex are engaged in emotional processing like appraisal processes and generation of emotional responses. The confluence of cognitive and emotional processing within the ACC seems to support the biological basis of the comparator function related to the BIS, encompassing mismatch or conflict detection and the state of anxiety as a consequence. However, more empirical data are needed to validate this assumption.

CONTROL PROCESSES RELATED TO THE BIS: BIOLOGICAL BASES

In the reformulated model (Corr, 2008; see Figure 1 above), activation of the BIS as a result of conflict detection leads to initiation of several cognitive processes (e.g., emotionally biased attention and memory) aimed at conflict resolution. The biological bases for these processes are not very clearly established within BIS theory. Corr (2010), based on the Miller and Cohen (2001) model, proposed that the dorsal stream of the prefrontal cortex is the cortical area related to the control function of the BIS (McNaughton & Corr, 2008). The role of the prefrontal cortex in conflict resolution was also studied within the conflict-control model of Botvinick and others (Botvinick, Braver, Barch, Carter, & Cohen, 2001; Kerns, 2006; Krug & Carter, 2012).

According to the conflict-control model (Botvinick et al., 2001), conflict detected by the ACC recruits control from the dorsolateral prefrontal cortex to resolve the conflict. The role of the dorsolateral prefrontal cortex in conflict resolution (producing the correct reaction) was confirmed in several experiments, with the Stroop or flanker tasks used to induce the process of conflict detection and resolution (Kerns, 2006; Krug & Carter, 2012). Botvinick et al. (2001) proposed that in the conflicting trials of a Stroop task the conflict is resolved by enhancing attention to the task-relevant stimulus or stimulus dimension (Enger & Hirsch, 2005).

Also, Miller and Cohen (2001) analyzed the control processes engaged in Stroop and the Wisconsin Card Sorting Test performance guided by rules and requiring either selective attention, behavioral inhibition, or working memory. The control processes related to top-down processing, "when behavior must be guided by internal states or intentions" (Miller & Cohen, 2001, p. 168), are linked to the function of the prefrontal cortex. Therefore top-down attentional processing is one of the primary processes related to cognitive control (see also Rueda et al., 2004).

BIS-RELATED COGNITIVE CONSEQUENCES OF CONFLICT DETECTION: ATTENTIONAL PROCESSING

The BIS is thought to be a goal-conflict detection/resolution device and as such is related to cognitive control (Botvinick et al., 2001; Corr, 2010). Corr (2010) links this comparator function to executive control on the basis of common neurological structures that share the BIS and executive control—namely, the prefrontal cortex (see Miller & Cohen, 2001). The concept of cognitive control contains a few higher-order cognitive processes related to "perceptual selection, response biasing, and the online maintenance of contextual information" (Botvinick et al., 2001, p. 624).

In the literature there are some other approaches referring to the notion of cognitive control, such as the concepts of executive attention (Rueda et al., 2004) and attentional control (Derryberry & Reed, 2002), all of which emphasize an important role of the attentional mechanisms in cognitive, emotional, and behavioral regulation. The concept of executive attention is one of the three attentional systems, in addition to the orienting and alerting systems, proposed by Rueda et al. (2004). Neurocognitive data support the role of the executive system of attention in conflict detection (Walsh, Buonocore, Carter, & Mangun, 2011), conflict-monitoring processes (Botvinick, 2007), and conflict resolution (Fernadez-Duque et al., 2000).

The processes of selective attention related to the executive system of attention are the main focus of this chapter. The control mechanism of selective attention guides the process of perception to filter out the stimulus salient for the sake of an active goal. To highlight the superior role of attentional processes over perception in cognitive control, the attentional processes are termed "perceptual attention" (Derryberry, 2002).

We postulate that if the BIS is related to conflict detection and monitoring, then the attention that selectively monitors and filters out the information about the state of discrepancy to the standard (current level of conflict) is a manifestation of the control mechanism related to the BIS. In other words, we suggest that discrepancy detection as a bottom-up attentional process establishes the top-down selective attention aimed at discrepancy or conflict monitoring. The detection of discrepancy occurs at an early stage of information processing, at the automatic level (see more evidence in the biological section of this chapter) involving a preattentive memory-based comparison process, with involuntary shift of attention (e.g., Yantis, 2008).

The discrepancy/conflict as potentially evolutionary salient information catch/engage the orienting mechanism of attention toward the source of a mismatch (e.g., Fernadez-Duque et al., 2000; Posner, 1994). Such attentional engagement might simultaneously evoke activation, resulting in engagement of the executive mechanism of attention (Fernadez-Duque et al., 2000; Posner, 1994). Executive attention is mostly employed in situations requiring voluntary selection among competing items, resolution of conflict among responses, and monitoring and correcting errors (Posner & Rothbart, 1998). The vigilance and orienting systems of attention are more reactive and closely related to motivational processes. Automatic processes regulate them until the executive system of attention is activated and starts to exert control over them in the service of ongoing needs and goals. Therefore involvement of the executive mechanism of attention changes the nature of cognition from automatic to controlled (Fan, McCandliss, Fossella, Flombaum, & Posner, 2005; Fernadez-Duque et al., 2000; Kolańczyk, 2004), probably with prioritizing the control over stimulus input.

The BIS operating as a comparator runs as a negative feedback system, in which the change of the output (at any level: emotional, cognitive, or physical) is aimed at countering any deviation of the input function from the reference value (no-conflict state; see Carver & Scheier, 1998). Thus the BIS as a comparator monitors any deviation from the standard value of no conflict, and as a result all incoming stimuli—which are different and might increase the discrepancy or the conflict—should be attended. In other words, the dissimilarity orientation, being a result of the engagement of the orienting system of attention by discrepancy detection, is sustained by the executive system of attention—selective top-down processing of dissimilarity in the service of active goal-discrepancy monitoring. Thus top-down selective attention serves a control function over bottom-up perceptual processes, modulating them according to an active standard.

We should expect that high BIS-sensitive subjects should be especially motivated to orient their attention toward dissimilarity, since individual differences in BIS sensitivity determine the threshold for the error-triggering mechanism (Corr, 2010). High BIS sensitivity being related to lower threshold—a kind of oversensitive, error-triggering mechanism—results in detecting minor discrepancies and experiencing a higher level of anxiety. By contrast, low BIS sensitivity should lead to impeded capability to detect the mismatch between expected and actual stimuli, resulting in increased tolerance of discrepancy and an absence or a low level of anxiety. Recently collected data provide some support for this hypothesis. Leue et al. (2012) confirmed the earlier findings of Amodio et al. (2008), showing that high-BIS individuals display high conflict-monitoring intensity to a low conflict level and do not adequately regulate the conflict-monitoring sensitivity in response to the variations in intensity of conflict level (more negative N2 amplitude as a response to a Go/NoGo task with a low conflict level); on the contrary, low trait-BIS individuals effectively adapt the comparator function of BIS (conflict-monitoring intensity) to the level of conflict (discrepancy).

Orientation to Dissimilarity

Dissimilarity focus and similarity focus are two types of comparative processes that play a crucial role in many psychological domains (Hassin, 2001). Perception of similarities or dissimilarities can be shaped by several factors like stimuli characteristics, task formulation, direction of comparison, and effective context (Tversky & Gati, 1978). Perceiving similarities is a positive function of common properties and negative function of distinctive properties (Tversky & Gati, 1978). The more the compared objects have in common, the more they are perceived as similar (Shepard & Arabie, 1979). On the other hand, when one of the compared objects has a characteristic that the other does not, the objects are perceived as dissimilar. Differences are easier to find for similar pairs than for dissimilar pairs (Genter & Markman, 1994). Characteristics of the standard also shape comparative processes. Extreme characteristics of the standard initiate a search for dissimilarities, while moderate characteristics trigger a search for similarities (Damisch, Mussweiler, & Plessner, 2006).

The attentional processes that underlie the similarity and dissimilarity perception are best represented in the search asymmetries, a part of feature integration theory of Treisman and Gelade (1980) that shows differences between two search conditions. In the target+ condition, the target is given an additional feature not contained in any of the nontargets. In the target- condition, a critical feature is removed from one (target) element and this feature is retained in all other nontarget elements. Thus, for instance, a target+ condition would be one in which the target is a Q and the nontargets are O's. In the target- condition, the mapping is reversed such that now O is the target and Q's are the nontargets (Quinlan, 2003).

The crucial finding of the search asymmetries is that the target present condition is easier than the target absent condition. Performance of the discrimination task where the target feature absent is more capacity demanding because of the memory imperative (Warm, Parasuraman, & Matthews, 2008). This task engages a successive discrimination, where the observer needs to compare current input with the standard retained in working memory to separate critical signals from nonsignal stimulus events. In the discrimination task where the target is present, simultaneous processing is involved. All the information needed to distinguish signals from nonsignals is present in the stimuli themselves and there is little involvement of recent memory for the signal feature.

Similar predictions can be derived from the social models of comparative judgments. Mussweiler and Epstude (2009) and Corcoran, Epstude, Damisch, and Mussweiler (2011) demonstrated that judging the similarity of two stimuli is faster and related to searching for less target information than judging the dissimilarity of two stimuli. Focusing on similarities thus appears to be the more efficient comparative thinking style and is activated as nonintentional process, which occurs during the "normal" course of processing and appears early in cognitive development (see discussion in Markman & Genter, 2005). Thus dissimilarity focus seems to be a more cognitively demanding strategy of information processing.

Biases in comparative processes range from an attentional level of processing to a conceptual one (Friedman & Förster, 2010; Gardner, 1953). Bias means that we are selectively concentrating either on stimuli that are similar and congruent to the comparative standard or on those that are dissimilar and incongruent (Carver & Scheier, 1998; Friedman & Förster, 2010; Mussweiler & Epstude, 2009). In addition to the stimuli and task characteristics, there are motivational processes that could bias the comparison.

Nussinson, Seibt, Häfner, and Strack (2011) presented a hypothesis that avoidance motivation leads to perceiving more differences between objects in the environment. In two experiments both avoidance and approach motivation were induced using the arm flexion procedure. Subjects rated the similarities and differences between eighteen pairs of objects related differently to each other. Results showed that manipulation of motivation differentiated the ratings of similarity in such a way that motivational states related to avoidance are related to the reduction of similarities perception (similarities/dissimilarities were a one-dimensional characteristic of comparative objects).

More indirect evidence comes from the studies of Förster (2009). He manipulated promotion and prevention focus and asked subjects to rate the similarities and differences between two pictures. Results revealed that subjects in a prevention state perceived more differences between objects than subjects in a promotion state or in the control group. They also perceived more differences than similarities as a within-group effect.

Looking for differences means that we selectively concentrate on features that are different from the standard or from other objects. Differences in terms of the feedback processes signal that something does not meet the standard or the expected value or an error occurs in ongoing processes (Carver & Scheier, 1998). Discrepancy itself is a state that evokes arousal (MacDowell & Mandler, 1989), negative affect (Carver, & Scheier, 1998; Hajcack & Foti, 2008), or affective consequences like surprise—a nonpropositional signal of the output of schema-discrepancy detector (Reisenzein, 2000). Therefore affective processes are strongly related to discrepancy detection (see also the biological part of the chapter). What is the role of affect in dissimilarity orientation?

Affect is a reaction of the organism to any change in the environment or organism, and as a "proto-emotion" is characterized only by the strength of activation and by the valence (positive or negative) that is based on basic biological processes, causing the tendency to be oriented toward or away from the source of change (e.g., Chen & Bargh, 1999; Kolańczyk, 2004; Neuman & Starck, 2000; Smith & Neuman, 2005). The role of affective processes in an error-detection mechanism might consist of automatic evaluation of what is going around. Affect is triggered before any controlled cognitive operations have been engaged and therefore operates subconsciously, providing basic information about the state of the environment or the organism (e.g., theory-based appraisal proposed by Clore & Ortony, 2000; Schwarz, 2002; Winkielman, Berridge, & Wilbarger, 2005).

Thus it is possible that unconscious detection of errors (Franssens & de Neys, 2009; Yantis, 2008) generates sufficiently strong negative affect (the higher sensitivity of BIS, the stronger the negative affect) to strengthen attention toward errors. In other words, negative affect provides basic information ("Watch out!") that intensifies the orienting system of attention, and in response the executive mechanism of attention is engaged with selective attention to mismatch.

THE BIS AND ATTENTIONAL ORIENTATION TO DISSIMILARITY: SYNOPSIS

The BIS working as a comparator is engaged in conflict detection and resolution. Conflict detection results in activation of the affective mechanisms (e.g., Hajcak & Foti, 2008), as well as the multilevel attentional mechanisms conclusively related to the executive attention system (cognitive control; Fernadez-Duque et al., 2000). Both types of mechanisms are aimed at conflict monitoring and conflict resolution (Aarts & Pourtois, 2010).

Taking all these data into account, we propose that orientation to dissimilarity is an attentional mode developed as one of the cognitive tools that supports conflict monitoring, the BIS-related comparator function. Therefore orientation to dissimilarity can be viewed as a part of cognitive control processes. The arguments supporting the theoretical status of orientation to dissimilarity are based on biological data, as well as cognitive and affective consequences of conflict detection.

Based on the cognitive and affective mechanisms activated as a result of conflict detection, which might be responsible for developing the BIS/dissimilarity focus relationship, we first examine the role of negative affect as a potential moderator of to the BIS/dissimilarity focus relationship. If this is true, then especially the high BIS sensitivity related to high negative affect should result in dissimilarity focus (Study 1). It is not entirely clear whether the BIS/dissimilarity focus relationship is the cognitive mechanism developed as a consequence of comparator function related to the BIS, or whether it developed as a consequence of affective reaction (anxiety) to conflict detection. The second hypothesis deals with the BIS relation to dissimilarity and similarity detection; we expect that BIS sensitivity should improve dissimilarity detection (Studies 2 and 3).

THE BIS AND ATTENTIONAL ORIENTATION TO DISSIMILARITY: SELECTED EMPIRICAL EVIDENCE

Below we present three empirical studies concerning the relation between the BIS as a dimension of individual differences and the attentional processes related to orientation to similarity versus dissimilarity.

To test selective attention to dissimilarity, we chose the d2 Test of Attention since it allows testing the process of objects selection according to the active goal provided by the instruction (select all objects similar or dissimilar to the target). During the process of objects selection, subjects need to focus on particular characteristics of objects while suppressing awareness of competing distractors (Brickenkamp & Zillmer, 1998). Moreover, studies on the structure of attention revealed that performing the d2 Test of Attention is related to the ability to switch the attentional focus from one stimulus dimension to another and the ability to divide attention between two stimulus dimensions (Goldhammer, Moosbruger, & Schweizer, 2007). Additionally, the condition of dissimilarity detection requires inhibition of the prompt reaction to signals similar to the target. All processes involved in the performance of the d2 Test are basic cognitive processes related to attentional control (Rueda et al., 2004).

Study 1. Does BIS Sensitivity or Negative Affect Improve Dissimilarity Orientation?

We hypothesized that the relation between the BIS and dissimilarity focus will be amplified by the intensity of negative affect.

The orientation to dissimilarity was tested with a paper-and-pencil d2 Test of Attention. The test consists of two subtests: objects selection of objects similar (d1) or dissimilar (d2) to the target (Brickenkamp & Zillmer, 1998; Polish adaptation by Dajek, 2003). In this study we used the second version—dissimilarity focus. Individual differences in BIS sensitivity were measured with the BIS/BAS scale (Carver & White, 1994; Polish adaptation by Müller & Wytykowska, 2005). First, 110 participants (64 females, $M = 21.6$, $SD = 1.9$) completed the BIS/BAS scale and later were randomly assigned to either the experimental or control condition. Twelve subjects were excluded from the analysis as outliers (Asendorpf, 2010).

In the experimental (failure) condition, participants played the well-known computer game Tetris for four minutes, which was programmed in such a way to make it almost impossible to create a horizontal line of ten blocks without gaps—hence they were bound to fail. In the control condition, participants rated ten pictures according to their quality. After finishing the computer task, they completed the PANAS short version (Watson, Clark, & Tellegen, 1988) and took the d2 Test of Attention (dissimilarity searching part). Individuals were expected to scan fourteen lines with 47 characters in each line and cross out all occurrences different from the letter *d* with two dashes in four minutes (inhibition and focusing on the dissimilarities condition), and were asked to "work as quickly as you can without making mistakes."

As an index of dissimilarity focus, we took the hit rate index reflecting the proportion of items correctly processed to the total number of items scanned. To avoid using letter symbols, we will call this index effectiveness of detection. Since this index is sensitive to the speed/accuracy trade-off, to control it we also tested the strategy of the test performance like skipping strategy, which is characterized by extremely high scores for processing speed—total number of items processed—but a correspondingly high percentage of errors, especially errors of omission. The omission type of error is mainly related to the speed/accuracy trade-off, since increased processing speed at the expense of processing accuracy results in an increase in errors of omission (Lobaugh, Cole, & Rovet, 1998; Zenger & Fahle, 1997).

First, the correlations between BIS measure and the performance indices were tested to check whether the index of effectiveness of detection could be reliably used. Additionally, the total of items processed as an index of speed of processing was analyzed. Results showed that the BIS positively correlates with hit rate $r(98) = 0.414$, $p < 0.01$, and negatively with skipping strategy $r(98) = -0.401$, $p < 0.01$; there was no significant relation to speed but the direction was negative. Therefore it seems that BIS sensitivity is related to processing strategy, manifested in sacrificing speed for accuracy.

Experimental manipulation was successful; the ANOVA analysis revealed that negative affect significantly differed between conditions $F(1, 95) = 8.640$, $p < 0.01$, $\eta^2 = 0.085$. In the stress condition the mean negative affect was 24.57, while in the control condition it was 20.53.

The ANOVA analysis showed that the experimental condition did not influence the hit rate in dissimilarity searching task $F(1, 98) = 0.30$, $p = 0.83$, $\eta^2 = 0.002$. The failure experience itself had no impact on effectiveness of dissimilarity detection. To test whether the BIS/dissimilarity focus relationship is dependent on the intensity of negative affect (measured after the failure experience), a hierarchical regression analysis was used. In the first step the BIS, NA, and experimental condition were entered as predictors, followed by the interaction of the BIS and NA in the next step and finally the interaction of the BIS and experimental condition. Even when the experimental condition was included in the regression analysis, the ANOVA was not significant, aimed at controlling the cognitive (worry) or motivational effects that might be not picked up by the NA scale. The first step of the regression model accounted for a significant portion of variance ($R^2 = 0.21$), $F(3, 94) = 7.98$, $p < 0.001$, with BIS ($ß = 0.509$, $p < 0.001$) as a significant predictor and both NA ($ß = -0.165$, $p = 0.124$) and experimental condition ($ß = 0.73$, $p = 0.46$) as nonsignificant. The second and third steps of the model did not account for an additional portion of variance. Therefore neither mood nor failure (experimental conditions) seem to moderate the BIS/effectiveness of dissimilarity detection relationship.

Hierarchical regression for skipping strategy as a dependent variable revealed that only the BIS accounted for a significant portion of variance ($R^2 = 0.19$), $F(3, 94) = 7.76$, $p < 0.001$, with BIS ($ß = -0.491$, $p < 0.001$). Neither NA and experimental conditions nor their interaction with the BIS appeared to be significant predictors.

Finally, we conducted hierarchical regression for speed (all items processed). Results showed again that only first model was significant ($R^2 = 0.08$), $F(3, 94) = 2.67$, $p < 0.05$. The significant predictors were BIS ($ß = -0.22$, $p < 0.05$) and NA ($ß = 0.225$, $p < 0.05$). The whole regression model appeared to be weak, however.

Results from the first study showed that BIS sensitivity promotes concentration on the accuracy rather than the speed of processing, which results in more effective detection of items different than the target. Negative affect appeared to be only slightly positively related to effectiveness of detection.

Studies 2 & 3. BIS Sensitivity and Dissimilarity Detection: A Stable Pattern of Relation?

The previous study suggests that the BIS is indeed related to orientation to dissimilarity. However, there are two modes of comparison processes: orientation to similarity versus orientation to dissimilarity. We hypothesized that the BIS should be particularly oriented to dissimilarity due to the fact that such orientation facilitates monitoring the discrepancies to the standard (no conflict) as one of the comparator functions. To test this prediction, we incorporated both types of detections—similarity and dissimilarity—into the next study.

The orientation to similarity versus dissimilarity was tested with the paper-and-pencil d2 Test of Attention and individual differences in BIS sensitivity were tested with the BIS/BAS scale. In Study 2, 99 participants after removing outliers (79 females, $M = 21.2$, $SD = 2.1$) across two sessions completed the BIS/BAS scale[1] and then took the first test of attention. Individuals were expected to scan fourteen lines with 47 characters in each line and cross out all occurrences of the letter *d* with two dashes while ignoring letters *d* or *p* marked with one, three, or four small dashes in four minutes (searching-for-similarities condition). After the distraction trial, they were asked to scan the lines and not cross out all occurrences of the letter *d* with two dashes while crossing out all other characters in four minutes (inhibition and focusing on the dissimilarities condition). The instruction again was "work as quickly as you can without making mistakes."

ANOVA with repeated measures within the hit rate as a within-subjects factor and BIS 3 (low vs. average vs. high) as a between-subjects factor was conducted. The significant result is shown in Figure 2.

Analysis of contrast effects showed that high BIS scores differ in effectiveness of detecting similarities versus dissimilarities, in such a way that high-BIS subjects are better at recognizing the items that are different than the target item (dissimilarity condition) than the items, which are the same as a target item (similarity condition) $F(1,96) = 5.41, p < 0.05, \eta^2 = 0.07$.

To control the speed/accuracy trade-off, the same ANOVA analysis was done for skipping strategy and speed. Analysis revealed the main effect of BIS for skipping strategy $F(2,95) = 3.61, p < 0.05, \eta^2 = 0.07$. Generally, the high-BIS ($M = 0.14$, $SD = 0.003$) and the average BIS ($M = 0.15$, $SD = 0.002$) subjects made less errors of omission than low-BIS subjects ($M = 0.23$, $SD = 0.003$). For the speed analysis, the results were nonsignificant.

The results partly confirmed predictions and suggested that high sensitivity of the BIS is related to more effective detection of dissimilar than similar signals.

[1] The sample was split into three groups according to the mean for the BIS scale ($M = 20.8$) and the 0.5 of the standard deviation ($SD = 4.2$) to the mean.

Such “specialization” was not observed in the groups with a low and medium level of BIS sensitivity. Nevertheless, this conclusion needs to be made with caution since the study design has one limitation. The search-for-similarities versus search-for-dissimilarities condition was not randomly distributed. All participants first completed the search-for-similarities task and after that the search-for-dissimilarities task; therefore the hit rate index might be a result of individual differences of the BIS, as well as the practice effect. However, even if the results mainly reflected the practice effect, this effect was significant only for the high-BIS group—which might suggest that subjects with high BIS sensitivity were particularly motivated to search for dissimilarities.

This line of reasoning is supported by the findings obtained by Nussinson et al. (2011). The effect of fatigue or ego-depletion processes is rather less, probably since the simple d2 Test takes only four minutes—in comparison with other popular tests that measure sustained attention (like the continuous performance test) that take five times longer. One more feature of the design of this study deserves our attention. There is a kind of set-switching element to the task since the second task required subjects to swap the stimulus-response mapping of the first task (G. Matthews, personal communication, 2014). Keeping in mind that the BIS is strongly related to the apprehension type of anxiety (Moser et al., 2013), the better detection of dissimilarity than similarity revealed only by high-BIS subjects seems to be inconsistent with Eysenck’s attentional control theory (ACT; Eysenck & Derakshan, 2011).

Eysenck and Derakshan (2011) claimed that anxiety mainly impairs processes related to executive functions of working memory like inhibition, updating, and

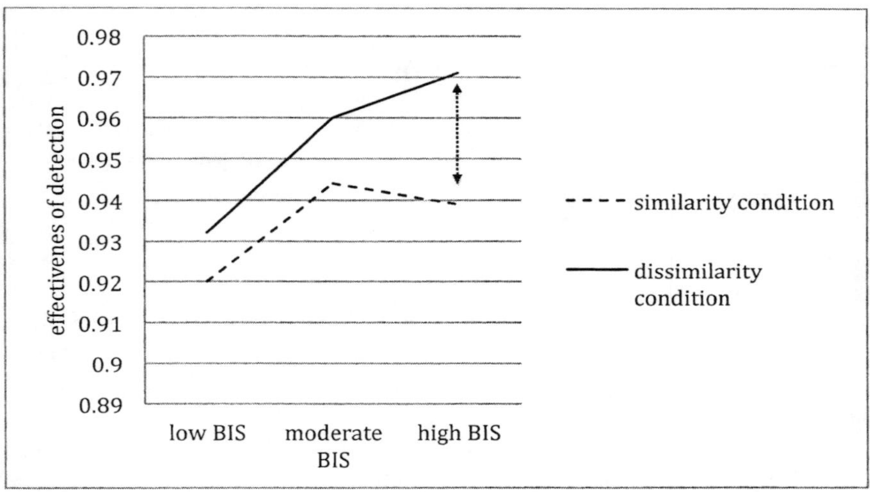

Figure 2. Effectiveness of similarity and dissimilarity detection as a within-group condition, depending on the BIS scores.

shifting. Therefore, in the case of shifting we should expect decreased—rather than improved—performance of the second task (dissimilarity detection) among high-BIS subjects. We might argue that the design of the study was not a standard design for testing the effectiveness of shifting (Eysenck & Derakshan, 2011) since there was a buffer task between both attentional tests. Therefore the 6–7 minutes of the buffer task might be long enough and sufficiently cognitively engaging to unlink the S–R association.

In the next study, the search for similarities and dissimilarities was a between-subject condition. A total of 108 participants (56 females, $M = 18.6$, $SD = 1.02$) across two sessions completed the BIS/BAS scale, then were randomly assigned to either the similarities or dissimilarities condition and took the Test of Attention.

Since the aim of the study was to test the relation between BIS sensitivity and effectiveness of similarities versus effectiveness of dissimilarity detection, two one-way ANOVA were conducted—one for the detection of similarities and the second for dissimilarities. The analysis of variance was chosen due to the fact that the BIS/dissimilarity detection relationship was curvilinear. The sample was split into three groups according to the mean for the BIS scale ($M = 20.25$) and the 0.5 of the standard deviation ($SD = 3.81$) to the mean.

Results showed that BIS sensitivity did not differentiate the effectiveness of similarity detection $F(2, 46) = 0.9$, $p = 0.4$. For the effectiveness of dissimilarity detection, the main effect of BIS was significant $F(2, 56) = 4.92$, $p < 0.05$, $\eta^2 = 0.18$. High-BIS subjects outperform ($M = 0.95$, $SD = 0.01$) moderate BIS subjects ($M = 0.91$, $SD = 0.01$), $p < 0.05$ and low-BIS subjects ($M = 0.93$, $SD = 0.01$), $p = 0.054$. In the similarities-detection condition, the BIS did not differentiate the effectiveness of similarity detection. The results are shown in Figure 3.

The results showed that indeed high BIS-sensitive subjects were more effective in detection of dissimilarities than their moderate and low BIS-sensitive counterparts. Additional analysis conducted for skipping strategy and speed did not reveal any significant results.

DISCUSSION

The main focus of this chapter is on the idea that, at the cognitive level, BIS sensitivity as a personality characteristic may result in developing the dissimilarity-oriented attentional mode that facilitates fulfilling the comparator function consisting of conflict detection and resolution. The idea is based on the analysis of the regulative function of the BIS operating according to the negative feedback loop.

We argued that if the BIS operates as a negative feedback system, then it needs to monitor any deviations from the standard value of the state of no conflict. As a result, all incoming stimuli (which are different than the standard and might increase the conflict) should be attended and therefore controlled. In other words, the dissimilarity orientation is a result of the engagement of the executive system of attention in the service of an ongoing goal—reduction of discrepancy to the state of no conflict to prevent a conflict (Botvinick et al., 2001).

We argued further that the data indicate two possible mechanisms responsible for the hypothesized dissimilarity focus/BIS relationship. The first mechanism is a cognitive one resulting from employment of the executive system of attention in response to conflict detection. The second mechanism is an affective one and stems from the affective response to conflict detection, in this case dissimilarity orientation developing as a consequence of the way in which negative affect shapes information processing. Finally, since we focus on the BIS as a personality characteristic, we claim that the mechanisms described above will develop into a relatively stable pattern of attentional processing mode.

The BIS and Dissimilarity Focus: Empirical Findings

We presented three studies more directly examining the relation between the attentional dissimilarity versus similarity focus and BIS sensitivity as a personality characteristic.

The pattern of the findings was generally in line with our proposal. High BIS-sensitive individuals, assigned according to the Carver and White (1994) scale, outperformed their low BIS-sensitive counterparts in the effectiveness of dissimi-

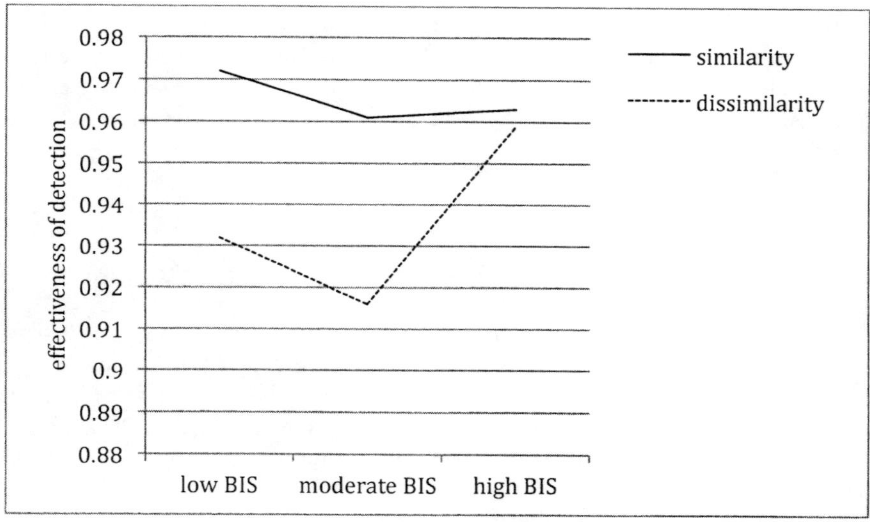

Figure 3. Effectiveness of similarity and dissimilarity detection, depending on the BIS scores.

larity detection across three studies. High-BIS individuals were more effective in detecting dissimilar stimuli to the target than low BIS-sensitive subjects (Studies 2 and 3). Also, Nussinson et al. (2011) recently collected data showing that avoidance motivation—induced by the arm flexion procedure—leads to perceiving more differences between objects. Keeping in mind that generally perceiving similarities is more imposed, quicker, and cognitively less demanding than perceiving dissimilarities (Förster, 2009; Markman & Gentner, 2005; Mussweiler & Epstude, 2009), we showed that high BIS sensitivity biased this rule toward dissimilarity preferences.

We hypothesized that the postulated BIS/dissimilarity orientation relationship may be developed as a result of the impact of the negative affect on information processing. The role of negative affect appeared to be statistically nonsignificant. However, the analysis suggests that to some extent negative affect might reinforce dissimilarity orientation, but only in low-BIS subjects since only those individuals benefited from intensive negative affect by improving the effectiveness of dissimilarity detection. Increase of negative affect for high BIS-sensitive individuals had no effect on their effectiveness to detect dissimilarities.

Therefore it seems that the affective mechanism might be important in developing dissimilarity orientation (e.g., Förster, Friedman, Özelsel, & Denzler, 2006) related to the BIS. However, it may not be reduced to it, which means that the BIS/dissimilarity focus relationship may not be explained only by the affective mechanisms. It is possible that for high-BIS individuals the low threshold for conflict detection results in engagement of cognitive and affective mechanisms at the same time. Since both mechanisms exert the same effect on attentional processing, they might mutually amplify their influence on attentional processing, resulting in development of the orientation to dissimilarity.

Neurocognitive data collected recently by Aarts and Poutois (2010) provide indirect support for this line of reasoning. They have showed that among high-anxious subjects (high BIS) the conflict created by a speeded Go/NoGo task produced higher sensitivity to errors (higher peak of error-related negativity), as well as an affective response to them at the very early stage of processing. Moreover, high-BIS participants felt more anxious. Aarts and Poutois concluded that this finding suggests that anxiety alters the configuration of the neural network activated during early error monitoring. The involvement of the rostral ACC may indicate that not only cognitive but also emotional monitoring effects were temporarily active in high-anxious participants during the early detection of response errors (Aarts & Poutois, 2010).

Dissimilarity Focus as a Control Function

For high-BIS subjects the dissimilarity orientation servers a control function over the stimulus incoming to the system. It enables monitoring any signals violating the standard but is also a more cognitively demanding method of information processing (Förster, 2009; Markman & Gentner, 2005; Mussweiler & Epstude, 2009).

Conditions in all the studies presented in this chapter were not highly demanding; hence high BIS could be more effective in dissimilarity detection. However, we could expect that when the experimental conditions are more stimulative, they would decrease the efficiency of dissimilarity detection (Wytykowska, 2011). Also, the studies on attentional control showed that trait anxiety does not impair attentional control processes until high cognitive demands (e.g., task difficulty) or high stimulating conditions (e.g., time pressure) are introduced (e.g., Derryberry, 2002; Eysenck, 2000; Eysenck, Derakshan, Santos, & Calvo, 2007).

The direct and indirect data presented concerning the BIS/dissimilarity focus relationship suggest that cognitive control is exerted primarily by control over an incoming stimulus. This suggestion is consistent with the part of ACT (Derakshan & Eysenck, 2009; Eysenck, Derakshan, Santos, & Calvo, 2007) where anxiety is proposed to be related largely to the stimulus-driven attention system and often at the expense of the goal-directed attention system. Moore et al. (2012) collected data showing the relation between individual differences in BIS sensitivity and theta waves during response to goal conflict. Subjects were presented with a continuous stream of digit sequences containing four single-integer digits in such a way that one digit was presented for one second, and after each digit sequence an *X* was presented. Subjects were asked to press the button containing four odd digits after each sequence. The registered pattern of theta responses seems to suggest that high- and low-BIS subjects might experience conflict within this task in a different manner. Specifically, low-BIS subjects seemed to experience conflict as a stimulus response, while for high-BIS subjects it was rather a stimulus-stimulus conflict.

Since we consider the dissimilarity orientation as an attentional control mechanism, we need to understand how it is related to ACT (Eysenck & Derakshan, 2011). Eysenck and Derakshan (2011) highlight three core components of attentional control: switching (mostly between the tasks), inhibition, and top-down selective attention. Based on empirical studies, they have demonstrated that anxiety impairs either processing efficacy (anxious individuals need to allocate more effort to perform the task) or impairs all three of these core components (performance effectiveness), mostly in more demanding situations. Also, BIS as a trait is negatively related to volitional attentional control (Fajkowska & Derryberry, 2010). The negative relation between anxiety and attentional control does not contradict the premise and empirical findings presented in this chapter. Dissimilarity orientation as a BIS-specific, selective top-down processing is governed by the need for control over the level of discrepancy (stimulation signaling standard disruption). The main regulative goal is to overcome the negative consequences resulting from the conflict. This positive relation is observed when the demands of the task do not exceed the cognitive resources of the individuals. However, if the task demands exceed the available cognitive resources, then the control mechanism becomes ineffective (Wytykowska, 2011).

Dissimilarity Focus: From the Attentional to the Conceptual Level of Processing

In a 1953 paper published in the *Journal of Personality*, Riley Gardner claimed that concentration on differences-dissimilarity focus is related to sensory judgment as well as conceptual judgment and is reflected in narrow categorization in free sorting tasks. Such a narrow categorization is suggested to be a mechanism to control external stimulation by

> attaching a greater importance to distinguishing between the objectively accurate and the more apparent qualities of stimuli (whichever is demanded at the moment) that result in building the representation of the world in terms of its reducible and classable features. (p. 230)

And Derryberry and Tucker (1994) observe that the detected relation between the BIS and dissimilarity orientation could have further consequences for information processing at the later stages, since the method of processing at the early stages (attentional processing) determines—to some extent—the method of processing at the later stages (conceptual processing).

The results supporting the control function of dissimilarity orientation at the conceptual level are presented by Mikulincer and associates (Mikulincer, Kedem, and Paz, 1990; Mikulincer, Paz, & Kedem, 1990). In their research anxious subjects formed not only narrower categories containing fewer objects in comparison with the breath of categories formed by nonanxious subjects, but they also perceived objects as less similar to the prototype (categorization task based on the approach by Rosch, 1978). High BIS sensitivity (BIS/BAS scale) also appeared to be related to concrete stimulus-based and narrow categorization (Wytykowska, 2005; Wytykowska & Smillie, 2009). These results showed that the BIS-dependent dissimilarity focus shapes more elaborate cognitive processes.

Limitations

First, there might be some reservations about using the d2 Test to examine dissimilarity orientation. Matthews (personal communication, 2014) pointed out that the difference between similarity and dissimilarity searching (especially in Study 1) might be a result of reversal of the S–R relationship rather than a change in stimulus processing—that is, when in the first test (similarity search) subjects had to detect all *d* with two dashes, then in the second test (dissimilarity search) the strategy might be "check whether it is *d* with two dashes and not respond." However, the results of Studies 2 and 3 suggest that the BIS-dissimilarity focus is not the case of the responding strategy. Nevertheless, more studies employing different attentional as well as more complex tasks are needed. Preliminary results of one study conducted by Wytykowska (in preparation) confirmed the BIS/dissimilarity focus relationship. Participants were asked to prepare a project according to some guidelines (standard) in limited time, after which they were provided with mixed feedback containing information that was both congruent and incongruent with the standard in their project. Results showed that the high-BIS subjects mainly focused on incongruent information.

Second, more studies are needed to clarify the exact status of dissimilarity orientation within the BIS model. On the one hand, it could be treated as a consequence of BIS activation and be placed beside the attentional and memory biases to threat. On the other hand, it could be a cognitive mechanism by which a comparator operates. If so, dissimilarity orientation should be placed within the model of the BIS as a comparator.

EPILOGUE: CHALLENGING ISSUES

The question now is how the relationship between the BIS and dissimilarity focus contributes to understanding the regulative role of the BIS as a comparator. The point on which we would like to focus is the standard value.

The standard of regulation is expressed as a state of no conflict. Corr (2008, 2010) claims that conflict detection results in BIS activation, which causes multilevel responses aimed at conflict resolution, returning to the state of no conflict. The function of dissimilarity orientation and negative biases in information processing is to monitor stimuli or action directions that might result in emerging and increasing conflict. These processes provide information about what needs to be avoided to prevent enlarging discrepancy. Cognitive control activated after the conflict detection contains conflict-monitoring and conflict resolution processes (e.g., Botvinick et al., 2004). Conflict-monitoring processes are reflected in "strategic adjustment of cognitive control, which serves to prevent conflict . . . and in detection of internal states signaling a need to intensify or redirect attention or control" (Botvinick et al., 2004, p. 539). Therefore it could be argued that dissimilarity orientation and negative biases in information processing initiated as a result of BIS activation might mainly control the inputs to prevent increasing the state of discrepancy or conflict, though they are related to conflict monitoring rather than conflict resolution.

There is also another aspect of conflict resolution related to the BIS that might be questioned. Provided that the BIS operates according to the negative feedback loop, the comparator should detect the state signaling conflict resolution to end the initiated process of regulation (Carver & Scheier, 1998). If so, the BIS should be sensitive to any input (external or internal) signaling the state of no conflict. For the sake of clarifying the argument presented, we will concentrate only on the emotional representation of the state of no conflict. If conflict detection is related to anxiety (Aarts & Pourtois, 2010; Hajcak, McDonald, & Simons, 2004), the state of conflict resolution or no conflict could be related to the emotion of relief or any other positive emotional state (e.g., joy). According to BIS theory (Corr, 2004, 2008), however, the BIS as a part of the punishment axis (along with the FFFS) is not sensitive to any state evaluated as positive or positive by the lack of negativity. Therefore it is difficult to show how the system knows that conflict is resolved. This creates a basic problem with the control function within the system (Carver & Scheier, 1998).

We may speculate that the BAS or FFFS might be responsible for conflict resolution. In this case the processes initiated after BIS activation (conflict detection) aiming at conflict monitoring reduce the discrepancy or anxiety to the extent that the inhibition of the BAS, exerted by the BIS, decreases enough to enable the BAS to take control over behavior. In other words, the regulatory function of the BIS would be based on confronting the circumstances to act quite safely under BAS regulation. In the other case, if the processes initiated by activation of the BIS are not processed successfully, the discrepancy will extend and the anxiety will increase—which reciprocally could enlarge activation within the FFFS (the BIS and FFFS are strongly connected and together form the punishment axis; Corr & McNaughton, 2008) and might result in the FFFS taking control over behavior. Thus, if the environment is not safe enough (discrepancy to the standard no conflict is still large, BIS regulation is not effective), it is better to run away (the FFFS controls the behavior).

The general line of argument given above suggests that the BIS is a system that monitors conflict and a system of prevention (like prevention regulatory focus; Higgins, 1997), while the conflict resolution process itself may be related either to the BAS or FFFS depending on the effectiveness of the regulatory function of the BIS and the state of the environment.

Acknowledgments

The studies presented in this chapter were supported by grant #MNiSW–N–N106 282839 from the National Science Center to Agata Wytykowska.

REFERENCES

Aarts, K., & Pourtois, G. (2010). Anxiety does not only increase, but also alters early error monitoring functions. *Cognitive, Affective, and Behavioral Neuroscience, 10*, 479–492.

Amodio, D. M., Master, S. L., Yee, C. M., & Taylor, S. E. (2008). Neurocognitive components of the behavioral inhibition and activation systems: Implications for theories of self-regulation. *Psychophysiology, 45*, 11–19.

Asendorpf, J. (2010, July). Robust statistics in personality research. Keynote address presented at the biennial meeting of the European Conference on Personality, Brno, Czech Republic.

Badre, D., & Wagner, A. D. (2004). Selection, integration, and conflict monitoring: Assessing the nature and generality of prefrontal cognitive control mechanisms. *Neuron, 41*, 473–487.

Bar-Haim, Y., Lamy, D., Pergamin, L., Bakermans-Kranenburg, M. J., & van Ijendoorn, M. H. (2007). Threat-related attentional bias in anxious and non-anxious individuals: A meta-analytic study. *Psychological Bulletin, 133*, 1–24.

Boksem, M. A., Tops, M., Wester, A. E., Meijman, T. F., & Lorist, M. M. (2006). Error-related ERP components and individual differences in punishment and reward sensitivity. *Brain Research, 1101*, 92–101.

Botvinick, M. M. (2007). Conflict monitoring and decision making: Reconciling two perspectives on anterior cingulate function. *Cognitive, Affective, and Behavioral Neuroscience, 7*, 356–366.

Botvinick, M., Braver, T., Barch, D. Carter, C., & Cohen, J. (2001). Conflict monitoring and cognitive control. *Psychological Review, 108*, 624–652.

Botvinick, M. M., Cohen, J. D., & Carter, C. S. (2004). Conflict monitoring and anterior cingulate cortex: An update. *Trends in Cognitive Sciences, 8*, 539–546.

Brickenkamp, R., & Zillmer, E. A. (1998). *d2 Test of Attention*. Göttingen, Germany: Hogrefe & Huber.

Bush, G., Luu, P., & Posner, M. I. (2000). Cognitive and emotional influences in anterior cingulate cortex. *Trends in Cognitive Science, 4*, 215–222.

Carter, C. S., Braver, T. S., Barch, D. M., Botvinick, M. M., Noll, D., & Cohen, J. D. (1998). Anterior cingulate cortex, error detection, and the online monitoring of performance. *Science, 280*, 747–749.

Carver, C. S., & Scheier, M. F. (1998). *On the self-regulation of behavior*. New York: Cambridge University Press.

Carver, C. S., Sutton, S. K., & Scheier, M. F. (2000). Action, emotion, and personality. Emerging conceptual integration. *Personality and Social Psychology Bulletin, 26*, 741–751.

Carter, C. S., & van Veen, V. (2007). Anterior cingulate and conflict detection: An update of theory and data. *Cognitive, Affective, and Behavioral Neuroscience, 7*, 367–379.

Carver, C. S., & White, T. (1994). Behavioral inhibition, behavioral activation, and affective responses to impending reward and punishment: The BIS/BAS scales. *Journal of Personality and Social Psychology, 67*, 319–333.

Chen, M., & Bargh, J. A. (1999). Nonconscious approach and avoidance behavioral consequences of the automatic evaluation effect. *Personality and Social Psychology Bulletin, 25*, 215–224.

Clore, G., & Ortony, A. (2000). Cognition in emotion: Always, sometimes, or never? In R. D. Lane & L. Nadel (Eds.), *Cognitive neuroscience of emotion* (pp. 24–61). New York: Oxford University Press.

Compton, R. J., Carp, J., Chaddock, L., Fineman, S. L., Quandt, L. C., & Ratliff, J. B. (2007). Anxiety and error monitoring: Increased error sensitivity or altered expectations? *Brain and Cognition, 64*, 247–256.

Corcoran, K., Epstude, K., Damisch, L., & Mussweiler, T. (2011). Fast similarities: Efficiency advantages of similarity-focused comparison. *Journal of Experimental Psychology: Learning, Memory, and Cognition, 37*, 1280–1286.

Corr, P. J. (2004). Reinforcement sensitivity theory and personality. *Neuroscience and Biobehavioral Reviews, 28*, 317–332.

Corr, P. J. (Ed.) (2008). *The reinforcement sensitivity theory of personality*. Cambridge, UK: Cambridge University Press.

Corr, P. J. (2010). Automatic and controlled processes in behavioural control: Implications for personality psychology. *European Journal of Personality, 24*, 376–403.
Corr, P. J., & McNaughton, N. (2008). Reinforcement sensitivity theory and personality. In P. J. Corr (Ed.), *The reinforcement sensitivity theory of personality* (pp. 155–187). Cambridge, UK: Cambridge University Press.
Corr, P. J., & McNaughton, N. (2012). Neuroscience and approach/avoidance personality traits: A two stage (valuation-motivation) approach. *Neuroscience and Biobehavioral Reviews, 36*, 2339–2354.
Dajek, E. R. (2003). *D2 – test do badania uwagi Brickenkamp & Zillmer* [D2: Test of attention of Brickenkamp & Zillmer]. Warsaw: Pracownia Testów Psychologicznych PTP.
Damish, L., Mussweiler, T., & Plessner, H. (2006). Olympic medals as fruits of comparison? Assimilation and contrast in sequential performance judgments. *Journal of Experimental Psychology: Applied, 12*, 166–178.
Derakshan, N., & Eysenck, M. W. (2009). Anxiety, processing efficiency, and cognitive performance: New developments from attentional control theory. *European Psychologist, 14*, 168–176.
Derryberry, D. (2002). Attention and voluntary self-control. *Self and Identity, 1*, 105–111.
Derryberry, D., & Reed, M. (2002). Anxiety-related attentional biases and their regulation by attentional control. *Journal of Abnormal Psychology, 111*, 225–236.
Derryberry, D., & Tucker, D. M. (1994). Motivating the focus of attention. In P. M. Niedenthal & S. Kitayama (Eds.), *Heart's eye: Emotional influences in perception and attention* (pp. 167–196). New York: Academic Press.
Dreisbach, G., & Fischer, R. (2012). Conflicts as aversive signals. *Brain and Cognition, 72*, 94–98.
Enger, T., & Hirsch, J. (2005). Cognitive control mechanisms resolve conflict through cortical amplification of task-relevant information. *Nature Neuroscience, 8,* 1784–1790.
Epstude, K., & Mussweiler, T. (2009). What you feel is how you compare: How comparisons influence the social induction of affect. *Emotion, 9*, 1–14.
Etkin, A., Egner, T., & Kalisch, R. (2011). Emotional processing in anterior cingulate and medial prefrontal cortex. *Trends in Cognitive Sciences,* 15, 85–93.
Eysenck, M. (2000). A cognitive approach to trait anxiety. *European Journal of Personality, 14*, 463–476.
Eysenck, M., & Derakshan, N. (2011). New perspectives in attentional control. *Personality and Individual Differences, 50*, 955–960.
Eysenck, M. W., Derakshan, N., Santos, R., & Calvo, M. G. (2007). Anxiety and cognitive performance: Attentional control theory. *Emotion, 7*, 336–353.
Fajkowska, M., & Derryberry, D. (2010). Psychometric properties of Attentional Control Scale: The preliminary study on a Polish sample. *Polish Psychological Bulletin, 41*, 1–7.
Falkenstein, M., Hoormann, J., Christ, S., & Hohnsbein, J. (2000). ERP components on reaction errors and their functional significance: A tutorial. *Biological Psychology, 51*, 87–107.
Fan, J., McCandliss, B. D., Fossella, J., Flombaum, J. I., & Posner, M. I. (2005). The activation of attentional networks. *NeuroImage, 26*, 471–479.
Fernandez-Duque, D., Barid, J. A., & Posner, M. I. (2000). Executive attention and metacognitive regulation. *Consciousness and Cognition, 9*, 288–307.

Förster, J. (2009). Relations between perceptual and conceptual scope: How global versus local processing fits a focus on similarity versus dissimilarity. *Journal of Experimental Psychology: General, 138*, 88–111.

Förster, J., Friedman, R., Özelsel, A., & Denzler, M. (2006). Enactment of approach and avoidance behavior influences the scope of perceptual and conceptual attention. *Journal of Experimental Social Psychology, 42*, 133–146.

Franssens, S., & de Neys, W. (2009). The effortless nature of conflict detection during thinking. *Thinking and Reasoning, 15*, 105–128.

Friedman, R., & Förster, J. (2010). Implicit affective cues and attentional tuning: An integrative review. *Psychological Bulletin, 136*, 875–893.

Gardner, R. W. (1953). Cognitive styles in categorizing behavior. *Journal of Personality, 22*, 214–233.

Gentner, D., & Markman, A. B. (1994). Structural alignment in comparison: No difference without similarity. *Psychological Science, 5*, 152–158.

Goldhammer, F., Moosbrugger, H., & Schweizer, K. (2007). On the separability of cognitive abilities related to Posner's attention components and their contributions to conceptually distinct attention abilities related to working memory, action theory, and psychometric assessment. *European Psychologist, 12*, 103–118.

Gomez, A., & Gomez, R. (2002) Personality traits of the behavioural approach and inhibition systems: Associations with processing of emotional stimuli. *Personality and Individual Differences, 32*, 1299–1316.

Gray, J. A., & McNaughton, N. (2000). *The neuropsychology of anxiety: An enquiry into the functions of the septo-hippocampal system* (2nd ed.). Oxford, UK: Oxford University Press.

Hajcak, G., & Foti, D. (2008). Errors are aversive: Defensive motivation and the error-related negativity. *Psychological Science, 19*, 103–108.

Hajcak, G., McDonald, N., & Simons, R. F. (2003). Anxiety and error-related brain activity. *Biological Psychology, 64*, 77–90.

Hajcak, G., McDonald, N., & Simons, R. F. (2004). Error-related psychophysiology and negative affect. *Brain and Cognition, 56*, 189–197.

Hajcak, G., Moser, J. S., Yeung, N., & Simons, R. F. (2005). On the ERN and the significance of errors. *Psychophysiology, 42*, 151–160.

Hassin, R. R. (2001). Making features similar: Comparison process affect perception. *Psychonomic Bulletin and Review, 8*, 728–731.

Higgins, E. T. (1997). Beyond pleasure and pain. *American Psychologist, 55*, 1280–1300.

Hoffman, W. (2010). Intersection "control": Bridging cognitive and personality psychology. *European Journal of Personality, 24*, 407–410.

Holroyd, C. B., & Coles, M. G. H. (2002). The neural basis of human error processing: Reinforcement learning, dopamine, and the error-related negativity. *Psychological Review, 109*, 679–709.

Kerns, J. G. (2006). Anterior cingulate and prefrontal cortex activity in an FMRI study of trial-to-trial adjustments on the Simon task. *NeuroImage, 33*, 399–405.

Kolańczyk, A. (2004). Procesy afektywne i orientacja w otoczeniu [Affective processes and orientation in surroundings]. In A. Kolańczyk, A. Fila-Jankowska, M. Fusiara-Pawłowska, & R. Sterczyński (Eds.), *Serce w rozumie. Afektywne podstawy orientacji w otoczeniu* (pp. 13–47). Gda sk, Poland: Gdańskie Wydawnictwo Psychologiczne GWP.

Krug, M. K., & Carter, C. S. (2010). Adding fear to conflict: A general purpose cognitive control network is modulated by trait anxiety. *Cognitive, Affective, and Behavioral Neuroscience, 10*, 357–371.

Krug, M. K., & Carter, C. S. (2012). Proactive and reactive control during emotional interference and its relationship to trait anxiety. *Brain Research,* 1481, 13–36.

Kumaran, D., & Maguire, E. (2006). An unexpected sequence of events: Mismatch detection in the human hippocampus. *PLoS Biology, 4*, 2372–2382.

Leue, A., Lange, S., & Beauducel, A. (2012). Reinforcement sensitivity and conflict processing: A study of principal components in the N2 time domain. *Journal of Individual Differences, 33*, 160–168.

Lobaugh, N. J., Cole, S., & Rovet, J. F. (1998). Visual search for features and conjunctions in development. *Canadian Journal of Experimental Psychology, 52*, 201–211.

Luu, P., Collins, P., & Tucker, D. M. (2000). Mood, personality, and self-monitoring: Negative affect and emotionality in relation to frontal lobe mechanisms of error monitoring. *Journal of Experimental Psychology: General, 129*, 43–60.

MacDowell, K., A., & Mandler, G. (1989). Constructions of emotion: Discrepancy, arousal, and mood. *Motivation and Emotion, 13*, 105–124.

Markman, A. B., & Gentner, D. (2005). Nonintentional similarity processing. In T. Hassin, J. Bargh, & J. Uleman (Eds.), *The new unconscious* (pp. 107–137). New York: Oxford University Press.

Matthews, G. (2008). Reinforcement sensitivity theory: A critique from cognitive science. In P. J. Corr (Ed.), *The reinforcement sensitivity theory of personality* (pp. 482–507). Cambridge, UK: Cambridge University Press.

McNaughton, N., & Corr, P. J. (2008). The neuropsychology of fear and anxiety: A foundation for reinforcement sensitivity theory. In P. J. Corr (Ed.), *The reinforcement sensitivity theory of personality* (pp. 44–94). Cambridge, UK: Cambridge University Press.

McNaughton, N., & Gray, J. A. (2000). Anxiolytic action on the behavioural inhibition system implies multiple types of arousal contribute to anxiety. *Journal of Affective Disorders, 61*, 161–176.

Mikulincer, M., Kedem, P., & Paz, D. (1990). Anxiety and categorization: 1. The structure and boundaries of mental categories. *Personality and Individual Differences, 11*, 805–814.

Mikulincer, M., Paz, D., & Kedem, P. (1990). Anxiety and categorization: 2. Hierarchical levels of mental categories. *Personality and Individual Differences, 11*, 815–822.

Miller, E. K., & Cohen, J. D. (2001). An integrative theory of prefrontal cortex function. *Annual Review of Neuroscience, 24*, 167–202.

Moore, R., Mills, M., Marshman, P., & Corr, P. (2012). Behavioural Inhibition System (BIS) sensitivity differentiates EEG responses during goal conflict in a continuous monitoring task. *International Journal of Psychophysiology, 85*, 135–144.

Moser, J. S., Moran, T. P., Schroder, H. S., Donnellan, M. B., & Yeung, N. (2013). On the relationship between anxiety and error monitoring: A meta-analysis and conceptual framework. *Frontiers in Human Neuroscience, 7*, 466.

Müller, J. M., & Wytykowska, A. M. (2005). Psychometric properties and validation of a Polish adaptation of Carver and White's BIS/BAS scales. *Personality and Individual Differences, 39*, 795–805.

Mussweiler, T., & Epstude, K. (2009). Relatively fast! Efficiency advantages of comparative thinking. *Journal of Experimental Psychology: General, 138*, 1–21.

Neuman, R., & Starck, F. (2000). Approach and avoidance: The influence of proprioceptive and exteroceptive cues on affective processing. *Journal of Personality and Social Psychology, 79*, 39–40.

Nussinson, R., Seibt, B., Häfner, M., & Strack, F. (2011). Cognitive consequences of motivational orientation: The effect on perceived similarity between objects. *Acta Psychologica, 138*, 39–44.

Posner, M. I. (1994). Attention: The mechanism of consciousness. *Proceedings of the National Academy of Sciences, 91*, 7398–7402.

Posner, M. I., & Rothbart, M. K. (1998). Attention, self-regulation and consciousness. *Philosophical Transactions of the Royal Society of London B, 353*, 1915–1927.

Quinlan, P. T. (2003) Visual feature integration theory: Past, present, and future. *Psychological Bulletin, 129*, 643–673.

Reisenzein, R. (2000). The subjective experience of surprise. In H. Bless & J. P. Forgas (Eds.), *The message within: The role of subjective experience in social cognition and behavior* (pp. 262–279). Philadelphia: Psychology Press.

Revelle, W., & Wilt, J. (2008). Personality is more than reinforcement sensitivity. *European Journal of Personality, 22*, 407–409.

Ridderinkhof, K. R., Ullsperger, M., Crone, E. A., & Nieuwenhuis, S. (2004). The role of medial frontal cortex in cognitive control. *Science, 306*, 443–447.

Rosch, E, H. (1978). Principles of categorization. In E. H. Rosch & B. B. Lloyd (Eds.), *Cognition and categorization* (pp. 27–48). Hillsdale, NJ: Erlbaum.

Rueda, M., Posner, M. I., & Rothbart, M. K. (2004). Attentional control and self-regulation. In R. F. Baumeister & K. D. Vohs (Eds.), *Handbook of self-regulation: Research, theory, and applications* (pp. 283–300). New York: Guilford Press.

Rutherford, E. M., MacLeod, C., & Campbell, L. W. (2004). Negative selectivity effects and emotional selectivity effects in anxiety: Differential attentional correlates of state and trait variables. *Cognition and Emotion, 18*, 711–720.

Schwarz, N. (2002). Situated cognition and the wisdom of feelings: Cognitive tuning. In L. B. Feldman & P. Salovey (Eds.), *The wisdom in feeling: Psychological processes in emotional intelligence* (pp.144–166). New York: Guilford Press.

Shepard, R. N., & Arabie, P. (1979). Additive clustering: Representation of similarities as combinations of discrete overlapping properties. *Psychological Review, 86*, 87–123.

Smith, E. R., & Neuman, R. (2005). Emotion processes considered from the perspective of dual-process models. In L. Feldman-Barrett, P. M. Niedenthal, & P. Winkielman (Eds.), *Emotion and consciousness* (pp. 287–311). New York: Guilford Press.

Spunt, R. P., Lieberman, M. D., Cohen, J. R., & Eisenberger, N. I. (2012). The phenomenology of error processing: The dorsal ACC response to stop-signal errors tracks reports of negative affect. *Journal of Cognitive Neuroscience, 24*, 1753–1756.

Treisman, A., & Gelade, G. (1980). A feature-integration theory of attention. *Cognitive Psychology, 12*, 97–136.

Tversky, A., & Gati, I. (1978). Studies of similarity. *Cognition and Categorization, 1*, 79–98.

van Veen, V., & Carter, C. S. (2005). Separating semantic conflict and response conflict in the Stroop task: A functional MRI study. *NeuroImage, 27*, 497–504.

Walsh, B. J., Buonocore, M. H., Carter, C. S., & Mangun, G. R. (2011). Integrating conflict detection and attentional control mechanisms. *Journal of Cognitive Neuroscience, 23*, 2211–2221.

Warm, J. S., Parasuraman, R., & Matthews, G. (2008). Vigilance requires hard mental work and is stressful. *Human Factors, 50*, 433–441.

Watson, D., Clark, L. A., & Tellegen, A. (1988). Development and validation of brief measures of positive and negative affect: The PANAS scales. *Journal of Personality and Social Psychology, 54*, 1063–1070.

Weinberg, A., Olvet, D. M., & Hajcak, G. (2010). Increased error-related brain activity in generalized anxiety disorder. *Biological Psychology, 85*, 472–480.

Weissman, D. H., Giesbrecht, B., Song, A. W., Mangun, G. R., & Woldorff, M. G. (2003). Conflict monitoring in the human anterior cingulate cortex during selective attention to global and local object features. *NeuroImage, 19*, 1361–1368.

Winkielman, P., Berridge, K. C., & Wilbarger, J. L. (2005). Emotion, behavior, and conscious experience: Once more without feeling. In L. Feldman-Barrett, P. M. Niedenthal, & P. Winkielman (Eds.), *Emotion and consciousness* (pp. 335–362). New York: Guilford Press.

Wiswede, D., Munte, T. F., Goschke, T., & Rüsseler, J. (2009). Negative affect induced by derogatory verbal feedback modulates the neural signature of error detection. *Social Cognitive and Affective Neuroscience, 4*, 227–237.

Wytykowska, A. (2005, July). Who and when is concrete? Who and when is abstract? Do individual differences modify the influence of mood state on categories construction process? Paper presented at the biennial meeting of the International Society for the Study of Individual Differences, Adelaide, Australia.

Wytykowska, A. (2011). Effect of energetic arousal and relaxation on the effectiveness of selective attention: The moderating role of BIS and BAS sensitivity. Unpublished manuscript.

Wytykowska, A. (in preparation). Positive evaluation of objects signaling lack of punishment is related to BIS, not to BAS.

Wytykowska, A., & Smillie, L. (2009). Lęk jako cecha, a proces kategoryzacji z różnych paradygmatach badawczych (Trait anxiety and categorization in different experimental paradigms]. In M. Fajkowska & B. Szymura (Eds.), *Lęk. Geneza–Mechanizmy–Funkcje* (pp. 346–375). Warsaw: Wydawnictwo Naukowe Scholar.

Yantis, S. (2008). Neural basis of selective attention: Cortical sources and targets of attentional modulation. *Current Directions in Psychological Science, 17*, 86–90.

Zenger, B., & Fahle, M. (1997). Missed targets are more frequent than false alarms: A model for error rates in visual search. *Journal of Experimental Psychology: Human Perception and Performance, 23*, 1783–1791.

PART II

Complex Models of Control

CHAPTER 4

Personality and Control

The Cognitive Orientation Approach

Shulamith Kreitler

CONTROL AS A KEY CONSTRUCT

Recent years have witnessed increasing awareness of the importance of control in the human sciences. Its role and manifestations have been identified in diverse domains of behavior including cognition, emotions, and behavior. To mention just a few examples, we find it in problem solving (e.g., Hains & Hains, 1988), in the expression of anger (e.g., Gailliot & Baumeister, 2007), in interpersonal relations (e.g. Fiske, 1993), in achievement behavior (e.g., Shapiro, 1981; Vohs & Schmeichel, 2003), in psychopathology (e.g., Tangney, Baumeister, & Boone, 2004), in physical health (e.g., Johnson, 1999; Martijn, Alberts, & de Vries, 2006; Ryff & Singer, 1998), and in one's sense of the meaningfulness of life (e.g., Feldman & Snyder, 2005). It plays a role in the initiation of an output and its discontinuation, in the rhythm or tempo of execution, and evidently in the processes of inhibition and excitation that accompany the performance of behavior.

Notably, there may even be a reservoir of resources for control, at least for self-control, so that when applied frequently it may actually undergo depletion (Baumeister, Vohs, & Tice, 2007; Sato, Harman, Donohoe, Weaver, & Hall, 2010; Vohs et al., 2008). Evidence for control is frequent also in the behavior of animals (Akre, Bakken, & Hovland, 2009; Auersperg, Laumer, & Bugnyar, 2013; Delgado,

Personality and Control edited by Philip J. Corr, Małgorzata Fajkowska, Michael W. Eysenck, and Agata Wytykowska. Eliot Werner Publications, Clinton Corners, New York, 2015.

1969; Grosch & Neuringer, 1981; Miller, DeWall, Pattison, Molet, & Zentall, 2012; Real, 1991). Further, the correlates of control have been identified on a neurological level (Brass & Haggard, 2007; Kühn, Haggard, & Brass, 2009; Kühn et al., 2011; Schilling et al., 2012). It appears that control also has biological roots. The basic processes of cell activities guided by feedback are only one example of the multitude of control processes that have been studied within the framework of biological control theory (Sontag, 2004).

Control has been considered an important construct in the psychology of personality since the early psychoanalytic period. In this theoretical framework, control has been conceptualized as a component or manifestation of ego strength—which is defined as the ability to integrate the demands of one's id, superego, and reality in order to satisfy one's desires with minimal pain and punishment (Hartmann, 1958). The issue of control has gained importance in research on personality, especially in the last two decades. There are several terms that have been used to refer to it such as self-regulation, delay of gratification, reasoned action, control, or simply regulation. Not surprisingly, control has come to play a major role in prominent theories of behavior and action. Examples include the theories of planned action (Ajzen, 1991), affect regulation (Larsen & Prizmic, 2004), regulatory focus (Higgins, 1997), dynamic process (Vancouver, 2008), and self-regulation (Carver & Scheier, 2011); the social cognitive theory of self-regulation (Bandura, 1991); or the goal systems approach (Kruglanski et al., 2002).

There are several common features shared by the different approaches to control. The major and most characteristic one is the underlying assumption that the individual is a self-regulating being. This assumption implies that individuals have a set of goals they desire to attain, consider several plans for attaining these goals, and tend to apply the one that is most advantageous in that it best serves their interests. Thus the major crux of the theories is to bridge goal representations with strategies for their implementation (Gollwitzer & Oettingen, 2011). The whole process is assumed to be attended by awareness and guided by rational decision making, cognitive evaluations, and perhaps even volition.

Some Critical Comments

Needless to say, this model of a rational, restrained, and reasonable human being does not quite match reality—at least not in all or most cases. Human beings have a lot of information about what is good and rational for them and for society but do not always adhere to these goals, despite the fact that they may concern the health, well-being, and happiness of themselves and those closest to them. A large body of research shows that people hardly behave according to the information they have about what is best for them (e.g. Stevens, Hatcher, & Bruce, 1994). Further, most of the models assume mistakenly that behavior elicitation is due to a person's deliberate decision. Again, the fact that we may be able to make decisions should not mislead us into assuming that most behaviors spring from decisions. Indeed, very few do and these are often based on unreasonable considerations (Kahneman, 2011; Kahneman, Slovic, & Tversky, 1982) and mostly do not represent the best alternative in terms of costs and benefits (Baron, 1994).

The apparent impression of rationality and self-regulation that is upheld by the models of self-regulation may be due in large part to the fact that these models are tested mostly in terms of cognitive outputs such as judgments, evaluations, attitudes, and reports about intended or self-attributed behaviors, but not in terms of actual observable behavior (e.g., Sharma et al., 2013; Stanojević, Jovanović, & Lajunen, 2013). Notably, many of the studies that deal with attitudes and behavior focus on behaviors that are not directly observable such as sexuality, eating (e.g., eating a certain amount of vegetables), or health habits (e.g., brushing one's teeth in a certain manner), so that it may not be immediately evident that behavior is actually only self-reported and not observed.

There is no reason to assume or expect that self-reports of behavior or intentions to behave in a certain way are identical with actual behavior. Mostly, they do not (e.g., Dumitrescu, Wagle, Dogaru, & Manolescu, 2011; Heckhausen & Kuhl, 1985; Scott, Eves, French, & Hoppé, 2007). The reason is that very different processes are involved in self-reports and actual behaviors. As noted by Baumeister, Vohs, and Funder (2007), self-reports are much more than behaviors under conscious control; are tailored to satisfy the requirements of experimenters as perceived by the subjects; and involve much less effort and risk, and fewer motivational tendencies and emotions. In sum, it appears reasonable to conclude that human beings may at times behave in line with the models mentioned, but not always and not necessarily so.

Some Preliminary Assumptions

The above examples about control and the manner of its handling in the human sciences warrant several conclusions.

First, it seems that control is not a universal characteristic. Nor is it likely to be an all-or-nothing phenomenon. Rather, it appears to be a graded variable, which may be manifested in different degrees. Hence it may be necessary to specify conditions under which control appears to dominate the scene to a greater or lesser extent.

Second, it seems that the mere maturity or evolutionary level of the individual is not the only—or perhaps not even a major—reason for more or less control, especially when we consider behaviors such as alcoholism, overeating, gambling, aggressiveness, and addictions that may persist despite the individual's repeated decisions to stop them.

Third, it appears that control does not always function on the level of awareness and not necessarily through reasoned decision-making acts. It is more likely that it also often functions outside awareness through automatic-procedural routines or various learned behaviors and strategies.

Possibilities of this kind suggest a fourth assumption that there may be multiple controls, perhaps of different kinds, on different levels, and attended by varying degrees of consciousness.

Finally, it is evident that control is manifested in different domains—emotions, thinking, and behavior, to mention only the major ones. There is no reason or justification to assume that control in these and other domains is of the same kind and that it functions in the same manner. It is more likely that in different domains one may identify controls that differ in their nature and form of functioning. Further, if one also considers controls on lower physiological levels, it may turn out that it is necessary to conceive of a hierarchical model of controls.

The above assumptions raise questions about the nature of control, its manner of functioning, and its manifestations. In order to analyze and perhaps find answers to these and further questions concerning control, it is necessary to start with a theory of motivation and behavior that is sufficiently comprehensive to accommodate behavior on different levels and in different domains. Cognitive orientation (CO) theory is a candidate that fulfills most of the stated requirements. A further argument in favor of applying this approach to the issue of control is that embedding a common and important theme—such as control—in a novel network of theoretical and methodological constructs may be expected to result in new insights that are likely to benefit both the embedded theme and the theory through which it is explored.

COGNITIVE ORIENTATION THEORY: INTRODUCTION

Cognitive orientation theory is a cognitive motivational theory of behavior designed to enable understanding, predicting, and changing behavior in different domains. It shares with other cognitive models of motivation the assumption that cognitive contents—viz. attitudes and beliefs—guide behavior, but does not share with them the assumption that rationality, realism, reasonableness, decision making, and volitional control determine behavior. Instead it focuses on meaning as a major construct and shows how behavior proceeds from meanings and clusters of orienting beliefs. The beliefs may orient toward rationality but may point also in other directions, and the outcome may seem rational or not regardless of the rationality or reasonableness of the beliefs that orient toward it. Further, the theory deals with predicting actual, observable overt behaviors as distinct from intentions, self-reported behaviors, and commitments or decisions to act.

According to CO theory, any act in the human system is a function of a motivational disposition and the actual implementation of that disposition. The disposition provides the directionality of behavior and answers the metaphorical questions "what to do" or "where to proceed," whereas the enactment of the output is the operational manifestation of the directionality and answers the metaphorical questions "how to perform the act" and "in which manner" or "with which means" to act. The motivational disposition and operational implementation differ greatly in their constituents and dynamics. Cognition plays a different role in regard to each of them (Kreitler, 2004; Kreitler & Kreitler, 1976, 1982).

Meaning is a concept that plays a major role in CO theory. It is defined as a pattern of cognitive contents (e.g., specifying shape, color, size, location, actions, or functions) focused on some input (e.g., a stimulus, a situation) that is expressed verbally or nonverbally, and together with the input constitutes a meaning unit—for example, "The sea – is blue" (Kreitler & Kreitler, 1990a). When formulated in the form of a sentence, a meaning unit forms a belief (e.g., "The sea is blue"). In a given context, meaning consists of a sequence of meaning units, each of which may be characterized in terms of the contents assigned to the input and relations between it and the input (e.g., its directness, generality). Meanings may vary in contents, structure, variety, and complexity and include a more interpersonally shared part as well as a more personal-subjective part. The various phases from input stimulation to behavioral output may be characterized in terms of different kinds of elaboration of meanings.

CO theory was first formulated in the late 1960s and underwent several extensions. Originally, it dealt only with molar observable behaviors such as reactions to success or failure, coming on time, and behaving honestly or deceitfully (Kreitler & Kreitler, 1982). In later phases the core of the theory was extended to further domains: cognitive performance such as problem solving, planning, curiosity, and creativity (Kreitler, 2013; Kreitler & Casakin, 2012; Kreitler & Kreitler, 1987, 1994; Kreitler & Margaliot, 2012; Rotstein, Maimon, & Kreitler, 2013); emotional behavior such as anger or fear (Kreitler, 2011a, 2012); psychopathological manifestations such as eating disorders, depression, and paranoia (Kreitler, 2011b; Kreitler & Kreitler, 1997); and physical health phenomena such as diabetes, cardiological disorders, and cancer (Drechsler, Brunner, & Kreitler, 1987; Kreitler & Kreitler, 1991; Kreitler, Kreitler, Len, Alkalay, & Barak, 2008; Kreitler, Weissler, & Nurymberg, 2004). All these extensions share the basic assumptions and processes of CO theory. In the present context, the major aspects of the core theory will be presented.

HOW DOES CO THEORY FUNCTION? MAJOR THEORETICAL STAGES

CO theory provides detailed descriptions of the processes intervening between input and output. These can be grouped into four stages, each characterized by metaphorical questions and answers.

Stage 1: Input Identification

The first stage is initiated by an external or internal input and is focused on the question "What is it?" It consists of identifying the input in terms of a limited and primary "initial meaning" as one of the following: (a) a signal for a defensive, adaptive, or conditioned response; (b) a signal for molar action; (c) as new or especially significant, and hence as a signal for an orienting response; or (d) as irrelevant in the present situation, and hence as something that may be overlooked or discarded.

The processes involved in input identification have been examined in a set of studies regarding different inputs. The findings showed that input identification is a joint function of a systematic processing of meaning values, which enables determination of the referent and its testing in view of further meaning values. Individual differences play an increasing role in regard to the perceived meaning values and referent endorsement in the phases following the initial response to the stimulus (Kreitler & Kreitler, 1984, 1986).

Stage 2: Extended Meaning Generation

The second stage is initiated by feedback indicating failure of coping with the situation by conditioned or unconditioned responses, or by a meaning signaling the need for molar action, or by an input that has failed to be sufficiently identified by means of the orienting response. It is focused on the question "What does it mean in general and what does it mean to or for me?" An enriched process of meaning generation sets in, based on extended elaboration of both interpersonally shared and personal kinds of meaning, in terms of meaning units that may take the form of different kinds of beliefs. By examining the extent to which the person's goals, norms, beliefs about self, and beliefs about others or reality are involved, meaning generation eventually leads to specification whether action is required or not. For example, action may be required if a goal (e.g., earning money) may be attained in the situation or a norm (e.g., one should help a person in need) is implicated.

Stage 3: Formation of the Motivational Disposition

If the outcome of the previous stage is that action is not required, the process ends at this point and the system is open for dealing with new inputs. A conclusion that action is required initiates the third stage that is focused on the question "What will I do?" The answer is sought by means of relevant beliefs of the following four types.

- Beliefs about goals that express actions or states desired or undesired by the individual (e.g., "I want to be respected by others").
- Beliefs about rules and norms that express ethical, esthetic, social, and other rules and standards (e.g., "One should be assertive").
- Beliefs about self that express information about oneself, such as one's traits, habits, behaviors, or feelings (e.g., "I often lose control of myself," "I like traveling").
- General beliefs that express information concerning others, the environment, or reality in general (e.g., "It is difficult to control others").

Formally, the beliefs differ in the subject (in beliefs about self and goals the subject is the self, in general beliefs and norms it is non-self) and in the relation between subject and predicate (in beliefs about self and general beliefs it is factual, in norms it is desirable, in goals it is desired).

The cognitive elaborations in the third stage refer to beliefs that represent deep, underlying meanings of the involved inputs rather than their obvious and explicit surface meanings. The meaning elaborations consist of matchings and interactions between beliefs ("belief clustering") based on clarifying the orienting direction of the beliefs (i.e., the extent to which they support the indicated course of action). If the majority of beliefs of a certain type support the action, that belief type is considered as positively oriented in regard to that action. However, a belief type may be negatively oriented or lack any orienting direction. If all four belief types support a certain action, or at least three support it whereas the fourth is neutral, a cluster of beliefs is formed (CO cluster) orienting toward a specific act. This cluster gives rise to a unified tendency orienting toward the performance of an action, which is called behavioral intent and can be considered as a vector representing the motivational disposition toward a given behavior.

No CO cluster will be formed if there are not enough beliefs in at least two belief types orienting toward the course of action. An incomplete CO cluster may include, for example, goal beliefs and beliefs about self-orienting toward a certain action but no beliefs about norms or general beliefs. An incomplete CO cluster of this kind could result in window shopping that is not followed by actual shopping. In the case of an action frequently performed by the individual, an almost complete CO cluster may be retrieved, which needs only to be minimally elaborated before the emergence of a motivational disposition. When there are two contradictory goals, two CO clusters may be formed that give rise to two behavioral intents (intent conflict). An interesting possibility is the formation of an inoperable CO cluster that includes "as if" beliefs in one or more belief types. A CO cluster of this kind may be manifested in the form of a daydream or guided imagery.

Stage 4: The Behavioral Program

The fourth stage sets in if a behavioral intent has been formed. It is focused on the question "How will I do it?" The answer is in the form of a behavioral program—namely, a hierarchically structured sequence of instructions controlling the performance of the act, including a more general strategy as well as more specific tactics. Programs of different kinds are involved in executing an overt molar act, a cognitive act, an emotional response, a daydreamed act, conflict resolution, a physiological disorder, etc. Four basic kinds of programs may be described.

- Innately determined programs (e.g., controlling reflexes and various physiological procedures).
- Programs determined both innately and through learning (e.g., controlling instincts and language behavior).
- Programs acquired through learning (e.g., controlling culturally shaped behaviors, such as running elections) or personal habits (e.g., cleaning one's room, sending birthday cards to one's friends, making notes for one's commitments).

- Ad hoc programs constructed by the individual in line with contextual requirements.

Programs of the first three kinds are retrieved in an almost complete state, whereas the ad hoc programs need first to be constructed, most probably from parts of other previously formed or enacted programs.

Implementing a motivational disposition by a program requires selecting and retrieving a program, and often adapting it to prevailing circumstances. When there are two equally adequate programs for implementing the same motivational disposition, a program conflict may occur. Another kind of program conflict may arise when there is one program still in operation while another program is about to be set into operation.

Figure 1 illustrates schematically the four stages of CO theory.

THE FOUR STAGES OF CO THEORY: AN ILLUSTRATION

The following example illustrates the four stages of CO theory in the case of helping a person in need. Let us imagine that a person walking in the street hears a loud noise. This input evokes the question "What is it?" thereby initiating the first stage of CO theory. Looking in the direction from which the sound came provides meaning values, such as "a person," "old," "on the street," leading to identification by means of the label "An old person fell." The primary identification indicates that the adequate response could not be by means of a conditioned or unconditioned response but calls for molar action.

The second stage is initiated by the question "What does it mean in general and for me?" which evokes a deeper and more comprehensive process of meaning generation by means of beliefs, such as *This person may not be able to get up*, *This person may need help*, *I usually help others*, *One should help a person in need*, *Helping someone may involve a person in something unpleasant*, or *I want to be able to provide help to others*. The evoked beliefs about goals, self, norms, and general beliefs show that the individual is involved; hence action is required.

Accordingly, the third stage is initiated with the question "Which action?" The belief that is likely to function as a focal belief in this context is "I want to be able to provide help to others." Deeper personal meanings of the action "helping others" are evoked—for example, *getting involved in something that does not concern oneself*, *losing time*, *making the world a safe place*, or *contributing to others*.

Concerning each of these themes, four types of beliefs are evoked. Each belief either orients toward helping or not. The beliefs are organized in terms of the four types, in line with their orienting direction. If there are enough beliefs (say, about half of those evoked in that belief type) orienting toward helping in at least three belief types, a CO cluster is formed. In the example presented, there were several beliefs in each belief type orienting toward helping but not enough toward not helping. Accordingly, a CO cluster is formed for helping the other. The action will be actually performed if an adequate behavioral program is available to that person.

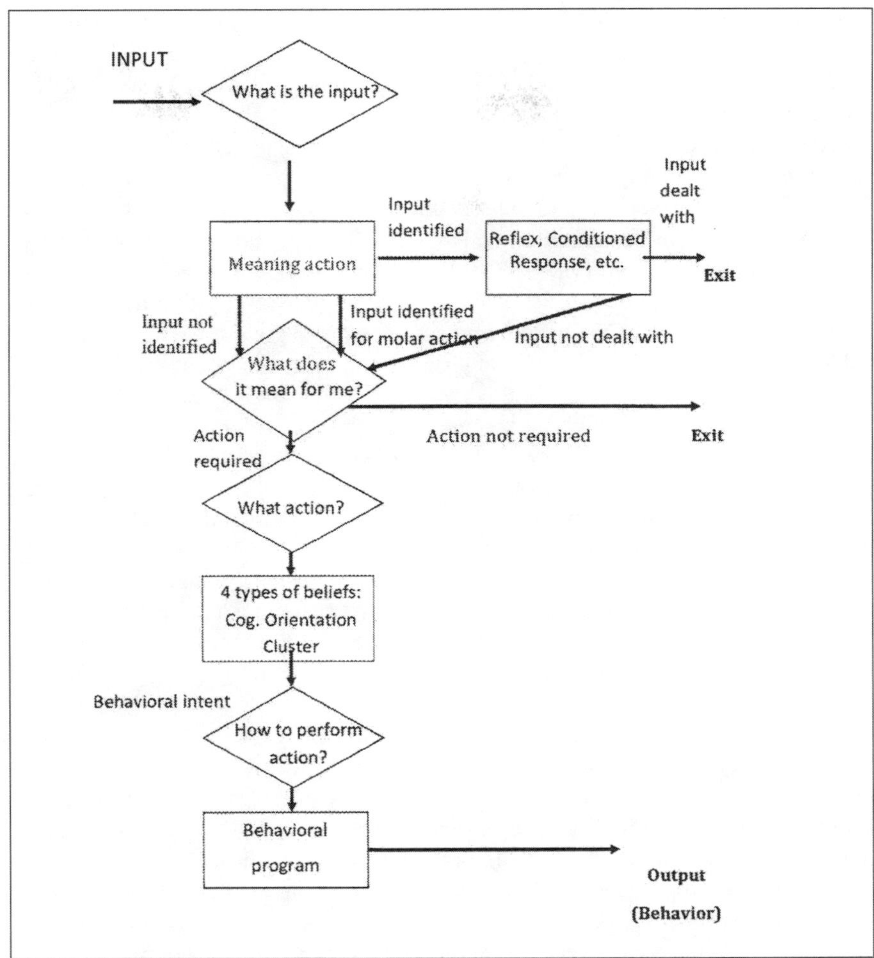

Figure 1. A schematic flow-chart of the CO model.

CO THEORY: PREDICTING AND CHANGING BEHAVIOR

A large body of research demonstrates the predictive power of CO theory in a variety of domains—for example, planning, conformity, coming on time, reactions to success and failure, curiosity, achievement, assertiveness, cheating, overeating, breastfeeding, cessation of smoking, self-disclosure, rigidity, defensive responses, undergoing tests for the early detection of breast cancer, sexual responses, compliance in diabetes patients, etc. All studies refer to actual observed behaviors. The participants were adults, adolescents, children, retarded individuals, schizophrenics, individuals with different physical disorders, and so on (Kreitler, Chaitchik,

Kreitler, & Weissler, 1994; Kreitler & Chemerinski, 1988; Kreitler & Kreitler, 1976, 1982, 1988, 1991, 1993, 1994; Kreitler, Schwartz, & Kreitler, 1987; Kreitler, Shahar, & Kreitler, 1976; Lobel, 1982; Nurymberg, Kreitler, & Weissler, 1996; Tipton & Riebsame, 1987; Westhoff & Halbach-Suarez, 1989).

All studies confirmed the hypothesis that behavior will occur if it is supported by at least three belief types and a behavioral program is available. The success of the predictions is based on applying the standardized procedure developed in the framework of CO theory (Kreitler & Kreitler, 1982). It consists of assessing the motivational disposition for the behavior (viz. behavioral intent) by means of a CO questionnaire and examining the availability of a behavioral program for implementing the intent. A CO questionnaire assesses the degree to which the individual agrees to relevant beliefs orienting toward the behavior in question or rejects those that do not orient toward it.

The beliefs differ in form and content. In form they refer to the four types of beliefs—namely, beliefs about goals, beliefs about rules and standards (or norms), beliefs about self, and beliefs about others and reality (or general beliefs). In contents they refer to themes that represent meanings underlying the behavior in question. Thus a CO questionnaire, which is used for predicting a behavior, usually consists of four parts presented together in random order—each representing one of the four types of beliefs (see Figure 2). Each part contains in random order beliefs referring to the different themes. The participant is requested to check on a four-point scale the degree to which each belief seems to him or her to be true (or correct).

The themes of the CO questionnaire are identified by means of a standard procedure applied to pretest subjects, some of whom manifest the behavior in question while others do not. The procedure consists of interviewing the participants about the personal-subjective meanings of the key terms and then in turn sequentially (three times) about the responses they have provided. Repeating the questions about meanings leads to deeper-layer meanings, out of which those that recur in at least 50% of the interviewees are selected for the final questionnaire. These deeper meanings are called themes and they constitute the subject matter represented by the beliefs in the CO questionnaire. The resulting CO questionnaire has to be examined for its psychometric properties—including reliability and validity—before it is ready for application.

Thus the beliefs in the questionnaire do not refer directly or indirectly to the behavior in question, but only to the themes that represent the underlying meanings. Hence, from the beliefs in a CO questionnaire it is impossible to determine the nature of the behavior to which these beliefs orient. Accordingly, an important advantage of the CO approach is that the link between the themes in the CO questionnaire and the assessed behavior is not evident and cannot be guessed by the respondent, so that the responses to the questionnaire are not tailored to fit one's conception about the assessed behavior.

It is noteworthy that although according to CO theory the major constructs involved in understanding and predicting behavior are cognitions, it cannot be con-

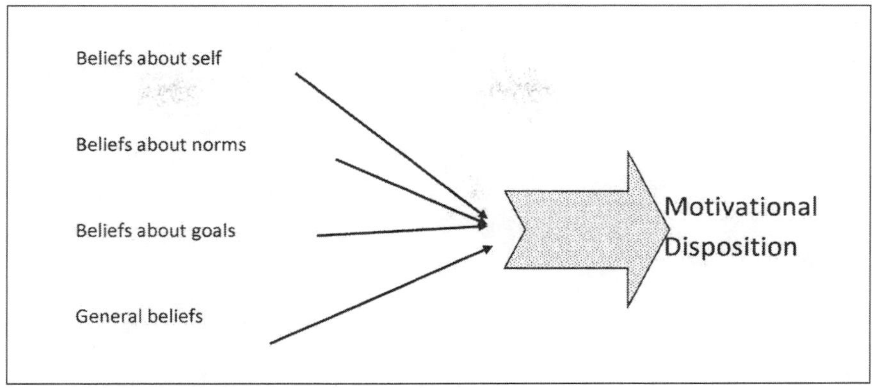

Figure 2. The vector of the four belief types representing the motivational disposition.

sidered as based on a rational, so-called "cool" system of information processing. The meanings and evoked beliefs in the different stages prior to the occurrence of a behavior are not assumed to be rational, and their combinations—which enable the emergence of the motivational disposition—do not necessarily conform to the rules of logic. The meanings, beliefs, and clusters that they form may be affected to varying degrees by emotions, desires, and veridical or nonveridical assumptions the individual may harbor, as a function of the nature of the behavior in question and its context. Hence, according to CO theory, both "cool" and "hot" cognition contribute in varying degrees to the formation of a motivational disposition. Figure 3 presents the matrix that consists of the four types of beliefs and the themes that together serve as the basis for the prediction of behavior.

It is evident that for every kind of behavior it is necessary to construct a specific CO questionnaire. However, if different behaviors share a sufficient number of themes, the same CO questionnaire will provide predictions of these behaviors—for example, the CO questionnaire of curiosity yielded significant predictions of fourteen different curiosity behaviors (Kreitler & Kreitler, 1994). Notably, the CO approach may be applied in regard to any behavior that can be assessed. Its application is straightforward and does not require the involvement of further criteria or constructs or the creation of particular conditions in regard to the predicted behavior, or any special mindset, preparation, intention, or even average intelligence on the part of the participants.

CO theory has also enabled successful modifications of behavior such as rigidity, impulsivity, and curiosity (Kreitler & Kreitler, 1988; 1990b; 1994; Zakay, Bar-El, & Kreitler, 1984). The essential components of the procedure consist of generating sufficient support for the desired course of action by evoking in the participant beliefs orienting toward this course of action. The intervention may be applied in regard to any behavior or kind of participant, and is likely to succeed when the evoked beliefs (a) refer to the themes (viz. underlying meanings of the action);

Themes	Beliefs about self	Beliefs about norms	Beliefs about norms	General beliefs
1) 2) 3) . . . n)				

Figure 3. Schematic representation of the matrix of beliefs predictive of behavior.

(b) refer to all four types of beliefs (viz. goals, norms, self, and general); and (c) have originated in the participant by a process of meaning generation (Kreitler & Kreitler, 1990b).

Both in the case of predicting behaviors as well as in regard to changing behaviors, it is necessary to consider the availability of a behavioral program for implementing the motivational disposition. The existence of behavioral programs may be established by means of questionnaires, observation, information from others, or role playing. New programs may be learned or constructed, if necessary.

CONTROL IN THE FRAMEWORK OF CO THEORY

In view of the approach of CO theory to motivation and the role of cognition in shaping behavior, it is evident that the manifestations and antecedents of control in the framework of CO theory are likely to differ from those in other theories. The issue of control may be analyzed from different perspectives: in terms of the four stages of CO theory and in the framework of predicting control behaviors.

Control Considered from the Point of View of the Four Stages of CO Theory

The following sections are devoted to embedding control in the framework of CO theory—first theoretically in terms of the CO model of the four stages describing the construction of a motivational disposition prior to the activation of a behavioral program, and then empirically by describing a study designed to construct and test a CO questionnaire for assessing the motivational disposition of control.

Stage 1 of CO of Control: Input Identification

In the first stage, the role of control largely depends on meanings. Thus whether control appears at all on the scene of action depends first and foremost on whether the construct exists in the individual's repertory in a verbal or nonverbal form. The meaning of control is a function of the separate items of contents relevant for control perceived by the individual in a given situation. These may include contents such as *power, predictable behavior, functional, smooth performance, leading to goal, expressing intention,* as well as *confusion, no direction, no order,* etc. Integrating several or all of these or similar meaning values may result in a label, such as "control."

The perception of the relevant meaning values depends mainly on the individual insofar as it is a function of two major factors: the availability of the meaning values relevant for control in the individual's cognitive repertory and the individual's attention at a given point in time. There is evidence that control may function already at this primary level of perception and that its manifestation is attended by neurological changes (Kühn et al., 2011).

Stage 2 of CO of Control: Extended Meaning Generation

If the construct of "control" resulted from the initial meaning action in the first stage, it was identified as requiring a molar action and hence in need of a more elaborate meaning generation. This consists of the evocation of different beliefs relating to control that result in an enriched network of meanings focused on control, such as "Control enables getting things done," "Control may harm one's relations with others," "When I am in control I feel good about myself," etc. The major point about the evoked beliefs is whether they imply directly or indirectly that the individual is involved in the situation in terms of action—namely, whether there is a goal that one may promote, or a norm that one should uphold, or some belief concerning oneself that implies a positive effect on one's self-image if an act is undertaken or a negative effect if it is not undertaken.

Notably, the fact that the individual easily retrieves beliefs about control suggests the existence of personality tendencies (mostly traits) involved with control. Previous studies showed that individuals scoring high on traits of control also have meanings and beliefs relating to control (Kreitler & Kreitler, 1990a). The resulting implication of the evoked beliefs may be that no action is required or desirable on the part of the individual, in which case the process ends. If, however, one or more beliefs indicate that an action by the individual is required or desirable, the indication for action initiates the third stage.

Stage 3 of CO of Control: Formation of the Motivational Disposition

The third stage focuses on the meaning elaboration of the focal beliefs about control that were evoked in the second stage. Beliefs with similar contents cluster into themes, such as "promoting success" or "saving time," that emerge in the course of meaning elaboration of control (see the next section for a discussion of the themes). Further beliefs of the four types are produced around the themes and concerning control. The process goes on until a sufficient number of beliefs of each of the four belief types is evoked—namely, at least one belief concerning each theme in each of the four belief types.

How many themes and how many beliefs of each of the four belief types are considered as meeting the criterion of sufficiency depends both on the salience of the construct of control for the specific individual, as well as on personality tendencies of the individual concerning (for example) intolerance of ambiguity and perfectionism. When a sufficient number of beliefs of each of the four types have been evoked, a motivational disposition orienting toward a control act is formed. No motivational disposition is formed if the evoked beliefs do not meet the criterion of sufficiency in a major respect—for instance, in regard to the four belief types or the identified themes.

At this point it may be necessary to emphasize that the beliefs discussed above concerning acts of control refer to meanings that are implied by control and support it (e.g., efficiency, saving time) but do not refer to it directly. Beliefs of this kind orient toward acts of control and need to be distinguished from beliefs that refer directly to control—for example, "I try to exercise control as often as possible," "I would like to avoid people who try to control me." Beliefs of the latter kind may fulfill a role as themes in the context of motivational dispositions that apparently have nothing to do with control, such as intolerance of ambiguity (Kreitler, Maguen, & Kreitler, 1975), cardiological disease (Kreitler, Weissler, & Brunner, 1991), or colorectal cancer (Kreitler et al., 2008).

Another aspect of control that may become manifest in the third stage concerns the management of beliefs and CO clusters themselves—as for example in regard to checking the degree of coherence and strength of the cluster prior to its closure, completing one CO cluster before launching another, avoiding contradictions within and conflicts between CO clusters, ordering CO clusters for enactment in terms of importance or preferences, and regulating the implementation of the CO clusters. This aspect of control may be a manifestation of cognitive control in the domain of self-control.

Stage 4 of the CO of Control: The Behavioral Program

The emergence of the motivational disposition initiates the fourth stage, which is devoted to retrieving an adequate behavioral program for implementing the act of control, adjusting it to the prevailing circumstances, and enacting it. Some individuals dispose of a large number of varied and specialized behavioral programs for enacting control. Their acquisition and enactment in practice is dependent on the individual's motivation and experience in regard to control. The behavioral programs of control include various habits concerning control that the individual may have acquired in different contexts.

Again, in the fourth stage control may be manifested in terms of checking the programs for adequacy, coherence, and efficiency prior to enactment; regulating the enactment of the different behavioral programs in a given period of time, so that they do not clash or overlap; guaranteeing the circumstances for the completion of the behavioral programs; and checking the end point of a program in terms of the attainment of the targeted goal. Notably, some of the enacted behavioral programs supposedly implementing control may actually not seem as subserving control, whereas programs that appear to manifest control may be enacted in order to implement a motivational disposition that is not control. Thus a dominant person in charge may manifest his or her control of subordinates through an apparently pleasant interaction with them, whereas a behavior of dictating orders may actually implement a motivational disposition of fear and anxiety.

Control Considered from the Point of View of Predicting and Changing Control

The question motivating this section is "How can we predict or change control behavior?" For this purpose it would be necessary to apply the procedure of CO theory for predicting behavior, and in the next step—in case it is so desired—to use the results for changing behavior, which may be characterized as control or noncontrol behavior.

The procedure for predicting would require constructing a CO questionnaire. For this purpose it would be necessary to apply the standard procedure for constructing a CO questionnaire. The first step in this procedure consists of interviewing pretest individuals so as to determine the themes constituting the relevant contents for the CO questionnaire. The interviewing proceeded in four consecutive steps, starting with the interpersonally shared meaning of "control" and proceeding to exploring the personal-subjective meanings of the responses provided by the interviewee three times in a row. The responses obtained in the final step were compared across subjects by three judges and those that recurred in at least 50% of the subjects in a positive or negative sense were selected as potential themes.

The interviews were conducted in individual sessions with fifteen pretest subjects. In the interviews we used as an initiating stimulus the term "control" without further specification. In performing the interviews, it turned out that some subjects naturally referred to self-control (i.e., of one's behavior, emotions, thoughts, addictions, habits), some to control of others, and some to control of situations and reality. Hence three separate pretests were carried out, focused on each of the kinds of control mentioned above. However, since there was a certain degree of overlap between the themes in the three sets of interviews (Table 1), the final set of themes selected for the CO questionnaire was based on all three sets together.

Thus the pretest interviews led to the construction of a CO questionnaire of control. The number of themes selected for the questionnaire was 22, and they included those shared by the three pretest tracks (e.g., predictability, security, having power) as well as an equal number of themes representing the three sets. Each theme was represented by one belief statement in each of the four types of beliefs (see Figure 3). Thus the questionnaire included four parts, one for each belief type (i.e., beliefs about self, beliefs about rules and norms, beliefs about goals, and general beliefs), with 22 items in each part. The items had the form of a statement (e.g., "I enjoy planning every act of behavior beforehand") and the subject was asked to check one of four response alternatives: very true, true, not true, not at all true. The questionnaire yielded four scores for the four belief types and in addition 22 scores for each of the themes.

A preliminary study was performed in order to explore the degree to which the CO questionnaire is relevant for assessing the motivational disposition of control. The number of subjects was 160, all undergraduate students in the social and behavioral sciences. They were administered the following nine questionnaires in random order.

(1) The CO Questionnaire of Control.

(2) The Action Control Scale (Kuhl, 1994). This scale includes three subscales: action orientation subsequent to failure versus preoccupation, prospective and decision-related action orientation versus hesitation, and action orientation during (successful) performance of activities (intrinsic orientation) versus volatility. Each subscale consists of twelve items describing particular situations. Each item has two alternative answers, one of which is scored as indicating action orientation and the other as indicating state orientation.

(3) The Life Control Scale (Bobak et al., 2000). This scale includes six items with responses rated on a five-point scale. It provides a total score designed to assess generalized perceived control of one's life.

(4) The Affective Control Scale (Williams, Chambless, & Ahrens, 1997). This scale includes 42 items with responses rated on a seven-point scale, providing scores for anger, depression, anxiety, and positive emotions in addition to a total score.

(5) The Dominance–Prestige Scales (Cheng, Tracy, & Henrich, 2010). This scale includes seventeen items rated on a seven-point scale, referring to controlling others, having one's way, being respected and admired by others, being considered an expert, providing advice to others, etc.

(6) The Locus of Control Scale (Rotter, 1966). This scale includes 29 items, each consisting of two alternatives—one of which presents the view that one controls situations and events, whereas the other presents the view that the determining factors are fate, circumstances, chance, and other eventualities. The former option is conceptualized as "internal control," the latter as "external control." Internal control expresses control over situations.

(7) The Need for Closure Scale (Roets & van Hiel, 2011), based on Kruglanski, Webster, and Klem (1993). This scale includes fifteen items referring to desire for predictability, preference for order and structure, discomfort with ambiguity, decisiveness, and closed-mindedness.

TABLE 1. Themes for the CO Questionnaire of Control

Themes for self-control	Themes for control of others	Themes for control of situations
Achieving success	Feeling security	Feeling security
Keeping balance	Being highly evaluated by others	Being in charge
Being strong, having strength	Having power	Feeling powerful
Avoiding self-harm	Minimizing the chances that others may harm you	Being able to plan
Maximizing predictability, avoiding surprises	Keeping emotional distance from others	Avoiding uncertainty
Respect/esteem for oneself	Responsibility in regard to others	Overcoming anxiety
Saving time	Preventing dependence on others	Feeling self-confidence
Priority for reason and logic	Preventing being controlled by others	Avoiding difficulties of making up one's mind, making decision making easy
Focusing primarily on oneself and one's needs	Taking care of others	Overcoming one's vulnerabilities
Making sure one would not do unreasonable things	Making sure things are done right, as they should be done	Overcoming chaos, feeling that all is logical and clear
Doing things according to the rules	Keeping things around you in harmony	Being able to understand in depth what is going on and why
Being able to rely on oneself	Being able to rely on others	Exploiting things for one's advantage

(8) The Brief Self-Control Scale (Tangney et al., 2004). This scale has thirteen items rated on a five-point scale, referring to issues such as self-indulgence, self-discipline, and acting without thinking through all the alternatives.

(9) The Attention Control Scale (Derryberry & Reed, 2002).This scale is designed to measure two major components of attention: attention focusing and attention shifting. It includes twenty items that are rated on a four-point Likert Scale from 1 (almost never) to 4 (always).

The questionnaires were selected for assessing different aspects of control: control of action and behavior (#2), control of one's life (#3), control of emotions (#4), control of others (#5), control of situations (#6), control of cognition, with an emphasis on contents of thoughts (#7), control of oneself (#8), and control of cognition, with an emphasis on attention (#9).

The major results of this preliminary study referred to the interrelations of the eight control questionnaires (#1–8) and the interrelations between them and the CO Questionnaire of Control. A confirmatory factor analysis was done in order to examine the degree to which all eight questionnaires actually assess the same construct. The results confirmed this expectation. The findings of the analysis were CMIN = 413.76, $df = 48$, CMIN/$df = 8.62$, $p < 0.001$; NFI = 0.986; TLI = 0.983; CFI = 0.988; RAMSEA = 0.053. Further, the standardized regression weights were all significant and were in the range 0.698–0.950. These indices indicate that the overall model is valid and that all eight scores representing the control questionnaires actually assess the same construct.

However, in addition to the shared component of variance, the eight questionnaires also assess further aspects. Of special interest is the indication by the results that the eight questionnaires tend to form two clusters: one representing mainly questionnaires #2–4, 8, and 9 and the other representing mainly questionnaires #5–7. The first cluster could be viewed as focused primarily on control in the personal sphere—referring to control of behavior, one's life, feelings, and cognitive performance—whereas the second cluster seems to be focused primarily on environmental control, including control of other people and external situations. Thus scores representing each of the clusters of questionnaires were also computed.

Concerning the CO questionnaire, the preliminary control analyses showed that it has an acceptable reliability (Cronbach's alpha in the range of 0.77 to 0.85) and provides scores that do not differ significantly for the genders and age groups in the range examined at this stage. An exploratory factor analysis of the themes yielded three major factors focused on predictability (or certainty), self-focus (or self-promotion), and strength (or power).

The most important results refer to the interrelations between the control questionnaires and the CO Questionnaire of Control. The findings show that the major factor of control representing the eight control questionnaires is related significantly to the four belief types, more to the beliefs about norms (0.68) and about oneself (0.57) than to the beliefs about goals (0.48) and general beliefs (0.50). Further, it is related significantly to the three factors representing the themes.

Specific analyses showed that the four belief types and the three theme factors of the CO Questionnaire of Control also predicted the scores of each of the eight questionnaires and the two clusters of questionnaires. A recurrent finding showed that beliefs about self and beliefs about goals contributed relatively more than norm beliefs and general beliefs to predicting the scores of the questionnaires representing control in the personal sphere (# 2–4, 8, and 9) separately or as a cluster. By contrast, beliefs about norms and general beliefs contributed relatively more than beliefs about self and beliefs about goals to predicting the scores of the questionnaires representing control of other people and situations (#5–7), both separately and as a cluster. Further, the theme factor of self-focus contributed relatively more to the prediction of the scores of the questionnaires and cluster of control in the personal sphere, whereas the theme factors of predictability and strength contributed relatively more to predicting the scores of the questionnaires and the cluster representing control of other people and situations.

The results of this preliminary study show that the different questionnaires assessing different aspects of control are sufficiently intercorrelated to justify the conclusion that there is a general latent factor of control. This statistical result is further confirmed by the finding of the study that the CO Questionnaire of Control predicted the scores of all the different control questionnaires and the clusters based on these questionnaires.

A major shortcoming of the study described is that it did not include any measure of control representing directly observed manifestations of control. As emphasized earlier, CO theory considers self-reports about behavior as distinct from directly observed behaviors and focuses on predicting the latter. This missing link will be completed in future studies of control now that the validity and reliability of the CO Questionnaire of Control have been established.

CONCLUSIONS: THE NATURE OF CONTROL

The theoretical explorations undertaken in this chapter and the findings of the preliminary study seem to warrant several general conclusions about the nature of control, which need to be discussed so as to clarify their theoretical and empirical implications.

Motivational Dispositions for Control: Their Nature and Kind

A major conclusion that seems to emerge from the preceding theoretical and empirical analyses is that there appears to exist a general tendency toward control that is basic, comprehensive, and adaptable to many goals, states, and situations. Confining ourselves at present to the psychological level, this tendency is manifested in the general motivational disposition toward control grounded in the individual's CO.

In addition, there are two further tendencies of control—one manifested in regard to the personal domain (e.g., feelings, thoughts) and the other in regard to the environment, including other people and situations. There may, however, be a third level of control tendencies, focused on specific domains within each of the more general kinds of control of self and control of others and the environment. The domains of the tendency for self-control would include control of emotions, thoughts, and behaviors. The domains of the tendency for environmental control may include control of other people, situations, and events. The kind and number of domains in regard to self-control or environmental control may be extended or limited in view of the individual's world of meaning, which is a function of one's cognitive system and is affected also by one's culture. Thus, for example, domains of environmental control may include control of higher powers (including God) or control of political events and social developments. Domains of self-control may include control of one's physical body and health or of one's state of consciousness.

Thus there are three aspects of the conceptualization and manifestations of control: the general tendency for control; tendencies in regard to control of self, others, and the environment; and control of particular domains within the spheres of control of self or of the environment. Each of these aspects is grounded in a motivational disposition produced by beliefs of the four types referring to themes relevant for the particular aspect examined, predicted, or chosen for change.

The suggested conceptualization of control parallels the conception developed in regard to cognition (Kreitler, 2013). In regard to cognition, studies performed over the last decade showed that there is a general tendency for cognition, and in addition tendencies for specific cognitive functions (e.g., memory, curiosity), further supplemented by tendencies for specific types of thinking (e.g., creativity, intuition, or logical reasoning) and tendencies for particular domains of contents (e.g., mathematics, psychology).

In regard to control, only three aspects have been conceptually defined up to now—in contrast to cognition, in which four aspects have been found. This may reflect differences in the nature of the construct or in the extent of available studies and information.

Motivational Dispositions for Control: Their Development and Evocation

The extent to which a particular tendency, say for cognition or control, may be further elaborated in terms of specific tendencies may be due to general evolutionary determinants and individual developmental factors. Thus it is likely that tendencies with evident evolutionary benefits, such as control or cognition, would be supplemented by further, more specific tendencies. Culture is another factor that may contribute to the elaboration of specific supplemental tendencies of the kind mentioned. In a culture setting a premium on control of the self, it is likely that many individuals would develop CO tendencies for control of the self and particular domains of the self. It may also be expected that culturally based themes promoting control of the self would be included in the matrix of themes constituting the motivational disposition of individuals in that culture.

Similar conceptualizations of a general tendency amplified by further, more specific tendencies may apply to other domains of psychology, such as addictions and psychopathology. There is already evidence that in regard to eating disorders there may be a general motivational disposition grounded in the individual's cognitive orientation, supplemented by CO tendencies for particular behaviors such as anorexia or bulimia (Kreitler, 2011b).

On the basis of studies performed on cognition and emotions (Kreitler, 2003, 2011a, 2013), it is possible to hypothesize about the determinants of the evocation of the different motivational dispositions in a given context. In line with the CO model, a motivational disposition is evoked when there is an input acting as a trigger in a given situation. However, it is also possible that the state of the individual's cognitive system in a given period of time may play a role in assigning meaning to the trigger and thus determining which of the relevant control tendencies would be evoked. The state of the cognitive system may be conceptualized as the state of consciousness characterizing the cognitive system (Kreitler, 1999, 2009; Rotstein et al., 2013). The state of consciousness of the system determines which cognitive contents and processes are readily available in a given situation. Hence it may affect the meaning assignment to the trigger that could be grasped as emotional or as affecting the self. In these circumstances it is likely that the evoked control tendency would be the general tendency supplemented by the tendency for control in regard to the self. States of consciousness may promote different images of reality that may promote meanings focused on the self, on reality, and on particular emotions or ideas.

Each of these and similar views could codetermine which control tendency is likely to be evoked in a given situation, if it is available in the individual's repertory.

A Hierarchical Model of Control

There may be different approaches to constructing a hierarchical model of control. One could consider the levels of physiology, psychology, and sociology whereby the manifestations of control in the cells or larger biological entities would form one level underlying the manifestations of control on the psychological level, which in turn could be underlying the manifestations of control in social entities, such as organizations and states. The approach we would like to outline is limited to psychology and has been inspired by the systemic theory of personality proposed by Fajkowska (2013). According to Fajkowska, personality can be conceptualized in terms of three levels— the first consisting of processes and mechanisms, the second of structures, and the third of behavioral acts. Thus the motivational dispositions for control defined by CO theory would correspond to the first level of processes.

The second level described by Fajkowska suggests the importance of detecting structural units that are relevant for the functioning of personality and psychopathology. In regard to control, it seems warranted to suggest structures that combine several of the described components and correspond to psychologically relevant constructs. Some examples are structures that consist of control of different aspects of the self. When tendencies for strict control of emotions and the body are included, the structure resembles anorexia (Kreitler, 2011a). When strict control of one's behaviors and thoughts are included, the structure resembles the obsessive-compulsive syndrome. Other examples are structures that consist of control of different aspects of the environment. When the tendencies are extreme, they may be manifested in the form of disturbed reality testing. When strict control of others and the environment are included, the resulting structure resembles paranoia (Kreitler & Kreitler, 1997; concerning the control of others, see also Fiske, 1993). Weak motivational dispositions for control of one's behavior may result in the impulsive syndrome, whereas weak motivational dispositions for control of one's emotions and physiological reactions may result in the hysteric syndrome.

Notably, in the present context it may be suggested that emotional reactions may provide additional support to the above-proposed distinction between control in regard to the self and control in regard to others and the environment. Deficits and failures in control in regard to the self seem to be related to anxiety responses, whereas deficits and failures in regard to control of others and the environment seem to be related to depression and depressive responses.

The third level described by Fajkowska (2013) refers to behaviors. This is the level of manifestations of control behaviors and control acts in different domains. In line with CO theory, this level is a function of behavioral programs and habits implementing control. As noted, it is likely that individuals differ in the number and variety of behavioral programs manifesting control and enabling the exercise of control in different domains. However, it should also be noted that a full-fledged act of control requires both a motivational disposition for control (general, particular, or domain-specific) as well as a behavioral program for implementing control.

In sum, accounting for an act of control manifested by an individual requires consideration of different psychological levels including motivational dispositions, structures, and behavioral programs responsible for behaviors. In addition, a more comprehensive understanding would also require analyzing biological levels—including physiological processes in the body and the brain—as well as sociological levels, including society and culture.

REFERENCES

Ajzen, I. (1991). The theory of planned behavior. *Organizational Behavior and Human Decision Processes, 50*, 179–211.

Akre, A. K., Bakken, M., & Hovland, A. L. (2009). Social preferences in farmed silver fox females (*Vulpes vulpes*): Does it change with age? *Applied Animal Behaviour Science, 120*, 186–191.

Auersperg, A. M. I., Laumer, I. B., & Bugnyar, T. (2013). Goffin cockatoos wait for qualitative and quantitative gains but prefer "better" to "more." *Biological Letters, 9*, 1–4.

Bandura, A. (1991). Social cognitive theory of self-regulation. *Organizational Behavior and Human Decision Processes, 50*, 248–217.

Baron, J. (1994). *Thinking and deciding* (2nd ed.). New York: Cambridge University Press.

Baumeister, R. F., Vohs, K. D., & Funder, D. (2007). Psychology as the science of self-reports and finger movements: Whatever happened to actual behavior? *Perspectives on Psychological Science, 2*, 396–403.

Baumeister, R. F., Vohs, K. D., & Tice, D. M. (2007). The strength model of self-control. *Current Directions in Psychological Science, 16*, 351–355

Bobak, M, Pikhart, H., Hertzman, C., Rose, R., Hertzman, C., & Marmot, M. (2000). Socioeconomic factors, material inequalities, and perceived control in self-rated health: Cross-sectional data from seven post-communist countries. *Social Science and Medicine, 51*, 1343–1350.

Brass, M., & Haggard, P. (2007). To do or not to do: The neural signature of self-control. *Journal of Neuroscience, 27*, 9141–9145.

Carver, C. S., & Scheier, M. F. (2011). Self-regulation of action and affect. In K. D. Vohs & R. F. Baumeister (Eds.), *Handbook of self-regulation: Research, theory, and applications* (2nd ed., pp. 3–21). New York: Guilford Press.

Cheng, J. T., Tracy, J. L., & Henrich, J. (2010). Pride, personality, and the evolutionary foundations of human social status. *Evolution and Human Behavior, 31*, 334–347.

Delgado, J. M. R. (1969). *Physical control of the mind: Towards a psychocivilized society.* New York: Harper & Row.

Derryberry, D., & Reed, M. (2002). Anxiety-related attentional biases and their regulation by attentional control. *Journal of Abnormal Psychology, 111*, 225–236.

Drechsler, I., Brunner, D., & Kreitler, S. (1987). Cognitive antecedents of coronary heart disease. *Social Science and Medicine, 24*, 581–588.

Dumitrescu, A.L., Wagle, M., Dogaru, B. C., Manolescu , B. (2011). Modeling the theory of planned behavior for intention to improve oral health behaviors: The impact of attitudes, knowledge, and current behavior. *Journal of Oral Science, 53*, 369–377.

Fajkowska, M. (2013). *Personality coherence and incoherence: A perspective on anxiety and depression.* Clinton Corners, NY: Eliot Werner Publications.

Feldman, D.B., & Snyder, C.R. (2005). Hope and the meaningful life: Theoretical and empirical associations between goal-directed thinking and life meaning. *Journal of Social and Clinical Psychology, 24*, 401–421.

Fiske, S. T. (1993). Controlling other people: The impact of power on stereotyping. *American Psychologist, 48*, 621–628.

Gailliot M. T., & Baumeister R. F. (2007). The physiology of willpower: Linking blood glucose to self-control. *Personality and Social Psychology Review, 11*, 303–327.

Gollwitzer, P. M., & Oettingen, G. (2011). Planning promotes goal striving. In K. D. Vohs & R. F. Baumeister (Eds.), *Handbook of self-regulation: Research, theory, and applications* (2nd ed., pp. 162–185). New York: Guilford Press.

Grosch, J., & Neuringer, A. (1981). Self-control in pigeons under the Mischel paradigm. *Journal of the Experimental Analysis of Behavior, 35,* 3–21.

Hains, A. A., & Hains, A. H. (1988). Cognitive-behavioral training of problem solving and impulse-control with delinquent adolescents. *Journal of Offender Counseling Services Rehabilitation, 12*, 95–113.

Hartmann, H. (1958). *Ego psychology and the problem of adaptation* (D. Rapaport, Trans.). Madison, CT: International Universities Press. (Journal of the American Psychoanalytic Association, Monograph Series, Vol. 1)

Heckhausen, H., & Kuhl, J. (1985). From wishes to action: The dead ends and short cuts on the long way to action. In M. Frese & J. Sabini (Eds.), *Goal-directed behavior: The concept of action in psychology* (pp. 78–94). Hillsdale, NJ: Erlbaum.

Higgins, E. T. (1997). Beyond pleasure and pain. *American Psychologist, 52*, 1280–1300

Johnson, I. E. (1999). Self-regulation theory and coping with physical illness. *Research in Nursing and Health, 22*, 435–448.

Kahneman, D. (2011). *Thinking fast and slow*. New York: Farrar, Straus & Giroux.

Kahneman, D., Slovic, P., & Tversky, A. (1982) *Judgment under uncertainty: Heuristics and biases*. New York: Cambridge University Press.

Kreitler, H., & Kreitler, S. (1976). *Cognitive orientation and behavior*. New York: Springer Publishing.

Kreitler, H., & Kreitler, S. (1982). The theory of cognitive orientation: Widening the scope of behavior prediction. In B. A. Maher & W. A. Maher (Eds), *Progress in experimental personality research* (Vol. 7, pp. 101–169). New York: Academic Press.

Kreitler, H., & Kreitler, S. (1986). Schizophrenic perception and its psychopathological implications: A microgenetic study. In U. Hentschel, G. Smith, & J. G. Draguns (Eds.), *The roots of perception* (pp. 301–330). Amsterdam: Elsevier.

Kreitler, H., & Kreitler, S. (1990b). Cognitive primacy, cognitive behavior guidance, and their implications for cognitive therapy. *Journal of Cognitive Psychotherapy, 4*, 151–169.

Kreitler, S. (1999). Consciousness and meaning. In J. L. Singer, J. A. Singer, & P. Salovey (Eds.), *At play in the fields of consciousness: Essays in honor of Jerome L. Singer* (pp. 175–206). Mahwah, NJ: Erlbaum.

Kreitler, S. (2003). Dynamics of fear and anxiety. In P. L. Gower (Ed.), *Psychology of fear* (pp. 1–17). Hauppauge, NY: Nova Science Publishers.

Kreitler, S. (2004). The cognitive guidance of behavior. In J. T. Jost, M. R. Banaji, & P. A. Prentice (Eds.), *Perspectivism in social psychology: The yin and yang of scientific progress* (pp. 113–126). Washington, DC: American Psychological Association.

Kreitler, S. (2009). Altered states of consciousness as structural variations of the cognitive system. In E. Franco (Ed.), *Logic perception, meditation, and altered states of consciousness* (pp. 407–434). Vienna: Oestrreichische Akademie der Wissenschaften.

Kreitler, S. (2011a). Anger: Cognitive and motivational determinants. In J. P. Welty (Ed.), *Psychology of anger: Symptoms, causes, and coping* (pp. 179–195). Hauppauge, NY: Nova Science Publishers.

Kreitler, S. (2011b). Cognitive orientation and eating disorders. In Y. Latzer, J. Merrick, & D. Stein (Eds.), *Understanding eating disorders: Integrating culture, psychology, and biology* (pp. 209–224). Hauppauge, NY: Nova Science Publishers.

Kreitler, S. (2013). The structure and dynamics of cognitive orientation: A motivational approach to cognition. In S. Kreitler (Ed.) *Cognition and motivation: Forging an interdisciplinary perspective* (pp. 32–61). New York: Cambridge University Press.

Kreitler, S., & Casakin, H. (2012). Motivation for creativity in design: Its nature, assessment, and promotion. In J. N. Franco & A. E. Svensgaard (Eds.), *Handbook on psychology of motivation: New research* (pp. 107–124). Hauppauge, NY: Nova Science Publishers.

Kreitler, S., Chaitchik, S., Kreitler, H., & Weissler, K. (1994). Who will attend tests for the early detection of breast cancer? *Psychology and Health, 9*, 463–483.

Kreitler, S., & Chemerinski, A. (1988). The cognitive orientation of obesity. *International Journal of Obesity, 12*, 471–483.

Kreitler, S., & Kreitler, H. (1984). Meaning assignment in perception. In W. D. Froehlich, G. J. W. Smith, J. G. Draguns, & U. Hentschel (Eds.), *Psychological processes in cognition and personality* (pp. 173–191). Washington, DC: Hemisphere.

Kreitler, S., & Kreitler, H. (1987). The motivational and cognitive determinants of individual planning. *Genetic, Social, and General Psychology Monographs, 113*, 81–107.

Kreitler, S., & Kreitler, H. (1988). The cognitive approach to motivation in retarded individuals. In N. W. Bray (Ed.), *International review of research in mental retardation* (Vol. 15, pp. 81–123). San Diego, CA: Academic Press.

Kreitler, S., & Kreitler, H. (1990a). *The cognitive foundations of personality traits*. New York: Plenum Press.

Kreitler, S., & Kreitler, H. (1991). Cognitive orientation and physical disease or health. *European Journal of Personality, 5*, 109–129.

Kreitler, S., & Kreitler, H. (1993). The cognitive determinants of defense mechanisms. In U. Hentschel, G. J. W. Smith, W. Ehlers, & J. G. Draguns (Eds), *The concept of defense mechanisms in contemporary psychology: Theoretical, research, and clinical perspectives* (pp. 152–183). New York: Springer-Verlag.

Kreitler, S., & Kreitler, H. (1994). Motivational and cognitive determinants of exploration. In H. Keller, K. Schneider, & B. Henderson (Eds.), *Curiosity and exploration* (pp. 259–284). New York: Springer-Verlag.

Kreitler, S., & Kreitler, H. (1997). The paranoid person: Cognitive motivations and personality traits. *European Journal of Personality, 11*, 101–132.

Kreitler, S., Kreitler, M., Len, A., Alkalay, A., & Barak, F. (2008). Psychological risk factors for colorectal cancer? *Psycho-Oncologie, 2*, 131–145.

Kreitler, S., Maguen, T., & Kreitler, H. (1975). The three faces of intolerance of ambiguity. *Archives of Psychology, 127*, 238–250.

Kreitler, S., & Margaliot, A. (2012). Motivation for cognition: The cognitive orientation approach. In A. M. Columbus (Ed.), *Advances in psychology research* (Vol. 95, pp. 97–118). Hauppauge, NY: Nova Science Publishers.

Kreitler, S., Schwartz, R., & Kreitler, H. (1987). The cognitive orientation of expressive communicability in schizophrenics and normals. *Journal of Communication Disorders, 20*, 73–91.

Kreitler, S., Shahar, A., & Kreitler, H. (1976). Cognitive orientation, type of smoker and behavior therapy of smoking. *British Journal of Medical Psychology, 49*, 167–175.

Kreitler, S., Weissler, K., & Brunner, D. (1991). Psychological and physiological risk factors for coronary heart disease. *Cardiovascular Risk Factors, 1*, 512–521.

Kreitler, S., Weissler, K., & Nurymberg, K. (2004). The cognitive orientation of patients with type 2 diabetes in Israel. *Patient Education and Counseling, 53*, 257–267.

Kruglanski, A., Shah, J. Y., Fishbach, A., Friedman, R., Chun, W.Y., & Sleeth-Keppler, D. (2002). A theory of goal systems. In M. P. Zanna (Ed.) *Advances in experimental social psychology* (Vol. 34, pp. 331–378). San Diego, CA: Academic Press.

Kruglanski, A. W., Webster, D. M., & Klem, A. (1993). Motivated resistance and openness to persuasion in the presence or absence of prior information. *Journal of Personality and Social Psychology, 65*, 861–876.

Kuhl, J. (1994). Action and state orientation: Psychometric properties of the Action Control Scale (ACS-90). In J. Kuhl & J. Beckmann (Eds.), *Volition and personality: Action versus state orientation* (pp. 47–59). Göttingen, Germany: Hogrefe & Huber.

Kühn, S., Haggard, P., & Brass, M. (2009). Intentional inhibition: How the "veto-area" exerts control. *Human Brain Mapping, 30*, 2834–2843.

Kühn, S., Schmiedek, F., Schott, B., Ratcliff, R., Heinze, H.-J., Düzel, E., et al. (2011). Brain areas consistently linked to individual differences in perceptual decision-making in younger as well as older adults before and after training. *Journal of Cognitive Neuroscience, 23,* 2147–2158.

Larsen, R. J., & Prizmic, Z. (2004). Affect regulation. In R. F. Baumeister & K. D. Vohs (Eds.), *Handbook of self-regulation: Research, theory, and applications* (pp. 40–60). New York: Guilford Press.

Lobel, T. (1982). The prediction of behavior from different types of beliefs. *Journal of Social Psychology, 118*, 213–233.

Martijn, A. C., Alberts, H. J. E. M., & de Vries, N. K. (2006). Maintaining self-control: The role of expectancies. In P. P. Verbeek & A. Slob (Eds.), *Self-regulation in health behavior* (pp. 169–192). Chichester, UK: Wiley.

Miller, H. C., DeWall, C. N., Pattison, K., Molet, M., & Zentall, T. R. (2012). Too dog tired to avoid danger: Self-control depletion in canines increases behavioral approach toward an aggressive threat. *Psychonomic Bulletin and Review, 19*, 535–540.

Nurymberg, K., Kreitler, S., & Weissler, K. (1996). The cognitive orientation of compliance in short and long-term type 2 diabetic patients. *Patient Education and Counseling, 29*, 25–39.

Real, L. A. (1991). Animal choice behavior and the evolution of cognitive architecture. *Science, 253*, 980–986.

Roets, A., & van Hiel, A. (2011). Item selection and validation of a brief, 15-item version of the Need for Closure Scale. *Personality and Individual Differences, 50*, 90–94.

Rotstein, Y., Maimon, O., & Kreitler, S. (2013). Cognitive effects of states of consciousness: Do changes in states of consciousness affect judgments and evaluations? In S. Kreitler & O. Maimon (Eds.), *Consciousness: Its nature and functions* (pp. 215–236). Hauppauge, NY: Nova Science Publishers.

Rotter, J. B. (1966). Generalized expectancies for internal versus external control of reinforcement, *Psychological Monographs: General and Applied, 80* (whole no. 609).

Ryff, C.D., & Singer, B. (1998) The contours of positive health. *Pychological Inquiry, 9*, 1–23.

Sato, T., Harman, B. A., Donohoe, W. M., Weaver, A., & Hall, W. A. (2010). Individual differences in ego depletion: The role of sociotropy-autonomy. *Motivation and Emotion, 34*, 205–213.

Schilling, C., Kühn, S., Romanowski, A., Schubert, F., Kathmann, N., & Gallinat, J. (2012). Cortical thickness correlates with impulsiveness in healthy adults. *NeuroImage, 59*, 824–830.

Scott, E. J., Eves, F. F., French, D. P., & Hoppé, R. (2007). The theory of planned behavior predicts self-reports of walking, but does not predict step count. *British Journal of Health Psychology, 12*, 601–620.

Shapiro, D. (1981). *Autonomy and rigid character*. New York: Basic Books.

Sharma, S., Dortch, K.S., Byrd-Williams, C., Truxillio, J. B., Rahman, G. A., Bonsu, P., et al. (2013). Nutrition-related knowledge, attitudes, and dietary behaviors among head start teachers in Texas: A cross-sectional study. *Journal of the Academy of Nutrition and Dietetics, 113*, 558–562.

Sontag, E. D. (2004). Some new directions in control theory inspired by systems biology. *Systematic Biology, 1*, 9–18.

Stanojević, P., Jovanović, D., & Lajunen, T. (2013). Influence of traffic enforcement on the attitudes and behavior of drivers. *Accident Analysis and Prevention, 52*, 29–38.

Stevens, V. M., Hatcher, J. W., & Bruce, B. K. (1994). How compliant is compliant? Evaluating adherence with breast self-examination positions. *Journal of Behavioral Medicine, 17*, 523–534.

Tangney, J. P., Baumeister, R. F., & Boone, A. L. (2004). High self-control predicts good adjustment, less pathology, better grades, and interpersonal success. *Journal of Personality, 72*, 271–324.

Tipton, R. M., & Riebsame, W. E. (1987). Beliefs about smoking and health: Their measurement and relationship to smoking behavior. *Addictive Behaviors, 12*, 217–223.

Vancouver, J. B. (2008). Integrating self-regulation theories of work motivation into a dynamic process theory. *Human Resource Management Review, 18*, 1–18

Vohs, K. D., Baumeister, R. F., Schmeichel, B. J., Twenge, J. M., Nelson, N. M., & Tice, D. M. (2008). Making choices impairs subsequent self-control: A limited-resource account of decision making, f-regulation, and active initiative. *Journal of Personality and Social Psychology, 94*, 883–898.

Vohs, K. D., & Schmeichel, B. J. (2003). Self-regulation and the extended now: Controlling the self alters the subjective experience of time. *Journal of Personality and Social Psychology, 85*, 217–230.

Westhoff, K., & Halbach-Suarez, C. (1989). Cognitive orientation and the prediction of decisions in a medical examination context. *European Journal of Personality, 3*, 31–71.

Williams, K. E., Chambless, D. L., & Ahrens, A.H. (1997). Are emotions frightening? An extension of the fear of fear concept. *Behaviour Research and Therapy, 35*, 239–248.

Zakay, D., Bar-El, Z., & Kreitler, S. (1984). Cognitive orientation and changing the impusivity of children. *British Journal of Educational Psychology, 54*, 40–50.

CHAPTER 5

Processes of Control in Musical Practice and Performance

An Integrative Approach

Joanna Kantor-Martynuska

INTRODUCTION

Music making is primarily a mental skill in which processes involved in technical operations carry out the higher level functions—e.g., planning (see Lehmann, Sloboda, & Woody, 2007). Musical expertise resulting from long-term training of mental and practical skills requires systematic practice—following precise technical cues—and developing and implementing the artistic interpretation of a piece. Musical expertise develops in accordance with the ability to exert control over the multiple processes and functions inherent in the planning, preparation, and execution of practice, as well as monitoring and valuating practice and performance (Galamian, 1964, as cited in Jørgensen, 2004).

The role of control in musical practice, as one of the performing arts, will be shown in light of several theories and illustrated with the relevant empirical evidence. Control is considered here as a capacity to resist distraction and inhibit impulsive action, but also as an ability to undertake and carry out self-initiated activity. Eventually, it may have a form of self-regulatory skills underlying a capacity to form and maintain habits of excellence.

Characteristics of Musical Performance

This chapter aims to demonstrate how control processes from many levels are integrated in most essential aspects of musicianship—comprising practicing an

Personality and Control edited by Philip J. Corr, Małgorzata Fajkowska, Michael W. Eysenck, and Agata Wytykowska. Eliot Werner Publications, Clinton Corners, New York, 2015.

instrument, mastering a piece of music, and delivering a performance. Musical training requires control on the elementary motor and cognitive levels of auditory processing and music making, higher levels of control comprising emotional and motivational self-regulation, and meta-cognitive control. Elementary and more complex processes of control are assumed to be interrelated and carry over to other domains of performance. Thus musical training is assumed to be an opportunity to develop and strengthen individual control capacity in a broader sense. This chapter illustrates the benefits and drawbacks of control and the risks of excessive depletion of control resources in musical practice. Since research concerning the role of control in musical practice is scarce, some speculations that follow may inspire further empirical work on the topic. Practical suggestions are drawn from the current state of the art in this domain, which may be interesting for both theorists and musicians.

Early beginning, high intensity, long duration, and regularity of training characterizes not only musicians, but also athletes and dancers. Yet what distinguishes musicians and singers from other performing professionals is using a sophisticated, expressive tool—namely, a musical instrument or voice. Highly specific technical requirements and the expressive potential of a musical instrument add complexity and difficulty to using one's body as a performing tool. Being a musician is more like being a puppeteer rather than an actor or an athlete. Musical practice is considered here as an exemplary domain of human activity in which processes of control are applied and developed.

This chapter begins by characterizing musical practice as a challenge to control processes at many levels. Then control processes inherent in musical practice are discussed, starting with the most elementary and moving to the more complex ones. The integrative role of meta-control functions for successful musical practice and performance is strongly emphasized. Self-regulatory functions are outlined with reference to the leading theories of action control (Kuhl, 1996), self-efficacy (Bandura, 1989), and self-control (Baumeister & Tierney, 2011). In light of these theoretical approaches, several speculations are presented concerning the role and effects of applying control within musical practice and performance. These speculations are accompanied with relevant empirical evidence and reference to the three theories of control processes. Perspectives for further research and practical conclusions follow.

CONTROL PROCESSES EMERGENT IN MUSICAL PRACTICE

Learning to play a musical instrument is a long-term commitment (Costa-Giomi, 2012), usually beginning at the age of five to seven. Regularity, continuity, and persistence of practice, flexibility in setting reasonable limits to the amount of practice (Wan, 2008), and switching between techniques and elements of musical production—all pose difficulty to young music students. At early stages of music education, children learn to cope with monotony, tediousness of musical practice, and their own inability to deliberately use practice techniques (Nathan, 2008), maintain task-focus, and apply an appropriate amount of effort in order to make progress.

Musical training coincides with the intense development of fine motor skills, inhibitory control, control of emotion, and volition. For instance, inhibitory control (i.e., the speed of stopping an already initiated speeded voluntary response) that performs the executive functions of the cognitive system (Schachar & Logan, 1990) and increases as children mature (Williams, Ponesse, Schachar, Logan, & Tannock, 1999) has a critical role in efficient musical practice.

At the elementary stages of musical training, children need encouragement and support from teachers and parents in developing self-regulatory skills critical for any advancement in music making (see Suzuki, 1983). These influential adults help them develop their own technical awareness and foster their "grit" (Duckworth, Peterson, Matthews, & Kelly, 2007). Students who follow teachers' cues for performance strategy, which also requires an ability to trust a teacher and follow his or her advice, achieve highest performance results (Barry, 1990).

Parents, actively participating in the process of learning, play an important role in children's satisfaction of their need to feel competent and experience autonomy, relatedness, and sense of purpose (Pomerantz, Grolnick, & Price, 2005). Parental style supporting children's autonomy, rather than controlling their activity, is influential also from the perspective of directing their attention toward effort rather than a fixed ability (McPherson, 2009). Such an instruction in self-regulatory attitude allows children to develop an internal locus of control (LOC) and an active approach to difficulties that they encounter. Parents also structure the environment in which learning takes place—as regards time and space—which may be decisive for children's ability to focus on practice.

Both musicians and researchers emphasize the importance of individually tailored practice and careful scheduling of practices. Practice should be mastery oriented and practice time must be well used in order to make progress and avoid overtraining. Building a technical foundation for the artistic growth at an elementary level of music education requires patience, determination, and the ability to set realistic short-term goals (Klickstein, 2009). From the very beginning of musical training, young music students learn to (a) develop technical skills and maintain them; (b) prepare a piece for performance involving its expressive aspect; and (c) give public performances, forming an interaction with the audience. Multiple processes of control must be involved in these complex tasks so that the satisfactory level of musical expertise and performance quality can be achieved.

Musicians' self-sufficiency concerning practice and its effectiveness grows as their skills develop. Self-regulated learning is a deliberate adaptive process (Butler & Winne, 1995) comprising setting goals for upgrading performance, monitoring the effects of engagement, and actively searching for strategies to make progress—all of which form the foundation even for improvisation (Weisberg, 1999). Besides the executive aspects of self-regulated learning, monitoring can refer to concentration, engagement in practice, and musical performance. Monitoring concentration and focusing on the activity allows the student to avoid mindless repetition (Jørgensen & Hallam, 2009).

In the course of rehearsing, it is crucial to identify the activities that are both highly demanding and have the highest potential to result in desired achievements, instead of extending the amount of time devoted to the domain-related activities. Regulating the engagement in practice is part of deliberate learning and control of practice schedule. Careful monitoring of performance is important to maintain motivation to practice that improves the quality of performance. Such training involves motor, cognitive, emotional, motivational, and meta-cognitive control, some of which have self-regulatory functions and will now be briefly outlined with reference to the leading theories of action control (Kuhl, 1996), self-efficacy (Bandura, 1989), and self-control (Baumeister & Tierney, 2011).

Control Processes in Musical Practice

There are three ways of maximizing performance quality, and minimizing physical effort and psychological tension, that could not be achieved if not for the ability to initiate and execute one's intentions and plans (see Kuhl, 1996), the sense of self-efficacy (Bandura, 1989), and self-control (Baumeister & Tierney, 2012). The respective theories point to the aspects of control that are of high relevance for musical practice. Theoretical references are accompanied by empirical evidence, forming the basis for the speculations constituting the integrative approach to control processes in musical practice.

Motor Control

Control of movement and monitoring its acoustic outcome are basic musical activities from the very beginning of musical training. Motor control, by which a technique is developed and maintained, is focused on ergonomics and precision in the way of sound making. At the first stage of training, students underrate the importance of meticulous motor control that is yet to be practiced by constant repetition in order to shape the desired correct movement sequences that are formed, mastered, combined, and applied within a specific piece of music.

Emotional Control

Emotional control in musicians is relevant to the practice hours, management of stress, and performance anxiety. It comprises using expressive cues during a performance, regulating emotion and arousal, and coping with stress. Motivational control requires monitoring one's energy associated with the activities and boosting it when necessary.

Cognitive Control

Control of attention, as an ability to (1) direct attention to a selected object, (2) sustain attention on task, or (3) resist to distractor interference (which have strong biological bases; Friedman & Miyake, 2004; Posner & Petersen, 1990), must go hand in hand with (4) voluntary attention shifting and (5) attentional flexibility that permit maintaining task-focus during a performance and simultaneously staying in touch with the audience. Memorization strategies and techniques are used to form the mental structure of a piece. Deliberate memorization of music helps develop a sense of control over the piece and diminishes performance anxiety.

Meta-Cognitive Control

Eventually, meta-cognitive control in musicians is predominantly manifested in the capacity to plan and monitor rehearsal, evaluate progress, and be aware of one's strengths and weaknesses (Hallam, 2001). Planning is inherent in scheduling practice sessions, determining memorization strategies, and developing a long-term approach to study. The facets of energy expenditure are alert to signals of overconcentration and overtraining and regulate arousal during performance. Metacognitive control and regulation-of-practice strategies shape the process of practice, which needs to be practiced itself (Jørgensen, 2004) in order to achieve maximum effectiveness. Stress coping strategies involve elementary levels of motor, cognitive, and affective control.

SELF-REGULATION, SELF-CONTROL, AND SELF-EFFICACY

In the model of action control (Kuhl, 1996), the ability to carry out one's intentions and plans is discussed as the domain of volition, willpower, self-regulation, and self-control. Self-regulation can be decomposed into more elementary mechanisms that people use to maintain their goals. Some of these are attention control, intention control, control of arousal, control of emotion and motivation, action control, coding control, reflective thinking, and planning (Kuhl & Goschke, 1994). These elements map very well onto such aspects of musical practice as motor, cognitive, emotional, motivational, and meta-cognitive activities.

Goal maintenance that sustains intentions over long periods of time (Kuhl, 1996) protects them against competitive action tendencies. In a self-regulatory ability, one of the forms of volition—self—is the agent of control, while in self-control self is the object of control (Kuhl, 1996). Both of these perspectives are relevant to musical practice. Self-regulation, fueled by proactive motivation, seems more adequate a term to use in the context of pursuing long-term goals such as mastering musical skills. Self-control appears to be more relevant to the control of motor activity or behavioral inhibition. It has stronger impact on avoiding or inhibiting undesired behaviors than on promoting desirable ones (de Ridder, Lensvelt-Mulders, Finkenauer, Stok, & Baumeister, 2012).

This function can be applied in resisting temptation to quit the long hours of rehearsing and switching to a more directly rewarding activity, rather than undertaking new artistic projects. Indeed, for young musicians it is often a personal and social challenge to organize their lives around musical practice by withdrawing from other types of activities. On the other hand, the social cognitive approach to self-regulated learning and performance (Zimmerman, 1995) points to self-initiated monitoring and controlling performance as crucial skills in the process of achieving a satisfactory level of performance (McPherson & Renwick, 2011).

Self-efficacy—comprising beliefs of control over potential threats—is associated with the consequent reduction of physiological symptoms of anxiety (Lehmann et al., 2007), while individuals with low levels of control efficacy suffer from self-doubt and anticipate failure (Bandura, 1991). It is plausible that anxiety and stress are moderated by perceived personal control of negative thoughts or environmental events (see Bandura, 1986), which is important considering that musicians experience stress and anxiety as states accompanying performance irrespective of the stage of their musical career (Kenny, 2011).

Another perspective on control is proposed in a concept of self-control that can be considered as "the capacity to alter or override dominant response tendencies and to regulate behavior, thoughts, and emotions" (de Ridder et al., 2012, p. 77), and forms the basis for self-regulation. Dispositional self-control, considered as a strength rather than a skill (Baumeister & Heatherton, 1996), is relatively stable across situations. It bears similarity to Thurstone's concept of intelligence as the ability to inhibit reflexive responses in order to better adapt to the environment (Sternberg, 1990, as cited in Nęcka, 2005). Self-control is manifested in good performance under the demands to delay gratification (Mischel, Shoda, & Peake, 1988) and while exerting control over behavior by its long-term consequences (Logue, 1996).

Within this concept self-control in musicians is implemented in the ability to focus on the desired and valuable outcome of their training that is yet delayed. Here the competing motives would be a growing capacity to produce music due to intense practice and a more immediate reward such as "easy pleasures" of going out with friends, watching television, or playing computer games (see Ainslie, 1975). The process of resisting such temptations both depletes self-control as a limited pool of willpower resources (Baumeister & Tierney, 2011) and strengthens it contributing to personality development (Muraven, Baumeister, & Tice, 1999). On the other hand, exerting self-control should be supported by such personality dispositions as conscientiousness (Chamorro-Premusic, 2006; Rothstein, Paunonen, Rush, & King, 1994) or low impulsiveness (Gray, 1981).

Theoretical Speculations About the Role of Control Processes in Musicians

This overview of the theories of control leads to several speculations that will guide the referencing of empirical data on the role of control processes, both in the efficient training and successful career of a practicing musician.

Speculation 1 (S1): Self-Regulatory Disposition as Carryover Effect of Musical Training

Apart from musical talent, an individual's apt self-control and meta-cognitive control applied to musical training facilitate the acquisition of musical skills. Since music education coincides with personality development, it should both engage and deplete willpower and self-control and contribute to their formation, strengthening willpower in the long run (Baumeister & Tierney, 2011; Muraven et al., 1999). It is plausible that the range of control processes operant in an individual broadens through training of a range of capacities involved in musical expertise. This proposition is complementary to ego depletion by performing activities calling for self-control (Baumeister & Tierney, 2011). While there are no empirical data to directly support this speculation, there is ample evidence of other mental functions being trained during musical practice and transferred to other domains of activity.

Speculation 2 (S2): Advantages of Control Flexibility

The ability to move easily between a highly controlled goal-focused approach and a relaxed, intuitive process-focused approach to practicing turns out to be most advantageous as a practice strategy. In the long term, such control flexibility leads to the highest proportion of successful performance outcomes and performance satisfaction. Its functional aspect will be discussed with reference to musicians' ability to avoid overpracticing and overcontrolling their performance on stage.

Speculation 3 (S3): Individual Differences in Ego Depletion

Willpower capacity varies individually, leading to individual differences in proneness to ego-depletion (Baumeister & Tierney, 2011). Musicians with more limited self-control resources, having invested in their professional activities with excessive control demands, should more eagerly compensate with activities posing no challenge in terms of control and allowing for the subjective release of control—such as drinking or using drugs. The empirical studies on musicians (Dobson, 2011) and evidence provided by their therapists (Sherman, 2012) support the theoretical assumptions concerning ego depletion (Baumeister & Tierney, 2011).

The above speculations will be further referenced with their symbols, for consideration in light of the empirical support provided throughout the chapter. The following part of the chapter presents control processes involved in musical practice, starting from its most basic elements—such as motorics, cognition, emotion, and motivation—to more complex ones involving self-regulation and stress-coping, such as practice scheduling, planning, rehearsing, and valuating practice. Consequently, mental processes and functions inherent in musical practice and performance (Galamian, 1964, as cited in Jørgensen, 2004) will be analyzed with reference to multiple facets of control processes.

THE ROLE OF CONTROL PROCESSES IN DEVELOPING MUSICAL SKILLS

Research demonstrates beneficial consequences of musical training on multiple intellectual functions, such as picking up prosodic information in speech (Thompson, Schellenberg, & Husain, 2003) and verbal memory (Roden, Kreutz, & Bongard, 2012); performance of such working memory components as articulatory loop and central executive (Roden, Grube, Bongard, & Kreutz, 2013) that may be due to enhanced ability to exert sustained cognitive control (Pallesen et al. 2010); and granularity of the emotional responses to music (Kantor-Martynuska & Bigand, 2013).

However, less is known about the effects of long-term musical training on more elementary control processes or trait self-control, mostly because personality contributes to undertaking and continuing music education (Corrigall, Schellenberg, & Misura, 2013) and develops simultaneously with long-term musical training. Practice in auditory-motor synchronization, which requires monitoring the relationship between auditory input and motor output, is related to better visual and auditory selective and sustained attention (Tierney & Kraus, 2013), suggesting a significant role of musical training in attentional control. Precision of motor behavior, control over attention, emotion, motivation, and interpretation of a piece of music—as well as planning and executing the planned actions—exemplify the elements of self-regulation (Kuhl & Goschke, 1994).

Motor Control

Motor control, as the most basic aspect of instrumental practice, is developed as a result of training in performing precise movement sequences. Control over motor activity is a challenge at the early stage of learning to play a musical instrument. Slow tempo inherent in the first months of practice is gradually increased, with simultaneous maintenance of motor control and the resulting performance quality. Forming correct technical habits, starting from the very beginning of music education (e.g., keystroke efficiency in pianists; Goebl & Palmer, 2013), is an important factor contributing to progress in performance. Finger movement control is improved throughout childhood as the latter stage of motor development, in which refined movements can be highly controlled and synchronized in both hands (see Henderson & Pehoski, 2006). This progress may also depend on self-control reservoirs (see de Ridder et al., 2012). Since involuntary slips or alterations of tempo due to imprecise movements manifest shortage of control, they result in a perceived lack of expertise and performance failure.

Skillful fine motor control on manual tasks is transferred to movement types that are not directly relevant to one's profession. An example is advantageous performance of fine motor control tasks in precision mechanics experts (Vieluf, Mahmoodi, Godde, Reuter, & Voelcker-Rehage, 2012), which can also be expected in instrumentalists (*S1*). Also, with reference to a study concerning sports activity

(Parschau et al., 2013), positive experience with previous musical activity should be associated with high self-efficacy, which fosters motor-control inherent in music making—but only in high action control individuals. This may exemplify how cognitive and motor skills work together to raise the level of competencies that contribute to a successful musical career.

While performing in public, best performance is observed at a lower level of fine motor action control, which allows focusing attention on the artistic aspect of the performance (Haslinger et al., 2004). Directing attention to the sonoric effects of finger movements—rather than to the movements themselves—leads to enhanced accuracy of motor performance in musicians (*S2*; Duke, Cash, & Allen, 2011). A unique balance between meticulous movement monitoring, motor control, and more intuitive sound making is desirable in mature musicianship as a result of flexible switching between these processes.

Control of Attention

Efficient musical training encompasses learning how to focus attention and developing an awareness of the distractors that might draw attention away from the main task. These skills underlie voluntary attention shifting, resulting in better recognition of the aspects of performance that are within and beyond control.

The advanced stage of musical practice comprises augmenting attentional engagement in the bits of experience inherent in the training process. Maintenance of attention to detail should persist even when the whole piece is being rehearsed. Part-whole transfer of training (Jørgensen & Hallam, 2009) consists of switching between playing difficult sections and the whole piece. Hearing the sections in context and apart, as figure and ground in Gestalt psychology, may be helpful in memorizing the piece, which enhances the role of attention for the efficient memorization of music.

In the formal perspective concerning performance, attention control proceeds along two dimensions—internal versus external and broad (extensive) versus narrow (intensive; see Kolańczyk, 2011). Dynamic regulation of broad versus narrow attention focus on the multiple aspects of performance situation is one of the predominant spheres in which musicians fail in high-pressure performance situations. An ability to redirect attention to task-relevant cues during a performance (after it has been drawn away) is enhanced by practice in identifying the phases of performance in which distraction is most frequent, and the factors that are most likely to attract it during performance (e.g., physical or human surroundings, past or future experiences, task-irrelevant thoughts).

An ability to disengage from emotional distraction and move the focus of attention to physical or mental objects—which are less harmful for performance—forms part of performing expertise (*S2*). Mastering attentional control comprises training in intentional and voluntary directing of attention to the selected elements of the environment, one's body or thoughts, and purposefully adding further sensations to the overall experience of the moment. Another option is shifting the focus between the objects that could be attended to (see Connolly & Williamon, 2004). A paradoxical way of augmenting attentional control is by becoming familiar with distraction, focusing on it deliberately, and viewing it positively (Nathan, 2008).

Regarding the carryover effects of musical aptitude on other skills, enhanced control over auditory processing (for a review see Strait & Kraus, 2011; Kraus & Chandrasekaran, 2010) has been linked to better linguistic aptitude in a range of subjects—from preschoolers through older children to adults with musical training. It comprises heightened perception of speech in noise in musicians compared with their untrained peers (*S1*; Parbery-Clark, Skoe, Lam, & Kraus, 2009; Strait, O'Connell, Parbery-Clark, & Kraus, 2013). While control over both technical and artistic aspects of performance results in the ability to structure mental activity carried out during music performance, when the level of stress increases, excessive amount of mental discipline may cause a decline in the quality of performance. Therefore, while the ability to focus attention and shift it between objects is crucial for musical aptitude (Williamon, Valentine, & Valentine, 2002), a preferred form of such a focused attention is "a relaxed state of being alert" (*S2*; Connolly & Williamon, 2008, p. 233).

Detrimental Effects of Overconcentration on Music Performance

Motor control can be within or beyond a musician's main focus while performing music. In the functional perspective, a continuum of concentration in music making is extended between the two extremes: (a) a focus on production and perception of sound with an open and relaxed posture and (b) the active concentration on the technical aspects and overt movements (Gellrich, 1991). Concentration as continuous attention during practice is recommended to prevent automatic repetitious practice without mental involvement (Wan, 2008; see also Bryant, 1999).

However, a performer may attempt to control everything from a single note to a series of movements, which most musicians experience at some point. Such focus can be stronger than necessary, leading to overconcentration. Excessively concentrated practice directs attention to the technical aspects of playing, resulting in a feeling of security but also risking loss of voluntary motor control due to extensive training. Such a manner of controlling the cognitive engagement in practice leads to increased tension and muscular contraction, localized in the parts of the body that are most involved in playing—especially if a musician has developed incorrect technique (*S2*; Wan, 2008). Overexertion may also cause or intensify anxiety (Wan, 2008) and contribute to risk of injury that inhibits physical movements (Gellrich, 1991). Resulting muscle dystonia, once developed, cannot be easily overcome (Wilson & Roland, 2002).

Musicians often insufficiently appreciate the importance of constant monitoring of the energy level and spotting the symptoms of fatigue in order to avoid overexertion and exhaustion (Ericsson, Krampe, & Tesch-Römer, 1993; Fry, 1986; Newmark & Lederman, 1987). To avoid injury one must control the duration and intensity of practice. Mindful practice involves taking breaks to allow the muscles to rest. Such a facet of self-regulation involves shifting attention from the precision of movements and expressive features of music onto one's bodily sensations and psychological state as valid cues for correct practice management. Thus the awareness of control intensity is crucial to form balance between a tense and a more relaxed approach to practice and performance. It is as important to know how long to pursue practicing as when to stop it (*S2*).

Preventing overtraining and overexertion is a means to efficient practice with consideration of the locus of control. Musicians' scores on the Locus of Control Inventory for Illness and Health (Lohaus & Schmitt, 1989), which estimates a tendency to take responsibility for one's health, were found highest on "internal" LOC (Spahn, Burger, Hildebrandt, & Seidenglanz, 2005). Musicians' scores on the LOC Inventory for Illness and Health were also higher than that of their peers and their lowest score was on "chance" LOC. Accordingly, musicians feel responsible for their health, and this topic may form grounds for argumentation underlying monitoring effort while practicing. The beneficial role of the internal locus of control and creativity can be sensed in young musicians' comments on how they deal with their practice routine. Making up stories, playing an imaginary film soundtrack, getting involved in fancy music making, and having fun while playing raise their capacity to deal with the challenges or overcome difficulties associated with performing in public (Nathan, 2008).

Deliberate Memorization

One of the major aspects of musical practice and preparation for performance is memorizing music in various ways and on different levels. Memorizing music can be focused on the structural, aesthetic, and expressive elements of the score. It is based on deep processing that comprises perceiving the functional relationships between smaller portions of the score. The ability to switch between attention to detail and attention to a larger passage contributes to successful memorization of music (*S2*). Deliberate and structured memorization of a piece of music requires attention control and meta-cognitive control skills, which suggests parallel action of several control modes.

Memorization proceeds in a different way in experts and novices. In chess players meaning and significance facilitate remembering chess position patterns (Chase & Simon, 1973). Experts engage their knowledge structure to interpret and memorize the meaningful entities within the domain of their expertise. It is a way to build a clear representation of the whole musical piece, with easy access to its particular elements.

Novices do not operate with this knowledge, and so their way to memorize is less systematic. Violinist Hilary Hahn recommends a memorizing technique that consists in marking the score of colors to divide it into sections "in a way that reflects the configuration of the music" (as quoted in Nathan, 2008, p. 65), in order to map the piece—meaning to build up its mental representation. From this perspective the sources of resistance to performance anxiety can be traced back to the very beginning of practice, which is focused on formation of the secure feeling of being well prepared. It is of high importance considering that memory slips are the most anxiety-producing aspect of live performances. Conscious memorization of a piece brings about a sense of sufficient preparedness and reduces performance anxiety (Wan, 2008). Here cognitive elements of self-regulation (Kuhl & Goeschke, 1994) contribute to managing the emotional aspect of performance, demonstrating the interdependence of cognition and emotion, and suggesting the integrative character of control processes in musical practice.

With reference to carryover effects of cognitive control in the memory domain, working memory for auditory material shows the effects of control processes involved in musical training. As compared with nonmusicians, musicians reveal enhanced memory for words (Chan, Ho, & Cheung, 1998) but not for visual images (Ho, Cheung, & Chan, 2003; Roden et al., 2012). They also show better performance of auditory working memory task, which may reveal their better ability to exert sustained cognitive control and may recruit more resources for cognitive control (Pallesen et al., 2010). These findings suggest that the skills acquired in the context of memorizing music get transferred onto the way other auditory stimuli are processed (*S1*). Acquisition of musical skills and mental rehearsal can be considered as manifestations of meta-cognitive control.

Mental Rehearsal

Mental strategies and focused practice form the basis for a successful performance. Mental practice consists of vividly imaging movement sequences (Altenmüller & Schneider, 2009) and rehearsing a skill (Barry & Hallam, 2002) without actual physical activity. Mental rehearsal techniques are as important an element of musical practice as playing an instrument, calling for cognitive control as a tool to proceed with the subsequent elements of training. Mental rehearsal encompasses refocusing attention during a performance in order to be aware of the selected aspects of performance. It enhances the role of more elementary processes of control for those of the higher level, supporting the validity of the integrative approach to control in musical practice. In the common practices of musical training with beginners, insufficient consideration of mental training results in mindless practice habits that reduce practice efficiency and may extend long into adolescence. Thus, besides actual instrumental rehearsal, putting more emphasis on mental training—including control flexibility—starting from the elementary stage of musical training would increase the efficiency of musical practice (*S2*).

Connolly and Williamon (2004) propose a set of procedures that may help develop control over mental rehearsal, encompassing development of bodily awareness, imagination exercises, focused and selective listening, and approaching an instrument with specific attitudes and perspectives. Musicians benefit from such a mental rehearsal on stage, since it allows skilled control over one's own technique and the optimum dose of contact with the audience (located dynamically between the extremes of isolation and distraction).

Considering relaxation practice, Connolly and Williamon (2004) mention several competencies—which contribute to successful relaxation—that mostly evoke deliberate attentional control, applied here to regulate emotion and arousal. One is the ability to voluntarily pay attention to the sounds and objects inside and outside the room, and to move the focus of attention onto one's thoughts or body (e.g., breathing exercises). Directing attention to different parts of the body and defocusing it while regulating tension and relaxation demonstrates the role of control flexibility, which allows for the optimum proportion of tension and relaxation in the performance situation (*S2*). Mental rehearsal also involves managing emotion and arousal in the context of practice and performance (Woody & McPherson, 2010) inherent in affective self-regulation.

Control of Emotion and Arousal

Practicing a musical instrument requires activity of both a "cold" cognitive system that serves long-term goals, and a "hot" system that seeks pleasure in the activities in which one is involved (see Logue, 1996). Achievement-focused musical training emphasizes technical virtuosity and hard work that will bring an expected outcome in the future. Another musical training style, focused on the process of skill development, refers to pleasure in evoking sound and personal involvement in making music (see Ablard & Parker, 1997). The combination of the two training styles should bring the best results considering students' individual differences in self-control and their varied ability to delay gratification (*S2, S3*).

Regarding practice strategies, individual differences in activity levels and emotionality may predispose individuals toward certain deliberate practice activities (Ericsson et al., 1993). The effectiveness of arousal control during performance should be moderated by temperament characteristics, including tonic level of arousal (e.g., extraversion; Eysenck, 1967), stimulation-processing capacity (Strelau, 2008), and rumination (Nolen-Hoeksema, 1998). These place limitations on the effectiveness of control processes in the context of musical training and performance (*S3*).

Another aspect of affective control in musical practice regards musical expression, which is "the way in which a musician brings a piece to life" (Clarke, Dibben, & Pitts, 2011, p. 35). It is based on personal interpretation of a piece of music and involves application of noticeable dynamic differences, changes in articulation, vibrato, and tempo fluctuations (Clarke et al., 2011) that give a piece a unique character while leaving it recognizable and structurally intact.

Giving a performance is often burdened with negative emotion, the control of which can be developed through practice in imagining oneself coming onto stage or looking at the audience in order to become familiar with multiple aspects of performance context. Emotional ambivalence, irrespective of the stage of music education, is grounded in having fun and developing self-efficacy in music making on one hand, and struggling with the stress, fatigue, and helplessness that cause tension on the other. Crafting performing confidence demands developing a positive attitude toward the audience and the act of performing, self-discipline in following a sensible preparation schedule, and caring for one's health and well-being (Klickstein, 2009). Such a contribution of self-regulatory mechanisms on multiple levels should foster intrinsic motivation that energizes musical activity (*S1*).

The slightest performance-associated anxiety and hesitation on stage can lead to nervous tension that is transmitted to different parts of the body (Grindea, 1995). In the context of performance preparation and the general practice schedule, relaxation techniques are used to manage the level of arousal before, during and after a performance—as well as to plan the proportions of effort and rest within each practice day. They imply both meticulous control of attention and a capacity to disengage from controlling motor actions involved in performance.

Control of Motivation: From External to Intrinsic Motivation

Music beginners need parental support to stabilize their motivation to practice (Pomerantz et al., 2005). Mastery-oriented musicians are intrinsically motivated by their goals and challenges (Lehmann et al., 2007) and experienced musicians find it easier to focus attention both on their goals and the means to carry them out (Jørgensen & Hallam, 2009).

At earlier stages of musical training, children are externally motivated to practice by concerts or auditions. Their motivation gradually earns a more internal character focused on playing at their most excellent (Nathan, 2008). The initial form of introjected regulation may be transformed into identified regulation, in which behavior is guided by conscious valuation of one's progress and performance. The final form of regulation to reach is integrated regulation, in which intrinsic motivation concerning the musical activity becomes an individual's central aim (see Austin et al., 2006). Young music students learn to boost their motivation to practice on a daily basis and there is a strong—if not perfect—correlation between the amount of time spent practicing and the level of expertise (Ericsson et al., 1993; Williamon & Valentine, 2000). It has tight links to practice strategies and mental rehearsal, which support the integrative approach to control processes in music making.

Upgrading students' motivation is one of a teacher's major tasks in musical training. In addition to natural talent, the amount of practice extended over a minimum of ten years is an indispensable factor in superior performance (Chi, Glaser, & Farr, 1988; Ericsson & Smith, 1991). Experts' performance preparation is characterized by a commitment to deliberate practice, a highly structured activity with the explicit aim to upgrade performance. It requires the ability to maintain motivation and overcome the periods of demotivation. This may be associated with deliberate focusing on long-term goals and consequences of behavior (Logue, 1996), or on a delayed but valuable outcome of one's effort (see Ainslie, 1975) and delaying gratification (Mischel et al., 1988). This perspective may be analyzed in the scope of self-regulatory mechanisms that are applied to self-initiated effort.

With reference to the speculation concerning the mutual relationship between personality and control in musical practice, on the one hand those with stronger personality predispositions toward such behaviors should find it easier to control their motivation (*S3*). On the other hand, long-term musical training should result in forming the skills or augmenting the dispositions that are called for during this process (*S1*).

Affective and Attentional Self-Regulation in Coping with Musical Performance Anxiety

Control over performance begins while starting working on a piece of music: organizing practice sessions, specifying goals, using memorization strategies, and preparing for the performance. Control processes contribute to how the piece is segmented, interpreted, and actively integrated. If any of these aspects is neglected or denied, a musician is likely to experience disappointment on stage. As flutist James Galway catastrophically put it, "Failing to prepare is like preparing to fail" (as quoted in Nathan, 2008, p. 74). Concern about possible failure manifests itself in intense performance anxiety, which is an exaggerated fear of performing in public. Performance anxiety has somatic, emotional, and cognitive components that can be subjected to coping strategies rooted in the application of control processes during preparation of a piece for performance and on stage.

Besides the high "local" self-efficacy concerning the level of preparation for a particular performance, there is a range of cognitive strategies that musicians use to attenuate their performance tension, implementing self-regulatory mechanisms. Throughout the process of rehearsing a piece, anxiety can be controlled by self-instruction and positive self-talk (e.g., "I can do it"), mental rehearsal, and imagery (McPherson & Zimmerman, 2011). Compared with setting performance outcome goals, recognition of learning-related or process-related goals contributes to enhanced enjoyment of performing music (Ablard & Parker, 1997), as relevant to the training styles described earlier in this chapter.

Multiple aspects of self-regulation allow for decreasing performance anxiety and maximizing the quality of performance. Exerting control over performance proceeds through (a) recognition of performance context and getting familiar with the hall, (b) awareness of what cannot be controlled (e.g., street noise from outside the hall), and (c) coming to terms with these factors. Performance routines such as planned warm-up on the instrument, focus on performance goals, and control of social interactions preceding performance (Wilson & Roland, 2002) are also the means of mapping a situation in which one is challenged to be at his or her most excellent. Most elementary processes of control at basic levels of musical practice contribute to more complex forms of control, which are important aspects of efficient musical practice and performance.

Attentional Control and Performance Anxiety

This theoretical assumption underlay research on the relationship between (a) the intensity of somatic tension and the negative feelings experienced in the performance context and (b) the ability to control attention in a form of resistance to distractor interference—indicated by the score on a flanker test—in teenage musicians (Kantor-Martynuska & Pastuszek-Lipińska, 2012). In the study performance anxiety was measured with the List of Symptoms and Consequences of Music Performance Anxiety (LSCMPA; Kępińska-Welbel, 1997), which comprises items related to physiological and psychological symptoms and consequences of music performance anxiety (MPA) throughout the performance.

Participants filled out the questionnaire in a neutral setting, reporting their tendency to experience trait MPA. Then they gave two public music performances within a few weeks, which were directly preceded and immediately followed by completing LSCMPA with reference to state MPA. The study revealed that participants who committed more errors on a flanker test also experienced weaker negative and stronger positive feelings during a performance. Participants whose reaction times in a flanker test were shorter—meaning better attentional control—showed less intense physiological symptoms of performance anxiety during performance. These findings indicate that the impulsive response style manifested in a flanker test is associated with less intense performance anxiety in teenage musicians.

In another study that employed music theater actors, dancers, and vocalists during a musical premiere, Kantor-Martynuska and Wlazłowska-Gorzko (in preparation) looked at the relationship between an artist's psychological and physiological state during a performance, his or her self-reported attentional control, and attentional control as resistance to distractor interference measured with a flanker test. As in the previous study, the participants filled out the LSCMPA a few days before giving a performance to report on their trait MPA. In the same session, they also completed the Attentional Control Scale (ACS; Fajkowska & Derryberry, 2010) and performed a flanker test (Eriksen & Eriksen, 1974). In another session, on the day of a musical premiere the participants filled out the LSCMPA, with reference to state MPA, three times: just before giving a performance, during an entr'acte, and immediately after a performance.

With regard to trait MPA, the results show that higher attentional control at a level of elementary cognitive processes is associated with fewer physiological symptoms of performance anxiety and less psychological tension. The intensity of positive feelings after a performance was higher in the participants whose reactions in a flanker test were more impulsive, which is consistent with the results of the previous study (Kantor-Martynuska & Pastuszek-Lipińska, 2012). In the natural setting of a musical premiere, higher self-reported attentional control was associated with (a) a lower level of negative feelings and physiological symptoms of performance anxiety before a performance; (b) a reduced tendency to negatively evaluate a performance; (c) a lower level of negative feelings experienced immediately after a performance; and (d) a higher level of self-reported positive feelings following a performance. The study suggested that in the context of giving a performance, self-reported ability to control attention is both somatically and psychologically beneficial for a musician.

The two studies reported above show that resistance to distractor interference as attentional control at the level of elementary cognitive processing is associated with less intense symptoms of music performance anxiety in a stressful performance situation. The level of attentional control manifested in processing simple visual stimuli may be diagnostic of a capacity to filter out task-irrelevant stimuli in a performance context. Those findings shed light on the importance of elementary attentional processes for dealing with the challenge of performing in public.

Risks of High Control Demands of Musical Performance

Successful control over motor action, cognition, emotion, and motivation inherent in performance should result in high self-efficacy (see Bandura, 1999). Conversely, if such control is either insufficient or consumes too much volitional effort, the self-perceived shortcomings of control over one's body and mental state during a performance may lead to perceived low self-efficacy—possibly generalized to low self-esteem—and the consequent overuse of alcohol, drugs, or prescription drugs (beta-blockers).

Musicians' common concern over their lack of job prospects and financial security makes them aware of the importance of reputation in the network of musicians in which they function (Dobson, 2011). A key means of advancing work prospects (Sherman, 2012) is socializing professionally, in which alcohol consumption often plays an important role. While research concerning musicians' use of alcohol is scarce (see Ginsborg, Spahn, & Williamon, 2012), alcohol or drug addiction among musicians seem to have multiple functions, such as protecting oneself under the excessive control demands or one's perceived inability to control his or her career. Drinking patterns are associated with the demands of performance, with alcohol consumption—probably more likely in males—arising as a consequence of either pressure or boredom (see Baumeister, Catanese, & Vohs, 2001).

Self-regulated musical training depletes willpower resources, posing requirements that are harder to meet for individuals whose level of self-control is low (*S1*). They should be particularly prone to seeking compensation in a form of impulsive carefree behavior or substance abuse (Baumeister & Tierney, 2012). Overusing alcohol and psychotropic drugs gives an illusory short-term reduction of responsibility and the experienced anxiety. Planning, preparation, and execution of musical practice, as well as monitoring and valuation of practice and performance (Galamian, 1964, after Jørgensen, 2004) as practice strategies, are constructive means of reducing performance tension. All of them involve a range of control processes presented below.

CONTROL PROCESSES IN PRACTICE STRATEGIES: FROM EXTERNAL TO INTERNAL CONTROL IN PRACTICE SCHEDULING

Mental skills concerning practicing a musical instrument involve planning and setting goals, expending effort to achieve these goals, monitoring progress, and assessing performance (Connolly & Williamon, 2004). A mastery-oriented perspective on preparing a performance entails control manifested in action planning, time scheduling, "chunking," rehearsing, and valuating practice. These are the ways to organize a regimen, emphasize excellence, and delve into details that form the basis for practicing deeply (Klickstein, 2009).

Deep practice comprises dividing the piece into sections, assimilating the ingredients, and merging the parts that require accuracy and exactitude (Klickstein, 2009). Such a precision of thought and action promotes mindful work on a piece. As in other performing arts and sports, deep practice protects musicians from routine and habitual repetitions, which contributes to a more sensitive interpretation of the piece. Structured practice is higher in effectiveness and raises a performer's perceived self-efficacy. The following part of the chapter elaborates on the processes of control within the subsequent elements of mastery-oriented rehearsing.

Planning and Time Scheduling

The ability to pursue deliberate practice involves taking intentional actions aimed at improving performance. They are always carried out in the context of individual capacities, limitations, and social interactions that support or hinder the process. The most basic strategy in practice is planning a practice session.

Planning a practice session is a thought strategy that may be applied intentionally with the engagement of control or become automatic if repeated (Jørgensen, 2004). In musical practice self-regulation is applied in both the structural and the purely musical domain. Musicians with higher levels of willpower have more resources left for practice itself (*S3*). Self-control may contribute to automatizing behavior (Baumeister & Alquist, 2009), which is suggested by medium to strong effects of self-control on automatic behaviors (de Ridder et al., 2012). Maintaining intentions concerning practice time habits and adhering to everyday practice regimens poses difficulties, particularly at the early stage of music education and for those with low self-control (*S3*; see de Ridder et al., 2012). Forming habits and maintaining routines relevant to musical training may be the strength of high-willpower musicians.

Planning practices can vary from a specific time each day and different times to split time (Nathan, 2008). The basic aspect of controlling practice at a global level is distributing the practice sessions throughout the week and during the day. The necessity to be alert determines that the most difficult aspects of the practice should be carried out in the morning (Lehmann & Ericsson, 1998). Executing such a schedule may be harder for individuals with high reactivity levels and a preferred supportive style of action, who engage in preparatory actions aimed at reducing their activation level so that it becomes optimal from the perspective of undertaking a difficult task of priority (see Strelau, 2008). Also, high impulsives may prefer to start practicing later in the day, since their activity levels increase during the day (see Revelle, Humphreys, Simon, & Gilliland, 1980).

The ability to match the practice schedule with the individual dynamics of activation is an advanced skill and a basic aspect of musicians' self-regulation. Such a capacity has hardly been an element of professional musical training and should be given more consideration at any stage of music education. Rehearsing methods guide the actual practice, comprising the processes of control mostly within the domains of motor activity and attention.

Rehearsing

Musical practice is more efficient when it implements the ability to pay attention to a large portion of music by referring to the formal structure of the piece in order to organize performance (see Chaffin & Lemieux, 2008). However, segmenting work into small portions allows limiting the number of inherent problems, which makes it possible to focus attention on specific problems and solve them.

One of the fundamental characteristics of musical excellence is the ability to concentrate fully on a task (Chaffin & Lemieux, 2004). Unlike mindless practice in which a piece can be played automatically, effective practice is "guided by thought" (Chaffin & Lemieux, 2004, p. 25). However, actually playing an instrument is only part of a professional musician's practice. A case study with an outstanding pianist participant (Chaffin & Imreh, 2002) shows that only a quarter of her practice time was devoted to playing the instrument, whereas three-quarters was spent thinking about the problems inherent in the piece of music and its structure. This study demonstrates a major role of deliberate mental effort in effective practice. Here self-initiated and self-regulated processes, rather than self-controlled collaboration or teamwork, are the basis of progress.

Habits of excellence include focused attention and constant valuation of progress (not to be mistaken for evaluation of performance by the audience; Runco & Chand, 1994). Valuation consists of intentional improvement of a work or performance and upgrading its artistic value in the process of creative thinking (Runco & Chand, 1994). In musical practice it evolves with practice and matures with experience.

Integrated regulation consists of managing emotion before and during a performance by eliminating negative affect and putting oneself in the emotional state that is optimal for a successful performance (Williamon, 2004). Emotions that performers experience while engaging in music form the beliefs about the value of their work (Austin, Renwick, & McPherson, 2006). Success in the domain of music performance involves realistic valuations of one's own performance. An ability to form a relevant opinion of one's musical production is yet another skill that calls for control in a form of self-regulation.

Valuating Practice: An Internal Perspective on the Quality of Practice and Performance

The process of valuation may be more constructive if it becomes more reflective and specific, focused on such precise valuations as "This is good," "This is bad," "I like that," or "It should be changed to . . ." (Runco & Chand, 1994). Such a specified valuation aims at always giving reasons for the judgments made so that they contribute to the improvement of performance quality.

Musicians gradually extend the awareness of the origin of errors in a broader context and develop strategies to manage repetition, as described above. Novices are less likely to identify errors: 60% of beginners leave errors uncorrected while learning a new piece and make them permanent by repetition (Hallam, 1997). Self-control in deliberate musical practice manifests in the awareness of one's own competencies, motivation, and cognitive processing, which provide grounds for judging how well the unfolding performance matches the standards one has adopted for the successful practice (Corno, 1993).

Orientation to mastery that leads to improving peformance quality is supported by a moderate level of perfectionism, while a strong perfectionist attitude may be a burden for a performing artist (Kenny, 2011). In professional artists high perfectionism combined with low personal control is associated with greater debilitating performance anxiety, increased somatic anxiety, and less goal satisfaction (Mor, Day, Flett, & Hewitt, 1995). A reason for that may be a competitive approach to music making that is widely enhanced at any stage of a musical career. Task-involved orientation versus ego-involved orientation protects musicians from being concerned about how others might evaluate their skills (Lehmann et al., 2007) and enhances the actual progress in the level of performance.

CONCLUSIONS

This chapter has presented the contribution of control processes to successful musical practice and performance. Control processes are inherent in the planning, preparation, and execution of practice; valuation of practice and performance; and energy expenditure during a performance. Musicians carry out their intentions and plans relevant to performing music with the implementation of practice strategies and self-regulation in a form of motor control, control of attention and emotion, structured memorization, time scheduling, and mental rehearsal. Control processes at most elementary technical levels of musical expertise contribute to efficiency of control in more complex aspects of musical practice, such as cognitive and affective self-regulation in public performance. At the same time, overcontrol may have detrimental effects on many aspects of practice and performance.

Musical training contributes to better performance of multiple nonmusical tasks (for a review see Schellenberg & Weiss, 2013), suggesting that musical expertise and outstanding performance per se should not be the only major aim of musical training. Documented structural and functional benefits of musical training suggest that regardless of musical talent, the very process of musical practice may be grounds for training multiple aspects of control whose application can extend to other domains. Possible carryover effects of control aptitude formed in the course of musical training to other domains, such as self-management in education and business, are awaiting empirical testing. Common and widespread music education could be an option for the widespread use of tablets and computer games that often have detrimental effects on their users' cognitive control (e.g., Gentile, Swing, Lim, & Khoo, 2012).

Individual differences in the effectiveness of control functions among professional musicians are expected to moderate the probability to attain a satisfactory level of performance. Presumably, individual self-control resources are depleted within the musical practice and performance context. More research is necessary to look into the long-term conditions of ego depletion and strengthening self-regulatory resources within the musical practice context. Such knowledge might help to work out cues for musicians concerning how to most effectively manage their control resources. Speculatively, musicians' deliberate application of control in the domains mentioned above, and their purposeful employment of an approach that allows technical imperfection and focuses on the pleasure of making music, should maximize the quality of performance. In combination with a focus on process-related goals and aesthetic pleasure, these mechanisms should contribute to raising the effectiveness of mindful practice and enjoyment of music making in professional and amateur musicians of all ages.

REFERENCES

Ablard, K. E., & Parker, W. D. (1997). Parents' achievement goals and perfectionism in their academically talented children. *Journal of Youth and Adolescence, 26*, 651–667.

Ainslie, G. W. (1975). Specious rewards: A behavioral theory of impulsiveness and impulse control. *Psychological Bulletin, 82*, 463–496.

Altenmüller, E., & Schneider, S. (2009). Planning and performance. In S. Hallam, I. Cross, & M. Thaut (Eds.), *The Oxford handbook of music psychology* (pp. 332–343). Oxford, UK: Oxford University Press.

Austin, J., Renwick, J., & McPherson, G. E. (2006). Developing motivation. In G. E. McPherson (Ed.), *The child as musician: A handbook of musical development* (pp. 213–238). Oxford, UK: Oxford University Press.

Bandura, A. (1986). *Social foundations of thought and action.* Englewood Cliffs, NJ: Prentice-Hall.

Bandura, A. (1989). Social cognitive theory. In R. Vasta (Ed.), *Annals of child development: Vol. 6. Six theories of child development* (pp. 1–60). Greenwich, CT: JAI Press.

Bandura, A. (1999). Social cognitive theory: An agentic perspective. *Asian Journal of Social Psychology, 2*, 21–41.

Barry, N. H. (1990). The effects of different practice techniques upon technical accuracy and musicality in student instrumental music performance. *Research Perspectives in Music Education, 1*, 4–8.

Barry, N. H., & Hallam, S. (2002). Practice. In R. Parncutt & G. E. McPherson (Eds.), *The science and psychology of music performance: Creative strategies for teaching and learning* (pp. 151–166). Oxford, UK: Oxford University Press.

Baumeister, R. F., & Alquist, J. L. (2009). Is there a downside to good self-control? *Self and Identity, 2 & 3*, 115–130.

Baumeister, R. F., Catanese, K. R., & Vohs, K. D. (2001). Is there a gender difference in strength of sex drive? Theoretical views, conceptual dimensions, and a review of relevant evidence. *Personality and Social Psychology Review, 5*, 242–273.

Baumeister, R. F., & Heatherton, T. F. (1996). Self-regulation failure: An overview. *Psychological Inquiry, 7*, 1–15

Baumeister, R. F., & Tierney, J. (2011). *Willpower: Rediscovering the greatest human strength*. London: Penguin Books.

Bryant, C. M. (1999). Memorizing: A science. *Clavier, 38*, 28–32.

Butler, D. L., & Winne, P. H. (1995). Feedback and self-regulated learning: A theoretical synthesis. *Review of Educational Research, 65*, 245–281.

Chaffin, R., & Imreh, G. (2002). Practicing perfection: Piano performance as expert memory. *Psychological Science, 13*, 342–349.

Chaffin, R., & Lemieux, A. F. (2004). General perspectives on achieving musical excellence. In A. Williamon (Ed.), *Musical excellence: Strategies and techniques to enhance performance* (pp. 19–39). Oxford, UK: Oxford University Press.

Chamorro-Premusic, T. (2006). Creativity vs. conscientiousness: Which is a better predictor of student performance? *Applied Cognitive Psychology, 20*, 521–531.

Chan, A. S., Ho, Y. C., & Cheung, M. C. (1998). Music training improves verbal memory. *Nature, 396*, 128.

Chase, W. G., & Simon, H. A. (1973). The mind's eye in chess. In W. G. Chase (Ed.), *Visual information processing* (pp. 215–281). New York: Academic Press.

Chi, M. T. H., Glaser, R., & Farr, M. J. (Eds.). (1988). *The nature of expertise*. Hillsdale, NJ: Erlbaum.

Clarke, E., Dibben, N., & Pitts, S. (2011). *Music and mind in everyday life*. Oxford, UK: Oxford University Press.

Connolly, C., & Williamon, A. (2004). Mental skills training. In A. Williamon (Ed.), *Musical excellence: Strategies and techniques to enhance performance* (pp. 221–245). New York: Oxford University Press.

Corno, L. (1993). The best-laid plans: Modern conceptions of volition and educational research. *Educational Researcher,* 22, 14–22.

Corrigall, K. A., Schellenberg, E. G., & Misura, N. M. (2013). Music training, cognition, and personality. *Frontiers in Psychology, 4*, 222.

Costa-Giomi, E. (2012). Music instruction and children's intellectual development: The educational context of music participation. In R. A. R. MacDonald, G. Kreutz, & L. Mitchell (Eds.), *Music, health, and wellbeing*. New York: Oxford University Press.

de Ridder, D. T. D., Lensvelt-Mulders, G., Finkenauer, C., Stok, F. M., & Baumeister, R. F. (2012). Taking stock of self-control: A meta-analysis of how trait self-control relates to a wide range of behaviors. *Personality and Social Psychology Review, 16*, 76–99.

Dobson, M. C. (2011). Insecurity, professional sociability, and alcohol: Young freelance musicians' perspectives on work and life in the music profession. *Psychology of Music, 39*, 240–260.

Duckworth, A. L., Peterson, C., Matthews, M. D., & Kelly, D. R. (2007). Grit: Perseverance and passion for long-term goals. *Journal of Personality and Social Psychology, 92*, 1087–1101.

Duke, R. A., Cash, C. D., & Allen, S. E. (2011). Focus of attention affects performance of motor skills in music. *Journal of Research in Music Education, 59*, 44–55.

Ericsson, K. A., Krampe, R. Th., & Tesch-Römer, C. (1993). The role of deliberate practice in the acquisition of expert performance. *Psychological Review, 100*, 363–406.

Ericsson, K. A., & Smith, J. (Eds.). (1991). *Toward a general theory of expertise: Prospects and limits.* Cambridge, UK: Cambridge University Press.

Eriksen, B. A., & Eriksen, C. W. (1974). Effects of noise letters upon the identification of a target letter in a nonsearch task. *Perception and Psychophysics, 16,* 143–149.

Eysenck, H. J. (1967). *The biological basis of personality*. Springfield, IL: Charles C. Thomas.

Fajkowska, M., & Derryberry, D. (2010). Psychometric properties of Attentional Control Scale: The preliminary study on a Polish sample. *Polish Psychological Bulletin, 41*, 1–7.

Friedman, N. P., & Miyake, A. (2004). The relations among inhibition and interference control functions: A latent-variable analysis. *Journal of Experimental Psychology: General, 133*, 101–135.

Fry, H. J. H. (1986). Incidence of overuse syndrome in symphony orchestra. *Medical Problems of Performing Artists, 1,* 51–55.

Galamian, I. (1964). *Principles of violin playing and teaching*. London: Faber & Faber.

Gellrich, M. (1991). Concentration and tension. *British Journal of Music Education, 8*, 167–179.

Gentile, D. A., Swing, E. L., Lim, C. G., & Khoo, A. (2012). Video game playing, attention problems, and impulsiveness: Evidence of bidirectional causality. *Psychology of Popular Media Culture, 1*, 62–70.

Ginsborg, J., Spahn, C., & Williamon, A. (2012). Health promotion in higher music education. In R. A. R. MacDonald, G. Kreutz, & L. Mitchell (Eds.), *Music, health, and well-being* (pp. 356–366). Oxford, UK: Oxford University Press.

Goebl, W., & Palmer, C. (2013). Temporal control and hand movement efficiency in skilled music performance. *PLoS One, 8*, e5090.

Gray, J. A. (1981). A critique of Eysenck's theory of personality. In H. J. Eysenck (Ed.), *A model for personality* (pp. 246–276). New York: Springer-Verlag.

Grindea, C. (1995). Tension in piano playing: Its importance and dangers. In C. Grindea (Ed.), *Tensions in the performance of musicians* (pp. 96–125). London: Kahn & Averill.

Hallam, S. (1997). Approaches to musical practice of experts and novices: Implications for education. In H. Jørgensen & A. C. Lehmann (Eds.), *Does practice make perfect? Current theory and research on instrumental music practice* (pp. 89–108). Oslo: Norges Musikkhøgskole.

Hallam, S. (2001). The development of metacognition in musicians: Implications for education. *British Journal of Music Education, 18*, 27–39.

Haslinger, B., Erhard, P., Altenmüller, E., Hennenlotter, A., Schwaiger, M., von Einsiedel, H. G., et al.(2004). Reduced recruitment of motor association areas during bimanual coordination in concert pianists. *Human Brain Mapping, 22*, 206–215.

Henderson A. T., & Pehoski, C. (Eds.) (2006). *Hand function in the child: Foundations for remediation* (2nd ed.) St. Louis, MO: Mosby-Elsevier.

Ho, Y. C., Cheung, M. C., & Chan, A. S. (2003). Music training improves verbal but not visual memory: Cross-sectional and longitudinal explorations in children. *Neuropsychology, 17*, 439–450.

Jørgensen, H. (2004). Strategies for individual practice. In A. Williamon (Ed.), *Musical excellence: Strategies and techniques to enhance performance* (pp. 87–122). New York: Oxford University Press.

Jørgensen, H., & Hallam, S. (2009). Practicing. In S. Hallam, I. Cross, & M. Thaut (Eds.), *The Oxford handbook of music psychology* (pp. 265–273). New York: Oxford University Press.

Kantor-Martynuska, J., & Bigand, E. (2013). Individual differences in granularity of the affective responses to music. *Polish Psychological Bulletin, 4*, 399–408.

Kantor-Martynuska, J., & Pastuszek-Lipińska, B. (2012, August). Symptoms and consequences of trait and state music performance anxiety in young musicians: The role of temperament and resistance to distractor interference. Poster presented at the Fourth Biennial Symposium on Personality and Social Psychology, Kazimierz Dolny, Poland.

Kantor-Martynuska, J., & Wlazłowska-Gorzko, E. (in preparation). Trema przed premierą a kontrola uwagowa [Performance anxiety at a premiere and attentional control].

Kenny, D. (2011). *The psychology of music performance anxiety*. New York: Oxford University Press.

Kępińska-Welbel J. (1997). *Trema egzaminacyjna u studentów Akademii Muzycznej im. F. Chopina*. [Music performance anxiety in the students of the F. Chopin Academy of Music]. Unpublished doctoral dissertation, Akademia Pedagogiki Specjalnej, Warsaw.

Klickstein, G. (2009). *The musician's way*. New York: Oxford University Press.

Kolańczyk, A. (2011). Uwaga ekstensywna. Model ekstensywno ci vs. intensywno ci uwagi [Extensive attention: A model of extensiveness vs. intensiveness of attention]. *Studia Psychologiczne, 49*, 7–27.

Kraus, N., & Chandrasekaran, B. (2010). Music training for the development of auditory skills. *Nature Neuroscience, 11*, 599–605.

Kuhl, J. (1996). Who controls whom when "I control myself." *Psychological Inquiry, 7*, 61–68.

Kuhl, J., & Goschke, T. (1994). A theory of action control: Mental subsystems, modes of control, and volitional conflict-resolution strategies. In J. Kuhl & J. Beckmann (Eds.), *Volition and personality: Action versus state orientation* (pp. 93–124). Gottingen, Germany: Hogrefe & Huber.

Lehmann, A. C., & Ericsson, K. A. (1998). Preparation of a public piano performance: The relation between practice and performance. *Musicæ Scientiæ, 2*, 67–94.

Lehmann, A. C., Sloboda, J. A., & Woody, R. H. (2007). *Psychology for musicians: Understanding and acquiring the skills*. Oxford, UK: Oxford University Press.

Logue, A. W. (1996). Self-control: An alternative self-regulation framework applicable to human and nonhuman behavior. *Psychological Inquiry, 7*, 68–72.

Lohaus, A., & Schmitt, G. M. (1989). *Fragebogen zur Erhebung von Kontrollüberzeugungen zu Krankheit und Gesundheit (KKG) Fragebogen und Manual* [Questionnaire to assess control beliefs concerning health and illness: Questionnaire and manual]. Test #01–060–01. Göttingen, Germany: Hogrefe & Huber.

McPherson, G. E. (2009). The role of parents in children's musical development. *Psychology of Music, 37*, 91–110.

McPherson, G. E., & Renwick, J. M. (2011). Self-regulation and mastery of musical skills. In B. Zimmerman & D. H. Schunk (Eds.), *Handbook of self-regulation of learning and performance* (pp. 234–248). New York: Taylor & Francis.

McPherson, G. E., & Zimmerman, B. J. (2011). Self-regulation of musical learning: A social cognitive perspective on developing performance skills. In R. Colwell & P. R. Webster (Eds.), *MENC handbook of research on music learning: Vol. 2. Applications* (pp. 130–175). New York: Oxford University Press.

Mischel, W., Shoda, Y., & Peake, P. K. (1988). The nature of adolescent competencies predicted by preschool delay of gratification. *Journal of Personality and Social Psychology, 54*, 687–696.

Mor, S., Day, H., J., Flett, G. L., & Hewitt, P. L. (1995). Perfectionism, control, and components of performance anxiety in professional artists. *Cognitive Therapy and Research, 19*, 207–225.

Muraven, M., Baumeister, R. F., & Tice, D. M. (1999). Longitudinal improvement of self-regulation through practice: Building self-control strength through repeated exercise. *Journal of Social Psychology, 139*, 446–457.

Nathan, A. (2008). *The young musician's survival guide*. New York: Oxford University Press.

Newmark, J., & Lederman, R. J. (1987). Practice doesn't necessarily make perfect: Incidence of overuse syndromes in amateur instrumentalists. *Medical Problems of Performing Artists, 2,* 142–144.

Nęcka, E. (2005). *Inteligencja. Geneza, struktura, funkcje* [Intelligence: Genesis, structure, functions]. Gdańsk, Poland: Gdańskie Wydawnictwo Psychologiczne.

Nolen-Hoeksema, S. (1998). The other end of continuum: The cost of rumination. *Psychological Inquiry, 9*, 216–219.

Pallesen, K. J., Brattico, E., Bailey, C. J., Korvenoja, A., Koivisto, J., Gjedde, A., et al. (2010). Cognitive control in auditory working memory is enhanced in musicians. *PLoS One, 5*, e11120.

Parbery-Clark, A., Skoe, E., Lam, C., & Kraus, N. (2009). Musician enhancement for speech-in-noise. *Ear and Hearing, 30*, 653–661.

Parschau, L., Fleig, L., Koring, M., Lange, D., Knoll, N., Schwarzer, R., et al. (2013). Positive experience, self-efficacy, and action control predict physical activity change: A moderated mediation analysis. *British Journal of Health Psychology, 18*, 395–406.

Pomerantz, E. M., Grolnick, W. S., & Price, C. A. (2005). The role of parents in how children approach achievement: A dynamic process perspective. In A. Elliot and C. W. Dweck (Eds.), *Handbook of competence and motivation* (pp. 259–278). New York: Guilford Press.

Posner, M. I., & Petersen, S. E. (1990). The attention system of the human brain. *Annual Reviews, 13*, 25–42.

Revelle, W., Humphreys, M. S., Simon, L., & Gilliland, K. (1980). The interactive effect of personality, time of day, and caffeine: A test of the arousal model. *Journal of Experimental Psychology: General, 109*, 1–31.

Roden, I., Grube, D., Bongard, S., & Kreutz, G. (2013). Does music training enhance working memory performance? Findings from a quasi-experimental longitudinal study. *Psychology of Music, 42*, 284–298.

Roden, I., Kreutz, G., & Bongard, S. (2012). Effects of a school-based instrumental music program on verbal and visual memory in primary school children: A longitudinal study. *Frontiers in Auditory Cognitive Neuroscience, 3*, Article 572, doi: 10.3389/fpsyg.2012.00572.

Rothstein, M. G., Paunonen, S. V., Rush, J. C., & King, G. A. (1994). Personality and cognitive ability predictors of performance in graduate business school. *Journal of Educational Psychology, 86*, 516–530.

Runco, M. A., & Chand, I. (1994). Creativity and its discontents. In M. P. Shaw & M. A. Runco (Eds.), *Creativity and affect* (pp. 102–123). Norwood, NJ: Ablex.

Schachar, R., & Logan, G. D. (1990). Impulsivity and inhibitory control in normal development and childhood psychopathology. *Developmental Psychology, 26*, 710–720.

Schellenberg, E. G., & Weiss, M. W. (2013). Music and cognitive abilities. In D. Deutsch (Ed.), *The psychology of music* (3rd ed., pp. 499–550). Amsterdam: Elsevier.

Sherman, D. (2012). Musician life coach Dave Sherman on what makes artists abuse drugs and alcohol. http://www.altpress.com/contributors/entry/musician_life_coach_ dave_sherman_021812, downloaded March 28, 2013.

Spahn, C., Burger, T., Hildebrandt, H., & Seidenglanz, K. (2005). Health locus of control and preventive behaviour among student of music. *Psychology of Music, 33*, 257–269.

Sternberg, R. J. (1990). *Metaphors of mind: Conceptions of the nature of intelligence*. Cambridge, UK: Cambridge University Press.

Strait, D., & Kraus, N. (2011). Playing music for a smarter ear: Cognitive, perceptual and neurobiological evidence. *Music Perception, 29*, 133–146.

Strait, D., O'Connell, S., Parbery-Clark, A., & Kraus, N. (2013) Biological impact of preschool music classes on processing speech in noise. *Developmental Cognitive Neuroscience, 6*, 51–60.

Strelau, J. (2008). *Temperament as a regulator of behavior: After fifty years of research*. Clinton Corners, NY: Eliot Werner Publications.

Suzuki, S. (1983). *Nurtured by love* (2nd ed.). (W. Suzuki, Trans.). Miami, FL: Summy-Birchard Publishing.

Thompson, F. T., Schellenberg, E. G., & Husain, G. (2003). Perceiving prosody in speech: Effects of music lessons. *Annals of the New York Academy of Sciences, 999*, 530–532.

Tierney, A, & Kraus, N. (2013). The ability to tap to a beat relates to cognitive, linguistic, and perceptual skills. *Brain and Language, 124*, 225–231.

Vieluf, S., Mahmoodi, J., Godde, B., Reuter, E.-M., & Voelcker-Rehage, C. (2012). The influence of age and work-related expertise on fine motor control. *GeroPsych, 25*, 199–206.

Wan, H. Y. A. (2008). *Physical and mental issues in piano performance: The interrelationships between physical tension, performance anxiety, and memorization strategies*. Saarbrücken, Germany: VDM Verlag Dr Müller.

Weisberg, R. (1999). Creativity and knowledge: A challenge to theories. In R. Sternberg (Ed.), *The handbook of creativity* (pp. 226–250). Cambridge, UK: Cambridge University Press.

Williamon, A. (2004). A guide to enhancing musical performance. In A. Williamon (Ed.), *Musical excellence: Strategies and techniques to enhance performance* (pp. 3–18). Oxford, UK: Oxford University Press.

Williamon, A., & Valentine, E. (2000). Quantity and quality of musical practice as predictors of peformance quality. *British Journal of Psychology, 91*, 353–376.

Williamon, A., Valentine, E., & Valentine, J. (2002). Shifting the focus of attention between levels of musical structure. *European Journal of Cognitive Psychology, 14*, 493–520.

Williams, B. R., Ponesse, J. S., Schachar, R. J., Logan, G. D., & Tannock, R. (1999). Development of inhibitory control across the life span. *Developmental Psychology, 35*, 205–213.

Wilson, G. D., & Roland, D. (2002). Performance anxiety. In R. Parncutt & G. E. McPherson (Eds.), *The science and psychology of music performance: Creative strategies for teaching and learning* (pp. 47–62). Oxford, UK: Oxford University Press.

Woody, R. H., & McPherson, G. E. (2010). Emotion and motivation in the lives of performers. In P. N. Juslin & J. A. Sloboda (Eds.), *Handbook of music and emotion: Theory, research, applications* (pp. 401–424). Oxford, UK: Oxford University Press.

Zimmerman, B. J. (1995). Self-regulation involves more than metacognition: A social-cognitive perspective. *Educational Psychologist, 30*, 217–221.

CHAPTER 6

Anxiety, Depression, and Cognitive Control

Michael W. Eysenck

INTRODUCTION

This chapter is mostly concerned with the negative emotional state of anxiety. More specifically, the emphasis is on trait anxiety. According to the definition provided by Spielberger, Gorsuch, and Lushene (1970), it "denotes relatively stable individual differences in anxiety proneness and refers to a general tendency to respond with anxiety to perceived threats in the environment" (p. 3).

The above definition has proved very influential but is limited in two important ways. First, it is not entirely true that individuals high in trait anxiety have excessive concerns about all types of environmental threats. Walsh, McNally, and Eysenck (2013) found that high-anxious individuals were more concerned than low-anxious ones about social and intellectual threats. However, the two groups did not differ with respect to threats to physical health or physical danger. Second, differences in anxiety proneness in response to threat are not limited to environmental or external threats. There is much evidence that high-anxious individuals have higher levels of state anxiety (currently experienced anxiety) than low-anxious ones in response to internal stimuli such as elevated heart rate (see Eysenck, 1997, for a review).

Personality and Control edited by Philip J. Corr, Małgorzata Fajkowska, Michael W. Eysenck, and Agata Wytykowska. Eliot Werner Publications, Clinton Corners, New York, 2015.

ANXIETY AND COGNITIVE CONTROL: THEORY

What is the relationship between anxiety and cognitive control? Prior to answering that question, it is necessary to consider the theoretical context out of which the current understanding of anxiety and control has arisen. Eysenck and Calvo (1992) proposed their processing efficiency theory, which represented an extension and development of the earlier theorizing of Eysenck (1979). According to processing efficiency theory, anxiety impairs the functioning of the working memory system proposed by Baddeley (1986). The working memory model originally consisted of three components: an attention-like central executive, a phonological loop for rehearsal and transient storage of verbal material, and a visuo-spatial sketchpad for visusal and spatial processing and brief storage. It was assumed that anxiety primarily impairs the functioning of the central executive rather than the other two components. Note that Baddeley (e.g., 2007) has developed the working memory model over the years.

When processing efficiency theory was introduced, there was a lack of consensus and clarity concerning the executive functions associated with the central executive. Subsequently, however, progress was made in identifying the main executive functions. For example, Miyake, et al. (2000) applied latent variable analysis to the data obtained from several executive tasks and obtained evidence for three executive functions. First, there was the inhibitory function, which controls processing of irrelevant stimuli and responses. Second, there was the shifting function, which controls switching of attention within and between tasks. In the words of Miyake et al. (2000), this function refers to "shifting back and forth between multiple tasks, operations, or mental sets" (p. 55). Third, there was the updating function, which is used to update and monitor whatever information is currently accessible within working memory.

Eysenck, Derakshan, Santos, and Calvo (2007) were strongly influenced by Miyake et al.'s (2000) seminal research in their attentional control theory. They argued that anxiety impairs the inhibition function, which is in broad terms associated with negative attentional control in that it is used to prevent task-irrelevant stimuli and responses from disrupting performance. Anxiety also impairs the shifting function, which is associated with positive attentional control in that it is used to allocate attention flexibly and optimally. It was assumed that the effects of anxiety on the updating and monitoring function were smaller in magnitude and would typically only be found in stressful conditions. Note that Eysenck and Derakshan (2011) subsequently added a few assumptions to attentional control theory.

An overarching assumption within attentional control theory is that there are two attentional systems—a goal-directed attentional system that exerts top-down control and a stimulus-driven attentional system that exerts bottom-up control. Of interest, Sylvester et al. (2012) incorporated exactly these theoretical assumptions in their theoretical approach but disappointingly did not acknowledge their indebtedness to Eysenck et al. (2007).

Several other theorists have argued that anxiety has adverse effects on attentional control. However, there is a major difference between attentional control theory and most other theories in this area (e.g., Williams, Watts, MacLeod, and Mathews, 1997). According to attentional control theory, anxiety has a *general* impairment effect on attentional and cognitive control. In other words, anxiety impairs attentional control in the presence of either threat-related or neutral stimuli. By contrast, other theories mostly focus on the notion that anxiety has a *specific* impairment effect in the presence of threat-related stimuli. Note that it is assumed within attentional control theory that the adverse effects of anxiety on processing and performance will typically be greater with threat-related than with neutral stimuli.

There is considerable empirical support for the notion that anxious individuals have an attentional bias for threat-related stimuli that involves attention being attracted to threat stimuli. For example, Bar-Haim, Lamy, Pergamin, Bakermans-Kronenburg, and van IJzendoorn (2007) found strong evidence for attentional bias with both supraliminal and subliminal stimuli. There is also evidence that anxiety produces difficulty in disengaging attention from threat stimuli (Cisler & Koster, 2010), which is another manifestation of impaired attentional control.

The most important commonality among the theoretical positions of Eysenck (1979), Eysenck and Calvo (1992), and Eysenck et al. (2007) is adherence to a distinction between performance effectiveness and processing efficiency. Performance effectiveness refers to the quality of an individual's task performance and can be assessed by conventional measures, such as the percentage of correct responses. Processing efficiency is a more complex notion depending on the relationship between performance effectiveness and the utilization of processing resources or effort.

The assumption based on the above distinction between performance effectiveness and processing efficiency is that anxiety typically impairs processing efficiency to a greater extent than performance effectiveness. This differential effect of anxiety is explained as follows. Task-irrelevant processing (e.g., worry) associated with anxiety impairs processing efficiency. However, impaired processing efficiency does not necessarily translate into reduced performance effectiveness. Individuals high in trait anxiety often utilize additional processing resources in order to compensate for the adverse effects of anxiety on processing efficiency. Use of these processing resources often prevents performance from being impaired.

It is now possible to provide an answer to the question concerning the relationship between anxiety and attentional control. It is assumed that anxiety impairs the efficiency of positive (shifting function) and negative (inhibitory function) attentional control. However, this may or may not lead to impaired performance depending on the extent to which anxious individuals make use of compensatory processes.

Processing Efficiency

How can processing efficiency be assessed? Ideally, four criteria will be fulfilled. First, there are two experimental conditions varying in the demands they impose on cognitive control in the form of the inhibitory or the shifting function. Second, interpretation of the findings is much simplified if anxiety has nonsignificant effects on performance effectiveness. Third, high-anxious individuals should show a greater increase in brain activity than low-anxious individuals in the more demanding condition compared with the less demanding one. Fourth, note that measures of brain activity cannot provide clear support for causal explanations. Accordingly, it is important that the increased brain activity associated with high versus low trait anxiety is located primarily in brain areas previously found to be associated with the relevant executive function. For example, there is plentiful evidence that the dorsolateral prefrontal cortex is associated with most executive functions (e.g., Braver, 2012).

Alternatively, techniques (e.g., event-related potentials) that possess excellent temporal resolution can be used. The prediction is that enhanced brain activity by high-anxious compared with low-anxious individuals should coincide with the stage of processing associated with the relevant executive function.

Alternative Viewpoints

Before discussing findings relevant to attentional control theory, it should be noted that other theorists have explained the adverse effects of anxiety in a very different way. Here we will focus on the theoretical approach of Bishop (2009; Forster, Elizalde, Castle, & Bishop, in press). According to this approach, there are several negative effects of high trait anxiety on cognitive processing. More specifically, Forster et al. argue that high trait anxiety is associated with increased worry, spontaneous self-relevant thoughts, task-unrelated mind wandering, and impoverished attentional control. In direct contrast to attentional control theory, it is assumed that high-anxious individuals make no use at all of any compensatory strategies.

What predictions follow from Bishop's theoretical approach? The most obvious prediction is that high-anxious individuals will invariably perform significantly worse than low-anxious ones. That is a striking prediction but one that (as we will see) has been disproved on numerous occasions. This theoretical approach also makes predictions concerning the relationship between trait anxiety and brain activity. According to Forster et al. (in press), high trait anxiety is associated with "reduced engagement of DLPFC [dorsolateral prefrontal cortex] in a frontal-thalamo-striatal network that supports the proactive control of attention, as well as reduced ACC [anterior cingulate cortex] and DLPFC engagement in reactive control." As indicated in the following discussion, these predictions have been disproved numerous times (including by Bishop, 2009).

ANXIETY AND COGNITIVE CONTROL: FINDINGS

The notion that anxiety is associated with impaired attentional control was tested by Ólafsson et al. (2011). They used the Attentional Control Scale developed by

Derryberry and Reed (2002) and identified two major factors in it. One was concerned with inhibition and focusing and resembles the inhibition function, whereas the other assessed the shifting function. Anxiety correlated –0.45 with the inhibition/focusing factor and –0.35 with the shifting factor.

Inhibition Function

Most of the research on anxiety and attentional or cognitive control has focused on the inhibition rather than the shifting function. Several studies have involved the performance of a cognitive task in the presence or absence of distracting stimuli. According to attentional control theory, high-anxious individuals should find it harder to inhibit the processing of these distractors and should manifest greater distractibility.

Eysenck et al. (2007) reviewed the evidence on the effects of distraction on task performance. Most of the evidence indicated that the performance of high-anxious individuals was more adversely affected by distraction than was the performance of low-anxious individuals. Further support for the theoretical prediction has been obtained in research published after the time period covered by Eysenck et al.'s review (e.g., Pacheco-Ungietti, Acosta, Callejas, & Lupia ez, 2010; Pacheco-Ungietti, Lupia ez, & Acosta, 2009).

Moser, Becker, and Moran (2012) recently reported a study involving a visual search task in which participants searched for a target in the presence or absence of a distractor. They obtained a correlation of +0.43 between trait anxiety and distractor cost, which provides strong support for attentional control theory.

According to attentional control theory, increased distractibility associated with high trait anxiety should in general be greater when task demands are high than when they are low. This prediction was tested by Sadeh and Bredemeier (2011) in a study in which the perceptual demands of a task were manipulated. As predicted, high anxiety was related to enhanced distractibility when the perceptual demands were high but not when they were low. This essentially replicates the findings from an earlier study by Eysenck and Graydon (1989).

Much of the behavioral research on anxiety and the inhibition function has made use of the antisaccade task. In essence, a visual cue is presented to one side of the fixation point and the task simply involves making an eye movement as rapidly as possible to the other side of the fixation point. The key measure is the latency of the first saccade directed to the appropriate side of the fixation point, which involves inhibiting eye movements toward the cue. The prediction from attentional control theory is straightforward: the latency of the first correct saccade should be longer in high-anxious than in low-anxious individuals. There is also a control condition (the prosaccade task) in which participants are instructed to fixate on the cue when it is presented. Performance on this task does not require the inhibition function and so high anxiety should not impair performance.

The findings from research using the antisaccade and prosaccade tasks have been remarkably consistent. As predicted, latency of the first correct saccade is negatively correlated with trait anxiety on antisaccade trials but is unrelated to trait anxiety on prosaccade trials (e.g., Ansari & Derakshan, 2010).

Processing Efficiency: Behavioral Studies

The simplest way of testing the theoretical assumption that anxiety impairs efficiency more than performance is to make use of subjective ratings of mental effort. The prediction is that high-anxious individuals should typically report greater mental effort than low-anxious ones in spite of having comparable or inferior levels of performance. This combination of high effort and moderate or poor performance is indicative of processing inefficiency.

There is much support for the above prediction (see Eysenck et al., 2007, for a review). Most of the research has involved the use of cognitive tasks but recently there has been increased interest in the effects of anxiety in sporting contexts. Consider, for example, a study by Canal-Bruland, Pijpers, and Oudejans (2010) in which participants threw darts at a target in low- and high-anxiety conditions. Performance was almost identical in the two conditions, but participants in the high-anxiety condition reported exerting substantially more mental effort than those in the low-anxiety condition. Thus high anxiety impaired processing efficiency but had no effect on performance effectiveness.

Another study focusing on the effects of anxiety on sporting performance was conducted by Causer, Holmes, Smith, and Williams (2011) on elite shotgun skeet shooters performing under conditions of low anxiety (practice) or high anxiety (competition). They were interested in what is known as quiet eye, which is the length of the final fixation in the direction of the target prior to pulling the trigger. Long duration of quiet eye predicts superior shooting performance and reflects good attentional control.

What did Causer et al. (2011) find? First, the level of performance was worse under anxious or stressful conditions than under nonanxious or practice conditions (62.9% hits vs. 74.6% hits, respectively). Second, the duration of the quiet eye was less under anxious than nonanxious conditions. Third, retrospective self-reports indicated that the mean level of mental effort expended was greater under anxious than nonanxious conditions (90.35 vs. 77.10, respectively, on a 150-point scale). These findings indicate that anxiety or stress reduced processing efficiency more than performance effectiveness. They also indicate that anxiety impaired attentional control as indexed by quiet eye duration.

Processing Efficiency: Dorsolateral Prefrontal Cortex

Studies in which brain activity—as well as performance—is assessed can provide a more precise test of attentional control theory, especially the assumption that anxiety impairs processing efficiency more than performance effectiveness. Most of this research has focused on activation within the dorsolateral prefrontal cortex (strongly associated with attentional control) or components of the event-related potential. We will start with research assessing dorsolateral prefrontal cortex activation and then proceed to event-related potential studies.

One of the earliest studies was by Bishop (2009). In the more demanding condition, participants detected a target letter with or without distraction. There were no effects of trait anxiety on speed or accuracy of performance, a finding that is more consistent with attentional control theory than with Bishop's theoretical approach.

Of most importance was the difference in activation in the dorsolateral prefrontal cortex between the distraction and nondistraction conditions. According to Bishop (2009), there should be a strong negative correlation between trait anxiety and dorsolateral activation given that anxiety is associated with "impoverished prefrontal control of attention" (p. 92). By contrast, it follows from attentional control theory that high-anxious individuals should have engaged in compensatory processes to offset the adverse effects of anxiety on processing efficiency. There was a correlation of +0.49 between trait anxiety and increases in dorsolateral prefrontal activation under distraction. This finding is diametrically opposed to Bishop's prediction and in line with attentional control theory. Bewilderingly, however, Bishop interprets her findings as supportive of her theoretical position!

Basten, Stelzel, and Fiebach (2011) also assessed activation in the dorsolateral prefrontal cortex when inhibitory control was required. They used the Stroop task on which words are printed in various colors and the task is to name the color rather than the word. There were congruent trials on which the color and the word's meaning were the same and incongruent trials on which the word's meaning differed from the color. There is plentiful evidence that inhibitory processes are required on incongruent but not on congruent trials. Basten et al. focused on activity in the dorsolateral prefrontal cortex, an area strongly associated with executive functioning.

What did Basten et al. (2011) find? Their key result was that participants high in trait anxiety showed a significantly greater increase in activation within the dorsolateral prefrontal cortex on incongruent trials, but not on congruent ones. Since the performance of the high-anxious participants was slightly inferior to that of the low-anxious ones, this indicates that the effects of anxiety were greater on processing efficiency than on performance effectiveness.

A similar study with similar findings was reported by Basten, Stelzel, and Fiebach (2012). Participants high and low in trait anxiety performed tasks that varied in the involvement of executive functions of the working memory system. The two groups did not differ in terms of performance (i.e., error rates or reaction times). Of most theoretical interest was the increased activation in the dorsolateral prefrontal cortex in the condition requiring executive processes, compared with the simpler control condition. As predicted, there was a greater increase in this dorsolateral activation in the high-anxious than the low-anxious group.

In sum, the typical pattern of findings is that there are no effects of trait anxiety on performance combined with greater dorsolateral activation in high-anxious than low-anxious individuals. There are occasional exceptions to that pattern (e.g., Forster et al., in press), but predominantly the findings provide strong support for the theoretical prediction that anxiety impairs efficiency more than effectiveness.

Processing Efficiency: Event-Related Potentials

The Sustained Attention to Response Task requires the use of the inhibition function. On this task participants are instructed to respond rapidly to every digit (Go trials), except that they should withhold or inhibit a response when a particular digit is presented (NoGo trials). Righi, Mecacci, and Viggiano (2009) used this task and also used event-related potentials. They were especially interested in the N2 component of the event-related potentials because that has been identified as most directly reflecting the use of inhibitory processes in NoGo trials.

Righi et al. (2009) found that there were no effects of trait anxiety on performance in either the Go or NoGo trials. However, the key finding was that high-anxious participants had a significantly larger N2 response than low-anxious ones in NoGo trials than in Go trials. Of importance, this enhanced N2 response was mostly located in the anterior part of the brain and so it plausibly reflects inhibitory processes occurring with the prefrontal cortex.

Sehlmeyer et al. (2010) carried out a similar study using the Go/NoGo paradigm while recording event-related potentials. Their findings closely resembled those of Righi et al. (2009). There were no differences between the high-anxious and low-anxious groups in the event-related potentials in Go trials, and only the N2 component (associated with inhibitory processes) showed a group difference in NoGo trials.

Savostyanov et al. (2009) also used Go and NoGo conditions and utilized the electroencephalogram (EEG) to provide an assessment of processing efficiency. Inhibitory processes were required in occasional and unpredictable NoGo trials in which an auditory signal indicated that participants should not respond to the task stimulus. There were no effects of trait anxiety on performance effectiveness in either the Go or NoGo conditions. Savostyanov et al. argued that their complex measure of EEG desynchronization reflected effort or use of processing resources. Their key finding was that high-anxious participants showed greater EEG desynchronization than low-anxious ones only in the NoGo condition. This enhanced desynchronization was found mostly after (rather than before) the warning signal indicating that the response should be inhibited, which strengthens the argument that it reflected inefficient use of the inhibition function.

In sum, the overall pattern of the findings provides reasonable support for the prediction of attentional control theory that anxiety impairs the efficiency of the inhibition function. It is notable that this support has been obtained using a variety of tasks and several different ways of assessing brain activity—for example, event-related potentials, EEG desynchronization, and functional magnetic resonance imaging (fMRI).

Shifting Functions

According to attentional control theory, high-anxious individuals use the shifting function inefficiently. Some support for this prediction was reported by Wilson, Vine, and Wood (2009). They assessed participants' eye movements while performing a basketball shooting task. The patterns of eye movements indicated that high-anxious participants used the shifting function less efficiently than low-anxious ones.

Miyake et al. (2000) identified the task-switching paradigm as perhaps the most direct way of assessing the shifting function. In the basic version of this paradigm, participants perform two tasks under two different conditions. In the control condition, participants perform only one of the tasks throughout each block of trials. By contrast, they perform both tasks (often alternating from trial to trial) throughout each block in the experimental condition. Since the shifting function is required in the experimental condition but not in the control condition, this paradigm permits assessment of the effects of trait anxiety on this function. Note, however, that interpreting the findings from the task-switching paradigm can be rather complex because of the range of processes involved (Monsell, 2003).

Derakshan, Smyth, and Eysenck (2009) used the task-switching paradigm with participants low and high in trait anxiety. As predicted by attentional control theory, there was a highly significant interaction between trait anxiety and task-switching condition. More specifically, the low-anxious individuals showed no effect of task-switching condition since their performance was comparable in the experimental and control conditions. By contrast, the high-anxious individuals performed considerably slower in the experimental condition than the control condition. Thus only the high-anxious participants incurred significant switching costs.

Santos, Wall, and Eysenck (2013) also made use of the task-switching paradigm and obtained measures of brain activity during task performance using functional magnetic resonance imaging. The tasks were simple and there were no effects of anxiety on task performance (reaction times or errors). The most important fMRI was based on the increase in brain activation, with rapid task switching minus activation in the no-switching condition. This increase (which involved the dorsolateral prefrontal cortex) was significantly greater for high-anxious than low-anxious individuals. When these findings are taken in combination, they indicate clearly that high anxiety was associated with impaired processing efficiency but not performance effectiveness.

Ansari, Derakshan, and Richards (2008) also tested the theoretical prediction that anxious individuals should use the shifting function less efficiently than nonanxious ones. They used the antisaccade task with antisaccade and prosaccade trials being presented in separate blocks or mixed within each block. The findings were somewhat more complex than had been expected. However, they suggested that high-anxious individuals did use the shifting function less efficiently.

According to attentional control theory, anxiety has a greater adverse effect on the inhibitory and shifting functions (concerned with attentional control) than on the updating and monitoring function (concerned with short-term memory). All of these theoretical assumptions were tested by Visu-Petra, Miclea, and Visu-Petra (2013) using several measures of verbal and spatial working memory, resistance to interference, negative priming, and task switching. As predicted by attentional control theory, the efficiency of inhibition and shifting were negatively related to trait and state anxiety. Also in line with the theory, trait anxiety was not negatively correlated with the updating and monitoring function; indeed, the correlation was positive.

In sum, there is insufficient research concerned with the effects of anxiety on the shifting function to reach any definitive conclusions. However, it can reasonably be argued that the findings that have been obtained to date are mostly consistent with the predictions of attentional control theory.

DEPRESSION AND ATTENTIONAL CONTROL

The precise relationship between anxiety and depression remains somewhat controversial. Part of the reason for this is that the distinction between them is often less clear at the empirical level than at the conceptual level. For example, there is a high level of comorbidity between anxious disorders and depression. As documented by Watson and Clark (1984), within the healthy population there are typically moderately high correlations between measures that allegedly assess depression (e.g., Beck Depression Inventory) and those that allegedly assess anxiety (State–Trait Anxiety Inventory).

At the conceptual level, anxiety is associated with active engagement and a future orientation, whereas depression is associated with passive disengagement and a past orientation (Eysenck, Payne, & Santos, 2006). Another important difference was emphasized by Clark and Watson (1991) in their tripartite model of anxiety and depression. In essence, they argued that anxiety and depression are similar in that negative affect is of central importance to both mood states. However, they are dissimilar in that anxiety is typically associated with moderate positive affect and high perceived physiological arousal, whereas depression is associated with low positive affect and low perceived physiological arousal.

In spite of the various differences between anxiety and depression, their effects on cognitive processes are often rather similar. De Raedt and Koster (2010) developed an ambitious conceptual framework for depression. In this framework depression is associated with reduced activity in prefrontal control circuits, leading to impaired ability to inhibit negative elaborate psychological processes underlying depressive rumination and a more general deficit in attentional control.

There is a substantial research literature showing that depressed individuals are susceptible to several cognitive biases and failures of cognitive control when tasks involve negative or threatening information (see Gotlib and Joormann, 2010, for a review). However, it is also important to assess the effects of depression on cognition in tasks involving neutral information. Research along these lines is theoretically important because it allows us to establish the extent to which the effects of depression are specific or general.

Findings

There is reasonable support for the above framework. For example, Fitzgerald, Laird, Maller, and Daskalakis (2008) carried out a meta-analysis of studies on brain activity at rest in depressed individuals. For present purposes the key finding was that there was decreased activation in dorsolateral prefrontal cortex and anterior cingulate cortex (both areas associated with executive functions) in depressed than in nondepressed individuals.

Siegle, Thompson, Carter, Steinhauer, and Thase (2007) gave depressed and nondepressed individuals a moderately complex executive task that involved digit sorting and updating. Of most importance, the depressed individuals had substantially less activation than the nondepressed ones in the left dorsolateral prefrontal cortex over a period of several seconds on each trial.

Fales, Barch, Rundle et al. (2008) asked depressed and nondepressed individuals to attend to (or to ignore) fear-related stimuli. Two of their findings are of interest here. First, nondepressed participants showed increased activation within the right dorsolateral prefrontal cortex when ignoring fear stimuli, but depressed individuals did not. Second, producing errors was followed by increased bilateral dorsolateral prefrontal cortex in nondepressed but not depressed individuals.

Research of more direct relevance to the anxiety studies discussed earlier was carried out by de Lissnyder, Koster, Derakshan, and de Raedt (2010). They used tasks designed to assess the inhibition and shifting functions and found that performance on these tasks was unrelated to depressive symptoms in general. However, when de Lissnyder et al. focused more specifically on rumination (a key component of depression), they found that it was related to impaired inhibitory processes and set shifting.

Conclusions

Findings in the depression literature are rather inconsistent and mixed. As a consequence it is difficult to make definitive statements about the effects of depression on attentional control and cognitive performance. However, the theoretical approach of de Raedt and Koster (2010) holds considerable promise. More specifically, their approach implies that depression is often associated with low motivation, hypoactivity within the brain, and inefficient attempts at control as indexed by low dorsolateral prefrontal activity. The research discussed earlier in this section is mostly consistent with those predictions.

Gotlib and Joormann (2010) considered the effects of depression on cognitive performance in a thoughtful review. They concluded that "[t]he bulk of the evidence points to depression-associated deficits in the control of attention" (p. 291).

How can we account for the frequent finding that depression is associated with impaired performance and hypoactivity? As Harvey et al. (2005) pointed out, it is difficult to establish causality. More specifically, impaired performance in depression might be a *consequence* of hypoactivity. However, impaired performance might alternatively be a *cause* of hypoactivity.

FUTURE DIRECTIONS

What does the future hold in terms of theorizing about the effects of anxiety and depression on cognitive control? It is generally hazardous to try to answer such questions. However, a theoretical approach that holds much promise for understanding the effects of anxiety on cognitive control is the dual mechanisms of control model put forward by Braver (2012). According to this model, cognitive control can be achieved in two different ways—namely, proactive control and reactive control. Proactive control involves the effortful anticipatory maintenance of task goals within lateral regions of the prefrontal cortex to enhance subsequent performance. By contrast, reactive control involves allocating attention to current goals in response to the detection of a problem (e.g., error, conflict).

How do the effects of anxiety relate to these two modes of control? Braver (2012) assumed that anxious individuals are distracted by worries that utilize resources needed for proactive control. As a consequence they rely mostly on reactive control. By contrast, low-anxious individuals alternate flexibly and efficiently between the proactive and reactive control modes.

Fales, Barch, Burgess et al. (2008) obtained findings that support this theoretical model. High-anxious and low-anxious participants performed a working memory task. The high-anxious participants had *reduced* sustained activity in brain areas associated with executive functions combined with *increased* transient activity in those areas. This pattern is indicative of a general reliance on reactive control with sporadic engagement of proactive control.

There are clear similarities between Braver's (2012) theoretical model and attentional control theory. More specifically, there is substantial overlap between the notion of reactive control and the stimulus-driven attention system within attentional control theory, and between proactive control and the goal-driven attention system identified within attentional control theory. However, Braver's model perhaps clarifies two issues. First, there is an emphasis on the switches between the two modes of control over time. Second, Braver discusses research findings showing that incentives and other motivational manipulations lead to increased use of proactive control. The notion that motivational factors and anxiety influence different types of attentional control is important and deserves to be explored in detail in future research.

There is another issue that has not as yet been investigated systematically. Implicit in attentional control theory is the notion that high anxiety causes a general impairment in the efficiency of attentional control. However, that is not necessarily the case. For example, it may be the case that high anxiety leads to a sporadic or intermittent impairment of attentional control; in other words, negative effects of anxiety on attentional control may occur on only a smallish fraction of trials.

There is a final point. As yet relatively few studies have directly compared the effects of anxiety and depression on attentional control and performance. In addition, the paradigms used in anxiety and depression research have often been rather different. As a result it is surprisingly difficult to make unequivocal statements about the similarities and differences in their effects. In terms of future research, what would be of great value would be systematic research programs in which the effects of anxiety and depression are compared on the same tasks in the same studies.

REFERENCES

Ansari, T. L., & Derakshan, N. (2010). Anxiety impairs inhibitory control but not volitional action control. *Cognition and Emotion, 24*, 241–254.

Ansari, T. L., Derakshan, N., & Richards, A. (2008). Effects of anxiety on task switching: Evidence from the mixed saccade task. *Cognitive, Affective, and Behavioral Neuroscience, 8*, 229–238.

Baddeley, A. D. (1986). *Working memory*. Oxford, UK: Clarendon Press.

Baddeley, A. D. (2007). *Working memory, thought, and action*. Oxford, UK: Oxford University Press.

Bar-Haim, Y., Lamy, D., Pergamin, L., Bakermans-Kronenburg, M.J., & van IJzendoorn, M.H. (2007). Threat-related attentional bias in anxious and nonanxious individuals: A meta-analytic study. *Psychological Bulletin, 133*, 1–24.

Basten, U., Stelzel, C., & Fiebach, C. J. (2011). Trait anxiety modulates the neural efficiency of inhibitory control. *Journal of Cognitive Neuroscience, 23*, 3132–3145.

Basten, U., Stelzel, C., & Fiebach, C. J. (2012). Trait anxiety and the neural efficiency of manipulation in working memory. *Cognitive, Affective, and Behavioral Neuroscience, 12*, 144–155.

Bishop, S. J. (2009). Trait anxiety and impoverished prefrontal control of attention. *Nature Neuroscience, 12*, 92–98.

Braver, T. S. (2012). The variable nature of cognitive control: A dual mechanisms framework. *Trends in Cognitive Sciences, 16*, 106–113.

Canal-Bruland, R., Pijpers, J. R., & Oudejans, R. R. D. (2010). The influence of anxiety on action-specific perception. *Anxiety, Stress, and Coping, 23*, 353–361.

Causer, J., Holmes, P. S., Smith, N. C., & Williams, A. M. (2011). Anxiety, movement kinematics, and visual attention in elite-level performers. *Emotion, 11*, 595–602.

Cisler, J. M., & Koster, E. H. W. (2010). Mechanisms of attentional biases towards threat in anxiety disorders: An integrative review. *Clinical Psychology Review, 30,* 203–216.

Clark, L. A., & Watson, D. (1991). Tripartite model of anxiety and depression: Psychometric evidence and taxonomic implications. *Journal of Abnormal Psychology, 100*, 316–336.

de Lissnyder, E., Koster, E. H. W., Derakshan, N., & de Raedt, R. (2010). The association between depressive symptoms and executive control impairments in response to emotional and non-emotional information. *Cognition and Emotion, 24*, 264–280.

de Raedt, R., & Koster, E. H. W. (2010). Understanding vulnerability for depression from a cognitive neuroscience perspective: A reappraisal of attentional factors and a new conceptual framework. *Cognitive, Affective, and Behavioral Neuroscience, 10*, 50–70.

Derakshan, N., Smyth, S., & Eysenck, M. W. (2009). Effects of state anxiety on performance using a task-switching paradigm: An investigation of attentional control theory. *Psychonomic Bulletin and Review, 16*, 1112–1117.

Derryberry, D., & Reed, M. A. (2002). Anxiety-related attentional biases and their regulation by attentional control. *Journal of Abnormal Psychology, 111*, 225–236.

Eysenck, M. W. (1979). Anxiety, learning and memory: A reconceptualization. *Journal of Research in Personality, 13*, 363–385.

Eysenck, M. W. (1997). *Anxiety and cognition: A unified theory*. Hove, UK: Psychology Press.

Eysenck, M. W., & Calvo, M. G. (1992). Anxiety and performance: The processing efficiency theory. *Cognition and Emotion, 6*, 409–434.

Eysenck, M. W., & Derakshan, N. (2011). New perspectives in attentional control theory. *Personality and Individual Differences, 50*, 955–960.

Eysenck, M. W., Derakshan, N., Santos, R., & Calvo, M. G. (2007). Anxiety and cognitive performance: Attentional control theory. *Emotion, 7*, 336–353.

Eysenck, M. W., & Graydon, J. (1989). Susceptibility to distraction as a function of personality. *Personality and Individual Differences, 10*, 681–687.

Eysenck, M.W., Payne, S., & Santos, R. (2006). Anxiety and depression: Past, present, and future events. *Cognition and Emotion, 20*, 274–294.

Fales, C. L., Barch, D. M., Burgess, G. C., Schaefer, A., Mennin, D. S., Gray, J. R., et al. (2008). Anxiety and cognitive efficiency: Differential modulation of transient and sustained neural activity during a working memory task. *Cognitive, Affective, and Behavioral Neuroscience, 8*, 239–253.

Fales, C. L., Barch, D. M., Rundle, M. M., Mintun, M. A., Snyder, A. Z., Cohen, J. D., et al. (2008). Altered emotional interference processing in affective and cognitive-control brain circuitry in major depression. *Biological Psychiatry, 63*, 377–384.

Fitzgerald, P. B., Laird, A. R., Maller, J., & Daskalakis, Z. J. (2008). A meta-analytic study of changes in brain activation in depression. *Human Brain Mapping, 29*, 683–695.

Forster, S., Elizalde, A. O. N., Castle, E., & Bishop, S. J. (in press). Unraveling the anxious mind: Anxiety, worry, and frontal engagement in sustained attention versus off-task processing. *Cerebral Cortex*.

Gotlib, I. H., & Joormann, J. (2010). Cognition and depression: Current status and future directions. *Annual Review of Clinical Psychology, 6*, 285–312.

Harvey, P.-O., Fossati, P., Pochon, J.-B., Levy, R., Lebastard, G., Lehéricy, S., et al. (2005). Cognitive control and brain resources in major depression: An fMRI study using the n-back task. *NeuroImage, 26*, 860–869.

Miyake, A., Friedman, N. P., Emerson, M. J., Witzki, A. H., Howerter, A., & Wager, T. (2000). The unity and diversity of executive functions and their contributions to complex "frontal lobe" tasks: A latent variable analysis. *Cognitive Psychology, 41*, 49–100.

Monsell, S. (2003). Task switching. *Trends in Cognitive Sciences, 7*, 134–140.

Moser, J. S., Becker, M. W., & Moran, T. P. (2012). Enhanced attentional capture in trait anxiety. *Emotion, 12*, 213–216.

Ólafsson, R. P., Ragnar, P., Smari, J., Guomundsdottir, F., Olafsdottir, G., Haroardottir, H. L., et al. (2011). Self-reported attentional control with the Attentional Control Scale: Factor structure and relationship with symptoms of anxiety and depression. *Journal of Anxiety Disorders, 25*, 777–782.

Pacheco-Ungietti, A. P., Acosta, A., Callejas, A., & Lupia ez, J. (2010). Attention and anxiety: Different attentional functioning under state and trait anxiety. *Psychological Science, 21*, 298–304.

Pacheco-Ungietti, A. P., Lupia ez, J., & Acosta, A. (2009). Attention and anxiety: Relationship between alertness and cognitive control with trait anxiety. *Psicologica, 30*, 1–25.

Righi, S., Mecacci, L., & Viggiano, M. P. (2009). Anxiety, cognitive self-evaluation and performance: ERP correlates. *Journal of Anxiety Disorders, 23*, 1132–1138.

Sadeh, N., & Bredemeier, K. (2011). Individual differences at high perceptual load: The relation between trait anxiety and selective attention. *Cognition and Emotion, 25*, 747–755.

Santos, R., Wall, M., & Eysenck, M. W. (2013). Anxiety and processing efficiency: fMRI evidence. Manuscript submitted for publication.

Savostyanov, A. N., Tsai, A. C., Liou, M., Levin, E. A., Lee, J.-D., Yurganov, A. V., et al. (2009). EEG correlates of trait anxiety in the stop-signal paradigm. *Neuroscience Letters, 449*, 112–116.

Sehlmeyer, C., Konrad, C., Zwitserlood, P., Arolt, V., Falkenstein, M., & Beste, C. (2010). ERP indices for response inhibition are related to anxiety-related personality traits. *Neuropsychologia, 48*, 2488–2498.

Siegle, G. J., Thompson, W., Carter, C. S., Steinhauer, S. R., & Thase, M. E. (2007). Increased amygdala and decreased dorsolateral prefrontal BOLD responses in unipolar depression: Related and independent features. *Biological Psychiatry, 61*, 198–209.

Spielberger, C. D., Gorsuch, R. L., & Lushene, R. E. (1970). *Manual for the State–Trait Anxiety Inventory*. Palo Alto, CA: Consulting Psychologists Press.

Sylvester, C. M., Corbetta, M., Raichle, M. E., Rodebaugh, T. L., Schlaggar, B. L., Sheline, Y. I., et al. (2012). Functional network dysfunction in anxiety and anxiety disorders. *Trends in Neurosciences, 35*, 527–535.

Visu-Petra, L., Miclea, M., & Visu-Petra, G. (2013). Individual differences in anxiety and executive functioning: A multidimensional view. *International Journal of Psychology, 48*, 649–659.

Walsh, J., McNally, M., & Eysenck, M. W. (2013). Interpretive bias and repressive coping. Manuscript submitted for publication.

Watson, D., & Clark, L. A. (1984). Negative affectivity: The disposition to experience negative aversive emotional states. *Psychological Bulletin, 96*, 465–490.

Williams, J. M. G., Watts, F. N., MacLeod, C. M., & Mathews, A. (1997). *Cognitive psychology and emotional disorders* (2nd ed.). Chichester, UK: Wiley.

Wilson, M. R., Vine, S. J., & Wood, G. (2009). The influence of anxiety on visual attentional control in basketball free throw shooting. *Journal of Sport and Exercise Psychology, 31*, 152–168.

CHAPTER 7

What Do Impulsive Aggression, Sensation Seeking, and Risk of Depression Have in Common?

Serotonergic Functioning and Dual Process Models of Behavioral Control

Charles S. Carver

INTRODUCTION

The collection of ideas described in this chapter began with a regulatory puzzle in personality psychology. Quite unexpectedly, this puzzle led to other puzzles in neurobiology and genetics. These latter topics, in turn, have led to what may be core issues in clinical psychology and psychopathology. All of these puzzles concern aspects of the dimension of reflexive reactivity versus constraint, or impulsive versus deliberative control of action.

The chapter begins by describing two general accounts of a basis for this dimension of variability from the literature on personality. It then turns to evidence that this dimension of variability is influenced by variation in serotonergic function. More specifically, it will be argued that certain brain regions that are serotonergically innervated may help moderate the expression in behavior of the outputs of more basic systems for approach and avoidance. Then the discussion turns to how this view may help in thinking about how deficits in serotonergic function could be involved in a broad set of social and emotional problems, ranging from antisocial behavior to depression.

Personality and Control edited by Philip J. Corr, Małgorzata Fajkowska, Michael W. Eysenck, and Agata Wytykowska. Eliot Werner Publications, Clinton Corners, New York, 2015.

IMPULSE AND CONSTRAINT

Personality as a field of study is home to great conceptual diversity. Textbook authors often deal with the diversity by describing various theoretical views as representing alternative perspectives on personality and its functions (e.g., Carver & Scheier, 2012). Sometimes the authors also try to synthesize across theoretical boundaries, pointing out themes that seem to emerge in one theory after another. Often enough, it turns out, diverse theories address similar themes—but do so in different ways.

One theme that emerges almost universally is the tension in life between impulsiveness and constraint. At least since Freud (e.g., 1962), this issue has been important to personality theories. It has been framed in terms of concepts such as delay of gratification, planfulness, socialization, and id versus ego. As it turns out, the concept of impulsiveness is actually quite broad. The term is used in diverse ways in different contexts. But the core of the concept within personality psychology is relatively straightforward. People often confront situations in which they can immediately express an impulse or desire, or they can overrule that impulse and evaluate more fully before acting.

It is important to acknowledge that both impulse and constraint have valuable characteristics in the appropriate contexts (Block & Block, 1980). When it is manifested as spontaneity, impulsiveness brings a sense of vigor and freedom to the human experience (e.g., Dickman, 1990; Hansen & Breivik, 2001). There are also occasions in which survival literally depends on the occurrence of impulsive action—occasions when a threat or an opportunity must be reacted to quickly.

However, impulses can also create problems. Impulsiveness can result in physical danger (e.g., impulsively chasing a bouncing ball into the street without looking for oncoming traffic). Impulses can interfere with attainment of longer-term goals (e.g., spending for today rather than saving for the future). Impulses can lead to violation of social norms (Cooper, Wood, Orcutt, & Albino, 2003; Lynam, 1996) and thereby can lead to interpersonal conflict and even legal problems. Potential adverse effects of impulsiveness include marital instability (Kelly & Conley, 1987), employment problems (Hogan & Holland, 2003), and disruption of health-maintaining behaviors (Bogg & Roberts, 2004; Hampson, Andrews, Barckley, Lichtenstein, & Lee, 2000; Hampson, Severson, Burns, Slovic, & Fisher, 2001; Skinner, Hampson, & Fife-Schaw, 2002). Being able to control impulsive reactivity is thus crucial to successful self-management (Vohs & Baumeister, 2011).

What forces tip the balance between impulse and constraint? What prevents impulses from always having free rein? Different theorists have posed different answers to these questions (for a broader treatment, see Carver, 2005).

Approach and Avoidance

One approach to this issue stems from the general view that incentives draw behavior toward them and threats inhibit or even reverse those actions (e.g., Cloninger, 1987; Davidson, 1984, 1998; Fowles, 1993; Gray, 1994a, 1994b; Lang, 1995). The incentive system is often termed a behavioral approach system (Gray, 1972, 1982, 1994a) or an activation or facilitation system (Depue & Collins, 1999; Fowles, 1980, 1987). When engaged by incentive cues, it yields approach and positive affect (Gray, 1994a, 1994b), including eagerness and desire. The threat system is also called a withdrawal system (e.g., Davidson, 1992, 1998). It earlier was called a behavioral inhibition system (BIS; Gray, 1972, 1982, 1994a), but this label has taken on different connotations today (Gray & McNaughton, 2000; McNaughton & Gray, 2000). When activated by threat cues, this system causes ongoing approach to be inhibited and may lead to behavioral withdrawal (Fowles, 1993; Gray, 1994a). It also underlies emotions such as fear (Carver & White, 1994; Davidson, 1992; Gray, 1982).

It can be argued that nothing more is needed to account for variability in impulsiveness than these basic approach and avoidance processes. The stronger the tendency to approach cues of incentives, the greater the likelihood of impulsive approach. Indeed, consistent with this idea, Gray (1994a) used "impulsivity" as his label for the personality dimension that he believed derives from sensitivity of the approach system. In the presence of threat cues, the threat system becomes active, stifling ongoing approach. One might think of this stifling of approach as being an overruling of the approach motive by the avoidance motive. (On the other hand, one might also think of a very reactive threat system as being itself impulsive, yielding reactive avoidance that is not down-regulated or overruled by the approach system.)

The competition between approach and avoidance is one starting point in thinking about impulse and constraint. But there are reasons to suspect that the competition between approach and avoidance is not the entire story. One reason is that in today's comprehensive trait models of personality, both the trait that reflects approach and positive emotions and the trait that reflects avoidance and negative emotions are distinct from the trait that reflects constraint (Clark & Watson, 1999; Depue & Collins, 1999; Zelenski & Larsen, 1999). That is, threat sensitivity, incentive sensitivity, and constraint are separate dimensions.

Another reason for believing that approach and avoidance are not the entire story is that it is relatively easy to point to situations in which constraint seems to be unrelated to anxiety or fear. Consider delay of gratification—foregoing a small reward now in order to obtain a larger one later (Mischel, 1974). Constraint in that situation does not seem to be based on avoidance of any threat, but rather about using time and planning to create more desirable overall outcomes.

Dual Process Models

A different viewpoint on these issues derives from contemporary dual process models of functioning. These models start with the idea that people process information in two somewhat distinct ways simultaneously. The two processing modes appear to use different aspects of the available information (Rudman, Phelan, &

Heppen, 2007). There is evidence that the two modes learn in different ways, and that the two patterns of learning create parallel influences on action that potentially compete with one another, thus requiring continuous arbitration (Daw, Niv, & Dayan, 2005). The more primitive mode of processing operates largely outside consciousness. The other is the familiar symbolic processor of the rational mind.

By now this idea and variations on it have been adopted as a useful conceptual framework in many areas of psychology (Barrett, Tugade, & Engle, 2004; Kahneman, 2011; MacDonald, 2008). The literature on personality psychology contains several such models. Epstein's (1973, 1985, 1990, 1994) cognitive-experiential self theory proposed that humans experience reality via a symbolic processor (the rational mind) and an associative and intuitive processor that functions automatically and quickly. Metcalfe and Mischel (1999), drawing on decades of work on delay of gratification, proposed a similar model. They posed a competition between a "hot" system (emotional, impulsive, reflexive, and connectionist) and a "cool" system (strategic, flexible, slower, and unemotional) to determine whether people restrain themselves.

The dual process idea has also been widely adopted in social psychology (Chaiken & Trope, 1999). The essence of such a view existed for decades in the literature on persuasion, but it has long since expanded beyond those bounds. Perhaps the most widely known dual process view in social psychology at present is Strack and Deutsch's (2004) reflexive-impulsive model (see Hofmann, Friese, & Strack, 2009). But the ideas have proliferated far more widely.

The dual process idea also has an important presence in developmental psychology. For example, Rothbart and her colleagues (e.g., Rothbart, Ahadi, & Evans, 2000; Rothbart, Ahadi, Hershey, & Fisher, 2001; Rothbart & Bates, 1998; Rothbart, Ellis, Rueda, & Posner, 2003; Rothbart & Posner, 1985) have argued for the existence of basic temperament systems for approach and avoidance, and a third temperament termed effortful control (see also Kochanska & Knaack, 2003; MacDonald, 2008; Marcovitch & Zelazo, 2009; Nigg, 2000, 2003, 2006). Before the capacity for effortful control emerges and stabilizes, behavior is a resultant of the influences of approach and avoidance temperaments (Figure 1). Greater sensitivity of the approach temperament makes reflexive action more likely; greater sensitivity of the avoidance temperament makes reflexive restraint more likely. Thus far this description closely resembles that outlined in the previous section.

Effortful control emerges later in development than the approach and avoidance temperaments. The label "effortful" conveys the sense that this is an executive, planful activity, entailing the use of cognitive resources to deter the tendency to react impulsively. Effortful control is said to rely on certain prefrontal brain areas (e.g., Eisenberg et al., 2004; Kochanska & Knaack, 2003; Nigg, 2001, 2003; Rothbart & Bates, 1998). Evidence from neuroimaging studies conducted on both adults and children supports that argument (e.g., Durston, Thomas, Worden, Yang, & Casey, 2002; Durston, Thomas, Yang et al., 2002).

Effortful control is superordinate to approach and avoidance temperaments (e.g., Ahadi & Rothbart, 1994; see also Clark, 2005). It thus can countermand

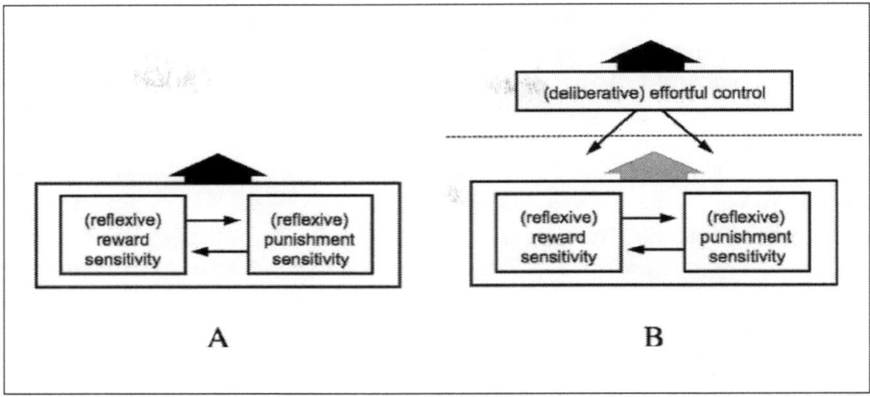

Figure 1. Three temperament influences on behavior, adapted from various statements by Rothbart, Eisenberg, and others. [A] A reactive system for approaching rewards and a reactive system for avoiding threats or punishment compete for ascendance; in the absence of effortful control, the resultant of that competition is expressed in behavior. [B] The engagement of an effortful control system permits the resultant arising from the competition of the reactive systems to be overridden, thus dampening the role of the reactive systems in determining behavior. Reprinted from "Serotonergic Function, Two-Mode Models of Self-Regulation, and Vulnerability to Depression: What Depression Has in Common with Impulsive Aggression" by C. S. Carver, S. L. Johnson, and J. Joormann, 2008, *Psychological Bulletin, 134*, p. 914. Copyright 2008 by the American Psychological Association. Reprinted with permission.

them. In that way it permits control over reactive behavior. That is, it permits the suppressing of tendencies that are triggered by either the approach or avoidance temperament, when doing so is situationally appropriate. If effortful control capacity is available, the jumping toward incentives promoted by a sensitive approach system can be restrained (Kochanska & Knaack, 2003; Murray & Kochanska, 2002). This child (or this adult) can delay gratification.

Although restraint of approach impulses is the most obvious manifestation of this process, it is important to point out other potential manifestations. Effortful control can also override a reflexive tendency toward avoidance when the avoidance temperament is especially active. Thus, for example, given sufficient effortful control resources, a person can remain in a tension-inducing social situation rather than flee from it. Furthermore, if the person's approach temperament is weak or relatively inactive, effortful control can override a reflexive tendency toward *inaction*. For example, it can get you to exercise when you don't really want to. Thus exerting effortful control can move a person toward either restraint or action, depending on which reflexive response is being overcome.

This argument casts a somewhat unusual light on the concept of impulsiveness. In this view what is impulsive is what is *reactive*, whether its outward display is of action or inaction. Impulsiveness as a concept has always been difficult to pin down (Barratt, 1985; Block, 2002; Dickman, 1990; Eisenberg, 2002; Nigg, 2000; Solanto et al., 2001; Stanford & Barratt, 1992; White et al., 1994; Whiteside & Lynam, 2001, 2003). It can take many forms, including jumping to acquire an incentive, being easily distracted by opportunities that arise while a current pursuit is ongoing, and reacting quickly to emotions. The aspect of impulsiveness emphasized in this chapter is that impulses are reactive—relatively immediate responses to some stimulus in disregard of other considerations. The key, in this view, is that whatever action property emerges represents a reactive, automatic association to the stimulus.

Complexity Introduced by Dual Process Views

Dual process models of influences on action seem to address issues that are not well handled by a viewpoint that considers only approach and avoidance. In dual process models, sometimes behavior is restrained because anxiety is stronger than desire (creating a kind of reflexive restraint); sometimes behavior is restrained because the effortful, reflective mode is acting to optimize longer-term outcomes. Thus the dual process view yields greater complexity of possibilities.

Characterizations of the two processing modes by various writers, though not identical, share many elements. The more basic mode is described by such terms as impulsive, reflexive, reactive, heuristic, and associative. It is said to be responsive to situational cues, schematic associations, and especially to strong emotions. Its strengths are its quickness and its low demand on processing resources. It can spontaneously create action when its schemas are sufficiently activated. It thus can act even with little information and high time urgency. The other mode is typically described by such terms as reflective, strategic, deliberative, and logical. Its strength is its ability to take into account circumstances that go beyond the immediate present. This mode requires more processing resources and thus loses efficiency when cognitive capacity is limited. Although there are differences among specific dual process conceptualizations that may be quite important, it is this shared common core that is the focus here.

SEROTONERGIC FUNCTION

Another viewpoint on personality that has become increasingly influential in recent years is based in biological systems—both brain structures and neurotransmitter systems. A number of people have begun to consider the possible roles played by different neurotransmitter systems in the management of behavior, and thus in the variations in human personality. One system that has been the subject of much investigation is the serotonergic system. This section of the chapter considers a potential role for serotonergic function in impulse and constraint.

Serotonin has been studied for some time, in both humans and other animals (for greater detail see Manuck, Kaplan, & Lotrich, 2006). It can be misleading to think only in terms of level of serotonin per se, because a good deal more is involved (e.g., Neumeister et al., 2006). On the other hand, some experimental manipulations do influence the level of serotonin that is available during a particular window of time. An example is a procedure called acute tryptophan depletion. Tryptophan is an amino acid that is a precursor to serotonin. It can be depleted by administering a drink (or capsules) containing high levels of other amino acids but no tryptophan. Several hours later behavioral effects of artificially lowered serotonin can be studied.

Another common methodological strategy is to relate behavior to genetic polymorphisms that have independently been linked to serotonergic function (Manuck et al., 2006). Most of this research has examined the gene that codes the serotonin transporter. Transcriptional activity of this gene is believed to be associated with a repetitive sequence in a region called 5-HTTLPR, which has a short version and a long version (i.e., with more repetitions). A variety of evidence links this polymorphism to variation in serotonergic function (reviewed in Carver, Johnson, & Joormann, 2008). It is now widely believed that the short allele is a marker of low serotonergic function (e.g., Canli & Lesch, 2007). Substantial research has tested what kinds of characteristics (behavioral, affective, cognitive, or personality) differ between persons with the short allele and those with the long allele.

The sections that follow provide a sense of some of the findings obtained using these methods and others. The position taken here is that this body of evidence tends to suggest that the serotonergic system functions (partly) to decrease reactivity and increase constraint.

Correlates of Serotonergic Markers in the Laboratory

Some of the evidence comes from laboratory studies, in which tryptophan depletion appears to impair constraint over automatic emotional responses. An example comes from a task in which specific cues are rewarded and for which the response thus becomes habitual. Then the rules change and this response is no longer rewarded. Tryptophan depletion impairs the ability to inhibit the responses after the rule changes (Cools et al., 2005; Park et al., 1994; Rogers et al., 2003). Tryptophan depletion has also led persons to report more sadness during exposure to uncontrollable noise stress, whereas the effect was only minor when the noise was controllable (Richell, Deakin, & Anderson, 2005). These types of studies suggest that the serotonin system can help inhibit responses to both rewarding and aversive stimuli.

Several studies have examined effects of tryptophan depletion on aggression. A very important conceptual point was made in a study by Cleare and Bond (1995). Participants were pre-assessed as being either high or low in aggression. Those pre-assessed as high in aggression became more aggressive, hostile, and quarrelsome after tryptophan depletion, but there was no effect for those assessed as low in aggression. Similar results were reported by Finn, Young, Pihl, and Ervin (1998). This pattern implies that effects of low serotonergic function on aggression are less about aggression per se and more about the release of existing habitual tendencies to be aggressive (see also Manuck et al., 2006; Spoont, 1992). A later study (Bjork, Dougherty, Moeller, & Swann, 2000) further reinforced this point: tryptophan depletion in this study led to more aggressive response to provocation among men high in aggressiveness, but had the opposite effect among those low in aggressiveness.

Correlates of Serotonergic Markers with Personality

A substantial number of studies have examined relationships of serotonergic function to personality self-reports, using several procedures to assess serotonergic function. Some of this work has focused on qualities pertaining to aggression and impulsiveness; others examined a broader range of qualities. Trait hostility has been related to low serotonergic function in several nonclinical samples (Cleare & Bond, 1997; Depue, 1995; Netter, Hennig, & Rohrmann, 1999). Depue (1995) related low serotonergic function as well to the Control–Impulsivity facet scale from the Constraint factor of the Multidimensional Personality Questionnaire (MPQ; Tellegen, 1985), the Aggression facet of the MPQ's Negative Emotionality factor (but not other facets), two sensation seeking subscales, and several other indices of impulsiveness.

There is also a substantial literature on the serotonin polymorphism and traits as assessed by broad-ranging inventories. These studies permit investigation of diverse possible associations, if facets as well as full factors are examined. Some years ago Lesch et al. (1996) found that the short allele (linked to low serotonergic function) related to higher neuroticism (by the Revised NEO Personality Inventory) and lower agreeableness. In facet analyses the neuroticism scales most closely linked to the short allele were Angry Hostility, Depression, and Impulsiveness. Greenberg et al. (2000) also related the short allele to both neuroticism and agreeableness, with an additional weaker association for conscientiousness. Analysis of neuroticism facets again revealed the strongest relations for Angry Hostility and Depression.

Many other studies, and even several meta-analyses, have since been done (for a review see Carver et al., 2008). Importantly, however, the meta-analyses have all focused on neuroticism, as has most of the developing literature. The consistent association with agreeableness has generally been disregarded.

Correlates of Serotonergic Markers with Impulsive Disorders

A good deal of research has also studied serotonergic function in people with clinical conditions that involve impulsive aggression (for a more extensive review, see Manuck et al., 2006). Lower serotonergic function has for some time been linked to history of fighting and assault (Coccaro, Kavoussi, Cooper, & Hauger, 1997), domestic violence (George et al., 2001), and impulsive aggression more generally (Cleare & Bond, 1997; Coccaro, Kavoussi, Hauger, Cooper, & Ferris, 1998).

Genetic evidence also connects serotonergic function to violent and antisocial behavior. For example, Dolan, Anderson, and Deakin (2001) linked low serotonergic function to higher impulsivity and higher aggression in male aggressive offenders. Interestingly, both impulsivity and aggression also related to higher anxiety in this sample. This particular finding argues persuasively against a path in which impulsive aggression is a product of low anxiety.

Characterizing the Pattern of Findings

The pattern of these findings (and others not reviewed here) appears consistent with the idea that serotonergic pathways are involved in impulse control (Depue, 1995; Depue & Collins, 1999; Depue & Spoont, 1986; Manuck, Flory, Muldoon, & Ferrell, 2003; Soubrié, 1986; Spoont, 1992; Zuckerman, 2005), particularly impulses that reflect strong emotions. High serotonergic function appears to relate to considering the future consequences of one's behavior (promoting conscientiousness) and to considering implications of one's behavior for positive social connection (promoting agreeableness).

This pattern can also be characterized in terms of the dual process viewpoint described in the preceding section (Carver et al., 2008). The basic, reactive mode of functioning was said to be impulsive and highly responsive to strong emotions. The reflective mode was said to be planful and less reactive to immediate emotional cues. Joining these descriptions with the kinds of findings described in this section, it seems plausible to suggest that serotonergic function may shift the balance of influence between these two modes of functioning. That is, it appears that lower serotonergic function may increase the influence of the reactive system or decrease the influence of the reflective system.

DEPRESSION AND SEROTONERGIC FUNCTION

And now a rather abrupt shift in focus, to the topic of depression. In the previous section, it was mentioned that depression as a facet scale of neuroticism has been linked repeatedly to the short allele of the serotonin transporter gene. There is also an accumulation of evidence from other studies linking serotonergic function to more clinically meaningful depression (for a review see Carver et al., 2008). Early studies looked for direct links from the polymorphisms to depression vulnerability. More recent work has focused on gene by environment interactions.

Caspi et al. (2003) first reported that the serotonin transporter polymorphism interacted with early maltreatment to predict depression diagnosis by early adulthood: negative life events had an adverse effect on those carrying at least one short allele, but not among those with two long alleles. A number of other studies followed and by now there have been several meta-analyses of this literature (Risch et al., 2009; Uher & McGuffin, 2008, 2010). The outcomes of the meta-analyses have varied as a function of selection criteria. However, Uher and McGuffin (2010) found that the serotonin transporter polymorphism interacted with early maltreatment to predict vulnerability to depression in each of the eleven studies that used objective or interview measures of maltreatment (see also Caspi, Hariri, Holmes, Uher, & Moffitt, 2010).

Impulsivity and Depression

Previous sections described studies linking low serotonergic function to high impulse expression, particularly impulsive reactions to emotional cues. Studies were also described linking low serotonergic function to behavioral problems in which a salient feature was poor control over impulsive action (e.g., impulsive aggression). The idea that high reactivity to emotions underlies impulsive violence, sensation seeking, attention deficit problems, and externalizing problems such as substance abuse is both intuitive and supported by a great deal of data (Cyders, Flory, Rainer, & Smith, 2009; Dick et al., 2010; Whiteside & Lynam, 2003).

In this section, by contrast, the topic is a link from low serotonergic function to vulnerability to depression. This idea may seem paradoxical in light of the others. Depression is not generally associated in people's minds with impulsive overt action. It is more often linked to lethargy, an absence of behavioral engagement (Sobin & Sackeim, 1997). What would account for this very substantial difference in presentation between impulsive aggression and depression?

To address this question, it is useful to return to the dual process models and the working definition of impulsiveness that was provided earlier in the chapter. Dual process models suggest that the reactive mode acts impulsively (reflexively) and is highly responsive to emotions. But these are "operating characteristics" of that mode of function. How the operating characteristics are manifested overtly depends on what emotions the person is experiencing and what reactive action impulse is thereby being triggered.

Most emotions call for outward action of some sort. Eagerness promotes approach. Fear promotes avoidance. But sadness is different from most others. Sadness—the affective core of depression—is a deactivating emotion. It represents a call for passivity, for giving up of effort (Frijda, 1986). If a person has an overresponsiveness to emotions in general, then applying that overresponsiveness to the specific emotion of sadness would promote the behaviors that sadness ordinarily triggers. Since the behavior that is triggered by sadness is *in*action, the result of being highly reactive to emotions in this case would be greater inaction. Interestingly, many aspects of depressed behavior reflect passivity and apparent difficulty in initiating action.

Paradoxically, then, the same functional property (behavioral reactivity to emotion) that can help release bursts of violence or acting out and sensation seeking may also help create virtually the opposite profile of behavior, in response to a different emotion. This argument seems rather circumstantial, though. It depends on a set of findings concerning correlates of the serotonergic system. Is there any further evidence to support the idea that depression is related to impulsiveness?

There is evidence from at least four studies. Three of them (Ekinci, Albayrak, & Caykoylu, 2011; Henna et al., 2013; Peluso et al., 2007) examined responses to the Barratt Impulsiveness Scale (Barratt, 1965) among persons with and without the diagnosis of major depressive disorder (MDD). In all of the studies, persons diagnosed with depression reported greater motor impulsivity than controls (e.g., "I act on the spur of the moment"); in two of them (Ekinci et al., 2011; Henna et al., 2013), a similar difference emerged for attentional impulsivity (e.g., "I often think about extraneous thoughts when thinking").

The Barratt Impulsiveness Scale is a relatively general measure. Its item content does not lend itself to attributing the impulsiveness that is being assessed to emotional versus nonemotional sources (though emotion is not explicitly mentioned in any of the items). However, we have recently collected additional data to explore more explicitly the possible association of depression with emotion-reactive impulsiveness (Carver, Johnson, & Joormann, 2013). The sample was college students, who completed a variety of questionnaires bearing on impulses versus control and also a diagnostic interview for lifetime episode of MDD.

Some of the self-report scales were chosen to pertain to reflexive reactivity to emotions. Some tended to focus on reactivity to negative emotions. Associations of these measures with lifetime MDD would be consistent with the widely held view that depression vulnerability is related to an enhanced experience of negativity (Bylsma, Taylor-Clift, & Rottenberg, 2011; Kendler, Neale, Kessler, Heath, & Eaves, 1993). However, the measures focused not on the frequency of occurrence of negative emotions, but on the tendency to respond relatively reflexively and automatically to them—either cognitively (e.g., by drawing further conclusions) or behaviorally.

We also included one scale that addressed impulsive behavioral reactions to emotions in general, and another scale that assessed impulsive reactions to positive emotions in particular (the Positive Urgency Measure; Cyders et al., 2007). Inclusion of these measures allowed us to go beyond measurement of reactivity to negative emotions, to measurement of reactivity to emotions more generally.

Although the focus was on reflexive responses to emotions, measures were also included to test the specificity of this reasoning. That is, some measures were used that pertain to better versus worse self-control without involvement of emotions. A measure of comorbid alcohol problems was also included, to test whether any associations of lifetime MDD with reactivity to emotions would actually be attributable to this commonly comorbid externalizing syndrome.

The impulse-related questionnaires used in this project were distilled to three underlying factors (Carver, Johnson, Joormann, Kim, & Nam, 2011). Factor 1 reflects a broad tendency for emotions to reflexively shape the person's orientation to the world: having one's worldview affected by temporary feelings, generalizing from negative events to the overall sense of self-worth, and reacting to sadness and fatigue with inaction. Factor 2 centers on the tendency to complete tasks versus being distracted by other things. This factor has no obvious involvement of reacting to emotion. Factor 3 centers on impulsive behavioral reactivity to emotions, including positive emotions.

Persons diagnosed with MDD lifetime proved to have higher scores on Factors 1 and 3 than did persons with negative diagnoses (Carver et al., 2013). There was no effect on Factor 2. Importantly, these differences between groups were robust to several kinds of analyses that controlled for effects of current depressive symptoms and externalizing symptoms.

The results of this study thus support the idea that lifetime MDD is related to impulsive reactivity to emotions in particular. The result is unsurprising with respect to Factor 1, because Factor 1 in part reflects reactions to negative emotions and fatigue, along with overtones of passivity and automatic coloring of one's view of the world from (mostly negative) events. The finding that the MDD group also endorsed a more general impulsive reactivity to emotions—including positive emotions—to a greater degree than did the control group is less intuitive, but far less ambiguous in supporting the dual process viewpoint. It is worth emphasizing that a link between history of MDD and reactivity to positive emotion would be very hard to predict from a perspective other than the dual process viewpoint underlying the study (for further evidence supporting this position, see Smith, Guller & Zapolski, 2013).

Further Influences: Approach Sensitivity and Dopamine

The idea that low serotonergic function is related to such diverse patterns as depression vulnerability, impulsive aggression, and sensation seeking has a further implication. It means that more has to be involved here than serotonergic function. The idea that low serotonergic function (and deficits in effortful control) have different effects in different kinds of people requires hypothesizing an interaction of some sort (see Depue & Lenzenweger, 2005). Something else must differ between the groups.

One candidate for this role is the sensitivity, or engagement, of the incentive approach system. When poor executive control is combined with high incentive sensitivity (a reactive approach system), the result is overt approach-related impulsiveness. When poor executive oversight is combined with low incentive sensitivity (a nonreactive approach system), the result is impulsive inaction—lack of effort toward potential rewards. In both cases the effects of variation in level of basic incentive sensitivity (high and low, respectively) are amplified by the absence of effortful override (see Figure 1 above).

In the case of depression vulnerability, a lack of incentive sensitivity means that the person is not strongly motivated to approach potentially rewarding contexts. A relative deficit in effortful control amplifies this problem, such that the person has greater difficulty overcoming this lack of motivations. This combination thus should yield apathy, passivity, and fatigue, which characterize many cases of depression.

Several sources of evidence suggest that depression is associated with a blunted approach system. For example, EEG laterality has been used to measure activity of the approach system. Behavioral and personality measures of approach motivation have been found to correlate with higher activation in left—rather than right—anterior cortical areas (e.g., Coan & Allen, 2003; Harmon-Jones & Allen, 1997; Sutton & Davidson, 1997). Previously depressed (Henriques & Davidson, 1990) and clinically depressed persons (Henriques & Davidson, 1991) have been found to have lower activation in left anterior cortical areas than nondepressed persons.

Behavioral research also links depression to blunted incentive sensitivity. For example, depressed persons are less responsive to reward than people who are not depressed (Henriques, Glowacki, & Davidson, 1994; Henriques & Davidson, 2000). Other evidence relates self-reports of low incentive sensitivity to depression (Campbell-Sills, Liverant, & Brown, 2004; Pinto-Meza et al., 2006). Indeed, three separate studies have found that self-reports of low incentive sensitivity predicted a worse course of depression over time (Campbell-Sills et al., 2004; Kasch, Rottenberg, Arnow, & Gotlib, 2002; McFarland, Shankman, Tenke, Bruder, & Klein, 2006).

Blunted approach motivation may also be manifested in low dopaminergic function. Dopaminergic pathways are believed to be critical in the engagement of goal-directed effort (Farrar et al., 2007; Salamone, Correa, Farrar, & Mingote, 2007; Salamone, Correa, Mingote, & Weber, 2005; Salamone, Correa, Mingote, Weber, & Farrar, 2006). A weakly functioning dopaminergic system yields less "wanting" for appetitive outcomes (Berridge, 2007) and less engagement of effort in pursuit of them (Salamone et al., 2005, 2006, 2007). A recent review—drawing from pharmacological, genetic, and dopamine challenge studies—reported a range of evidence for deficits in the function of dopamine among depressed persons (Dunlop & Nemeroff, 2007).

TOWARD TRANSDIAGNOSTIC VULNERABILITY

The preceding section emphasized depression, partly because the prediction that vulnerability to depression would be related to impulsive reactivity to emotions is highly counterintuitive. Many externalizing problems have been related to this sort of reactivity, including vandalism, risky sexual behavior, gambling, and drug use (Cyders et al., 2007; Zapolski, Cyders, & Smith, 2009), but there is less evidence regarding its role in internalizing problems. This raises an interesting question. Across how broad a spectrum of disorder is reactivity to emotion—even positive emotion—a contributor?

A little more information is available on this question. The three factors described above have also been studied in other psychopathology-related contexts. One study found that manic temperament, measured by the Hypomanic Personality

Scale, was correlated significantly with Factor 3 but not with the other two factors (Johnson, Carver, Mulé, & Joormann, 2013). Thus reports of an overresponsiveness to positive emotions and emotions in general appears to relate to mania vulnerability as well as depression vulnerability. Another study has related Factor 3 to a wider variety of psychopathology-related self-reports (Johnson, Carver, & Joormann, 2013), including aggression, anxiety, borderline tendencies, and an index of suicidality. This pattern suggests that the involvement of overreactivity to emotion may be quite wide ranging.

The possibility that the broad spectrum of psychopathologies may be characterized by a more limited number of features that are actually transdiagnostic, rather than diagnosis-specific, has been raised in a number of places in recent years (e.g., Cuthbert, 2005; Harvey, Watkins, Mansell, & Shafran, 2004). It is worth asking whether an impulsive overreactivity to emotions may be one such transdiagnostic feature (see also a related argument made by Johnson-Laird, Mancini, & Gangemi, 2006, about the role of emotional overresponsiveness in psychopathology). This is a possibility that certainly deserves further attention.

An interesting question more generally is the extent to which diverse psychopathologies may relate to insufficiency of reflective override processes. It is possible that the dual process models may have more to offer this part of psychology than has yet been realized.

PERSONALITY AND CONTROL: DUAL PROCESS MODELS

How behavior is controlled is a complex problem. It is clear that the competition between approach and avoidance tendencies is an important contributor to determining what action occurs at any given moment. It is also clear that the answer involves greater complexity than that. This chapter adopted a view of behavioral control that is being widely explored in personality, social, developmental, and cognitive psychology, in which two modes of processing are assumed—one more basic and reactive, the other more deliberative. This dual process orientation is being used as a conceptual tool by others to address a wide range of problems.

This chapter also addressed the possibility that one influence on which mode of functioning dominates and directs behavior is the functioning of the serotonergic system. There is evidence linking low serotonergic functioning to a substantial range of impulsive behaviors (including impulsive violence), consistent with the idea that parts of the serotonergic system have the potential to constrain outputs of the approach system. There is also evidence linking low serotonergic functioning to depression, however—which at first seems paradoxical, since depression is so unlike the externalizing problems that are also linked to low serotonergic functioning.

This apparent paradox was addressed conceptually by arguing that depression entails impulsive reactivity to a deactivating emotion. The apparent paradox was also addressed more directly, by data indicating that depression vulnerability is in fact related to self-report measures of impulsiveness. Finally, the possibility was raised that an inability to control basic impulses may actually represent a transdiagnostic feature of psychopathology, serving to exaggerate and amplify reactivity to emotions, driving behavior in different directions as a function of differences in emotions. Throughout the chapter the general framework of dual process models seems to have provided a reasonable, broad orientation to the issues under discussion. I recommend the ideas to others for their own exploration.

REFERENCES

Ahadi, S. A., & Rothbart, M. K. (1994). Temperament, development and the big five. In C. F. Halverson, Jr., G. A. Kohnstamm, & R. P. Martin (Eds.), *The developing structure of temperament and personality from infancy to adulthood* (pp. 189–207). Hillsdale, NJ: Erlbaum.

Barratt, E. S. (1965). Factor analysis of some psychometric measures of impulsiveness and anxiety. *Psychological Reports, 16*, 547-554.

Barratt, E. S. (1985). Impulsive subtraits: Arousal and information processing. In J. T. Spence & C. E. Izard (Eds.), *Emotion and personality* (pp. 137–146). New York: Elsevier.

Barrett, L. F., Tugade, M. M., & Engle, R. W. (2004). Individual differences in working memory capacity and dual-process theories of the mind. *Psychological Bulletin, 130,* 553–573.

Berridge, K. C. (2007). The debate over dopamine's role in reward: The case for incentive salience. *Psychopharmacology, 191*, 391–431.

Bjork, J. M., Dougherty, D. M., Moeller, F. G., & Swann, A. C. (2000). Differential behavioral effects of plasma tryptophan depletion and loading in aggressive and nonaggressive men. *Neuropsychopharmacology, 22*, 357–369.

Block, J. (2002). *Personality as an affect-processing system: Toward an integrative theory.* Mahwah, NJ: Erlbaum.

Block, J. H., & Block, J. (1980). The role of ego-control and ego-resiliency in the organization of behavior. In W. A. Collins (Ed.), *Development of cognition, affect, and social relations* (Minnesota Symposia on Child Psychology, Vol. 13, pp. 39–101). Hillsdale, NJ: Erlbaum.

Bogg, T., & Roberts, B. W. (2004). Conscientiousness and health-related behaviors: A meta-analysis of the leading behavioral contributors to mortality. *Psychological Bulletin, 130*, 887–919.

Bylsma, L. M., Taylor-Clift, A., & Rottenberg, J. (2011). Emotional reactivity to daily events in major and minor depression. *Journal of Abnormal Psychology, 120*, 155–167.

Campbell-Sills, L., Liverant, G. I., & Brown, T. A. (2004). Psychometric evaluation of the Behavioral Inhibition/Behavioral Activation scales in a large sample of outpatients with anxiety and mood disorders. *Psychological Assessment, 16*, 244–254.

Canli, T., & Lesch, K. (2007). Long story short: The serotonin transporter in emotion regulation and social cognition. *Nature Neuroscience, 10*, 1103–1109.

Carver, C. S. (2005). Impulse and constraint: Perspectives from personality psychology, convergence with theory in other areas, and potential for integration. *Personality and Social Psychology Review, 9*, 312–333.

Carver, C. S., Johnson, S. L., & Joormann, J. (2008). Serotonergic function, two-mode models of self-regulation, and vulnerability to depression: What depression has in common with impulsive aggression. *Psychological Bulletin, 134*, 912–943.

Carver, C. S., Johnson, S. L., & Joormann, J. (2013). Major depressive disorder and impulsive reactivity to emotion: Toward a dual process view of depression. *British Journal of Clinical Psychology, 52*, 285–299.

Carver, C. S., Johnson, S. L., Joormann, J., Kim, Y., & Nam, J. (2011). Serotonin transporter polymorphism interacts with childhood adversity to predict aspects of impulsivity. *Psychological Science, 22*, 589–595.

Carver, C. S., & Scheier, M. F. (2012). *Perspectives on personality* (7th ed.). Upper Saddle River, NJ: Pearson Education.

Carver, C. S., & White, T. L. (1994). Behavioral inhibition, behavioral activation, and affective responses to impending reward and punishment: The BIS/BAS scales. *Journal of Personality and Social Psychology, 67*, 319–333.

Caspi, A., Hariri, A. R., Holmes, A., Uher, R., & Moffitt, T. E. (2010). Genetic sensitivity to the environment: The case of the serotonin transporter gene and its implications for studying complex diseases and traits. *American Journal of Psychiatry, 167*, 509–527.

Caspi, A., Sugden, K., Moffitt, T. E., Taylor, A., Craig, I. W., Harrington, H., et al. (2003). Influence of life stress on depression: Moderation by a polymorphism in the 5-HTT gene. *Science, 301*, 386–389.

Chaiken, S. L., & Trope, Y. (Eds.). (1999). *Dual-process theories in social psychology*. New York: Guilford Press.

Clark, L. A. (2005). Temperament as a unifying basis for personality and psychopathology. *Journal of Abnormal Psychology, 114*, 505–521.

Clark, L. A., & Watson, D. (1999). Temperament: A new paradigm for trait psychology. In L. A. Pervin & O. P. John (Eds.), *Handbook of personality: Theory and research* (2nd ed., pp. 399–423). New York: Guilford Press.

Cleare, A. J., & Bond, A. J. (1995). The effect of tryptophan depletion and enhancement on subjective and behavioural aggression in normal male subjects. *Psychopharmacology, 118*, 72–81.

Cleare, A. J., & Bond, A. J. (1997). Does central serotonergic function correlate inversely with aggression? A study using D-fenfluramine in healthy subjects. *Psychiatry Research, 69*, 89–95.

Cloninger, C. R. (1987). A systematic method for clinical description and classification of personality variants: A proposal. *Archives of General Psychiatry, 44*, 573–588.

Coan, J. A., & Allen, J. J. B. (2003). Frontal EEG asymmetry and the behavioral activation and inhibition systems. *Psychophysiology, 40*, 106–114.

Coccaro, E. F., Kavoussi, R. J., Cooper, T. B., & Hauger, R. L. (1997). Central serotonin activity and aggression: Inverse relationship with prolactin response to d-fenfluramine, but not CSF 5-HIAA concentration, in human subjects. *American Journal of Psychiatry, 154*, 1430–1435.

Coccaro, E. F., Kavoussi, R. J., Hauger, R. L., Cooper, T. B., & Ferris, C. F. (1998). Cerebrospinal fluid vasopressin levels: Correlates with aggression and serotonin function in personality-disordered subjects. *Archives of General Psychiatry, 55*, 708–714.

Cools, R., Blackwell, A., Clark, L., Menzies, L., Cox, S., & Robbins, T. W. (2005). Tryptophan depletion disrupts the motivational guidance of goal-directed behavior as a function of trait impulsivity. *Neuropsychopharmacology, 30,* 1362–1373.

Cooper, M. L, Wood, P. K., Orcutt, H. K., & Albino, A. (2003). Personality and the predisposition to engage in risky or problem behaviors during adolescence. *Journal of Personality and Social Psychology, 84*, 390–410.

Cuthbert, B. N. (2005). Dimensional models of psychopathology: Research agenda and clinical utility. *Journal of Abnormal Psychology, 114*, 565–569.

Cyders, M. A., Flory, K., Rainer, S., & Smith, G. T. (2009). The role of personality dispositions to risky behavior in predicting first-year college drinking. *Addiction, 104*, 193–202.

Cyders, M. A., Smith, G. T., Spillane, N. S., Fischer, S., Annus, A. M., & Peterson, C. (2007). Integration of impulsivity and positive mood to predict risky behavior: Development and validation of a measure of positive urgency. *Psychological Assessment, 19*, 107–118.

Davidson, R. J. (1984). Affect, cognition, and hemispheric specialization. In C. E. Izard, J. Kagan, & R. Zajonc (Eds.), *Emotion, cognition, and behavior* (pp. 320–365). New York: Cambridge University Press.

Davidson, R. J. (1992). Prolegomenon to the structure of emotion: Gleanings from neuropsychology. *Cognition and Emotion, 6*, 245–268.

Davidson, R. J. (1998). Anterior electrophysiological asymmetries, emotion, and depression: Conceptual and methodological conundrums. *Psychophysiology, 35*, 607-614.

Daw, N. D., Niv, Y., & Dayan, P. (2005). Uncertainty-based competition between prefrontal and dorsolateral striatal systems for behavioral control. *Nature Neuroscience, 8*, 1704–1711.

Depue, R. A. (1995). Neurobiological factors in personality and depression. *European Journal of Personality, 9*, 413–439.

Depue, R. A., & Collins, P. F. (1999). Neurobiology of the structure of personality: Dopamine, facilitation of incentive motivation, and extraversion. *Behavioral and Brain Sciences, 22*, 491–517.

Depue, R. A., & Lenzenweger, M. F. (2005). A neurobiological dimensional model of personality disturbance. In M. F., Lenzenweger & J. F. Clarkin (Eds.). *Major theories of personality disorder* (2nd ed., pp. 391–453). New York: Guilford Press.

Depue, R. A., & Spoont, M. R. (1986). Conceptualizing a serotonin trait: A behavioral dimension of constraint. *Annals of the New York Academy of Sciences, 487*, 47–62.

Dick, D. M., Smith, G., Olausson, P., Mitchell, S. H., Leeman, R. F., O'Malley, S. S., et al. (2010). Understanding the construct of impulsivity and its relationship to alcohol use disorders. *Addiction Biology, 15*, 217–226.

Dickman, S. J. (1990). Functional and dysfunctional impulsivity: Personality and cognitive correlates. *Journal of Personality and Social Psychology, 58*, 95–102.

Dolan, M. C., Anderson, I. M., & Deakin, J. F. W. (2001). Relationship between 5-HT function and impulsivity and aggression in male offenders with personality disorders. *British Journal of Psychiatry, 178*, 352–359.

Dunlop, B. W., & Nemeroff, C. B. (2007). The role of dopamine in the pathophysiology of depression. *Archives of General Psychiatry, 64*, 327–337.

Durston, S., Thomas, K. M., Worden, M. S., Yang, Y., & Casey, B. J. (2002). The effect of preceding context on inhibition: An event-related fMRI study. *NeuroImage, 16*, 449–453.

Durston, S., Thomas, K. M., Yang, Y., Ulug, A. M., Zimmerman, R. D., & Casey, B. J. (2002). A neural basis for the development of inhibitory control. *Developmental Science, 5*, F9–F16.

Eisenberg, N. (2002). Emotion-related regulation and its relation to quality of social functioning, In W. W. Hartup & R. A. Weinberg (Eds.), *Child psychology in retrospect and prospect* (Minnesota Symposia on Child Psychology, Vol. 32, pp. 133–171). Mahwah, NJ: Erlbaum.

Eisenberg, N., Spinrad, T. L., Fabes, R. A., Reiser, M., Cumberland, A., Shepard, S. A., et al. (2004). The relations of effortful control and impulsivity to children's resiliency and adjustment. *Child Development, 75*, 25–46.

Ekinci, O., Albayrak, Y., & Caykoylu, A. (2011). Impulsivity in euthymic patients with major depressive disorder: The relation to sociodemographic and clinical properties. *Journal of Nervous and Mental Disorder, 199*, 454-458.

Epstein, S. (1973). The self-concept revisited: Or a theory of a theory. *American Psychologist, 28*, 404–416.

Epstein, S. (1985). The implications of cognitive-experiential self theory for research in social psychology and personality. *Journal for the Theory of Social Behavior, 15*, 283–310.

Epstein, S. (1990). Cognitive-experiential self-theory. In L. Pervin (Ed.), *Handbook of personality: Theory and research* (pp. 165–192). New York: Guilford Press.

Epstein, S. (1994). Integration of the cognitive and the psychodynamic unconscious. *American Psychologist, 49*, 709–724.

Farrar, A. M., Pereira, M., Velasco, F., Hockemeyer, J., Müller, C. E., & Salamone, J. D. (2007). Adenosine A_{2A} receptor antagonism reverses the effects of dopamine receptor antagonism on instrumental output and effort-related choice in the rat: Implications for studies of psychomotor slowing. *Psychopharmacology, 191*, 579–586.

Finn, P. R., Young, S. N., Pihl, R. O., & Ervin, F. R. (1998). The effects of acute plasma tryptophan manipulation on hostile mood: The influence of trait hostility. *Aggresssive Behavior, 24,* 173–185.

Fowles, D. C. (1980). The three arousal model: Implications of Gray's two-factor learning theory for heart rate, electrodermal activity, and psychopathy. *Psychophysiology, 17*, 87–104.

Fowles, D. C. (1987). Application of a behavioral theory of motivation to the concepts of anxiety and impulsivity. *Journal of Research in Personality, 21*, 417–435.

Fowles, D. C. (1993). Biological variables in psychopathology: A psychobiological perspective. In P. B. Sutker & H. E. Adams (Eds.), *Comprehensive handbook of psychopathology* (2nd ed., pp. 57–82). New York: Plenum Press.

Freud, S. (1962). *The ego and the id* (J. Strachey, Trans.). New York: Norton.

Frijda, N. H. (1986). *The emotions*. Cambridge, UK: Cambridge University Press.

George, D. T., Umhau, J. C., Phillips, M. J., Emmela, D., Ragan, P. W., Shoaf, S. E., et al. (2001). Serotonin, testosterone, and alcohol in the etiology of domestic violence. *Psychiatry Research, 104*, 27–37.

Gray, J. A. (1972). The psychophysiological basis of introversion-extraversion: A modification of Eysenck's theory. In V. D. Nebylitsyn and J. A. Gray (Eds.), *The biological bases of individual behavior* (pp. 182–205). New York: Academic Press.

Gray, J. A. (1982). *The neuropsychology of anxiety: An enquiry into the functions of the septo-hippocampal system.* Oxford, UK: Oxford University Press.

Gray, J. A. (1994a). Personality dimensions and emotion systems. In P. Ekman & R. J. Davidson (Eds.), *The nature of emotion: Fundamental questions* (pp. 329–331). New York: Oxford University Press.

Gray, J. A. (1994b). Three fundamental emotion systems. In P. Ekman & R. J. Davidson (Eds.), *The nature of emotion: Fundamental questions* (pp. 243–247). New York: Oxford University Press.

Gray, J. A., & McNaughton, N. (2000). *The neuropsychology of anxiety: An enquiry into the functions of the septo-hippocampal system* (2nd ed.). Oxford, UK: Oxford University Press.

Greenberg, B. D., Li, Q., Lucas, F. R., Hu, S., Sirota, L. A., Benjamin, J., et al. (2000). Association between the serotonin transporter promoter polymorphism and personality traits in a primarily female population sample. *American Journal of Medical Genetics (Neuropsychiatric Genetics), 96*, 202–216.

Hampson, S. E., Andrews, J. A., Barckley, M., Lichtenstein, E., & Lee, M. E. (2000). Conscientiousness, perceived risk, and risk-reduction behaviors: A preliminary study. *Health Psychology, 19*, 496–500.

Hampson, S. E., Severson, H. H., Burns, W. J., Slovic, P., & Fisher, K. J. (2001). Risk perception, personality factors and alcohol use among adolescents. *Personality and Individual Differences, 30*, 167–181.

Hansen, E. B., & Breivik, G. (2001). Sensation seeking as a predictor of positive and negative risk behaviour among adolescents. *Personality and Individual Differences, 30*, 627–640.

Harmon-Jones, E., & Allen, J. J. B. (1997). Behavioral activation sensitivity and resting frontal EEG asymmetry: Covariation of putative indicators related to risk for mood disorders. *Journal of Abnormal Psychology, 106*, 159–163.

Harvey, A., Watkins, E., Mansell, W., & Shafran, R. (2004). *Cognitive behavioural processes across psychological disorders: A transdiagnostic approach to research and treatment.* Oxford, UK: Oxford University Press.

Henna, E., Hatch, J. P., Nicoletti, M., Swann, A. C., Zunta-Soares, G., & Soares, J. C. (2013). Is impulsivity a common trait in bipolar and unipolar disorders? *Bipolar Disorders, 15*, 223–227.

Henriques, J. B., & Davidson, R. J. (1990). Regional brain electrical asymmetries discriminate between previously depressed and healthy control subjects. *Journal of Abnormal Psychology, 99*, 22–31.

Henriques, J. B., & Davidson, R. J. (1991). Left frontal hypoactivation in depression. *Journal of Abnormal Psychology, 100*, 535–545.

Henriques, J. B., & Davidson, R. J. (2000). Decreased responsiveness to reward in depression. *Cognition and Emotion, 14*, 711–724.

Henriques, J. B., Glowacki, J. M., & Davidson, R. J. (1994). Reward fails to alter response bias in depression. *Journal of Abnormal Psychology, 103*, 460–466.

Hofmann, W., Friese, M., & Strack, F. (2009) Impulse and self-control from a dual-systems perspective. *Perspectives on Psychological Science, 4*, 162–176.

Hogan, J., & Holland, B. (2003). Using theory to evaluate personality and job performance relations: A socioanalytic perspective. *Journal of Applied Psychology, 88*, 100–112.

Johnson, S. L., Carver, C. S., & Joormann, J. (2013). Impulsive responses to emotion as a transdiagnostic vulnerability to internalizing and externalizing symptoms. *Journal of Affective Disorders, 150*, 872–878.

Johnson, S. L., Carver, C. S., Mulé, S., & Joormann, J. (2013). Impulsivity and risk for mania: Toward greater specificity. *Psychology and Psychotherapy: Theory, Research, and Practice, 86*, 401–412.

Johnson-Laird, P. N., Mancini, F., & Gangemi, A. (2006). A hyper-emotion theory of psychological illnesses. *Psychological Review, 113*, 822–841.

Kahneman, D. (2011). *Thinking, fast and slow*. New York: Farrar, Straus & Giroux.

Kasch, K. L., Rottenberg, J., Arnow, B. A., & Gotlib, I. H. (2002). Behavioral activation and inhibition systems and the severity and course of depression. *Journal of Abnormal Psychology, 111*, 589–597.

Kelly, E. L., & Conley, J. J. (1987). Personality and compatibility: A prospective analysis of marital stability and marital satisfaction. *Journal of Personality and Social Psychology, 52*, 27–40.

Kendler, K. S., M. C. Neale, Kessler, R. C., Heath, A. C., & Eaves, L. J. (1993). A longitudinal twin study of personality and major depression in women. *Archives of General Psychiatry 50,* 853–862.

Kochanska, G., & Knaack, A. (2003). Effortful control as a personality characteristic of young children: Antecedents, correlates, and consequences. *Journal of Personality, 71*, 1087–1112.

Lang, P. J. (1995). The emotion probe: Studies of motivation and attention. *American Psychologist, 50*, 372–385.

Lesch, K-P., Bengel, D., Heils, A., Sabol, S. Z., Greenberg, B. D., Petri, S., et al. (1996). Association of anxiety-related traits with a polymorphism in the serotonin transporter gene regulatory region. *Science, 274*, 1527–1531.

Lynam, D. R. (1996). Early identification of chronic offenders: Who is the fledgling psychopath? *Psychological Bulletin, 120*, 209–234.

MacDonald, K. B. (2008). Effortful control, explicit processing, and the regulation of human evolved dispositions. *Psychological Review, 115*, 1012–1031.

Manuck, S. B., Flory, J. D., Muldoon, M. F., & Ferrell, R. E. (2003). A neurobiology of intertemporal choice. In G. Loewenstein, D. Read, & R. F. Baumeister (Eds.), *Time and decision: Economic and psychological perspectives on intertemporal choice* (pp. 139–172). New York: Russell Sage Foundation.

Manuck, S. B., Kaplan, J. R., & Lotrich, F. E. (2006). Brain serotonin and aggressive disposition in humans and nonhuman primates. In R. J. Nelson (Ed.) *Biology of aggression* (pp. 65–102). New York: Oxford University Press.

Marcovitch, S., & Zelazo, P. D. (2009). A hierarchical competing systems model of the emergence and early development of executive function. *Developmental Science, 12*, 1–25.

McFarland, B. R., Shankman, S. A., Tenke, C. E., Bruder, G. E., & Klein, D. N. (2006). Behavioral activation system deficits predict the six-month course of depression. *Journal of Affective Disorders, 91*, 229–234.

McNaughton, N., & Gray, J. A. (2000). Anxiolytic action on the behavioral inhibition system implies multiple types of arousal contribute to anxiety. *Journal of Affective Disorders, 61*, 161–176.

Metcalfe, J., & Mischel, W. (1999). A hot/cool-system analysis of delay of gratification: Dynamics of willpower. *Psychological Review, 106*, 3–19.

Mischel, W. (1974). Processes in delay of gratification. In L. Berkowitz (Ed.), *Advances in experimental social psychology* (Vol. 7, pp. 249–292). New York: Academic Press.

Murray, K. T., & Kochanska, G. (2002). Effortful control: Factor structure and relation to externalizing and internalizing behaviors. *Journal of Abnormal Child Psychology, 30*, 503–514.

Netter, P., Hennig, J., & Rohrmann, S. (1999). Psychobiological differences between the aggression and psychoticism dimension. *Pharmacopsychiatry, 32*, 5–12.

Neumeister, A., Hu, X., Luckenbaugh, D. A., Schwarz, M., Nugent, A. C., Bonne, O., et al. (2006). Differential effects of 5-HTTLPR genotypes on the behavioral and neural responses to tryptophan depletion in patients with major depression and controls. *Archives of General Psychiatry, 63*, 978–986.

Nigg, J. T. (2000). On inhibition/disinhibition in developmental pychopathology: Views from cognitive and personality psychology as a working inhibition taxonomy. *Psychological Bulletin, 126*, 220–246.

Nigg, J. T. (2001). Is ADHD a disinhibitory disorder? *Psychological Bulletin, 127*, 571–598.

Nigg, J. T. (2003). Response inhibition and disruptive behaviors: Toward a multiprocess conception of etiological heterogeneity for ADHD combined type and conduct disorder early-onset type. *Annals of the New York Academy of Sciences, 1008,* 170–182.

Nigg, J. T. (2006). Temperament and developmental psychopathology. *Journal of Child Psychology and Psychiatry, 47,* 395–422.

Park, S. B., Coull, J. T., McShane, R. H., Young, A. H., Sahakian, B. J., Robbins, T. W., et al. (1994). Tryptophan depletion in normal volunteers produces selective impairments in learning and memory. *Neuropharmacology, 33,* 575–588.

Peluso, M. A. M., Hatch, J. P., Glahn, D. C., Monkul, E. S., Sanches, M., Najt, P., et al. (2007). Trait impulsivity in patients with mood disorders. *Journal of Affective Disorders, 100,* 227–231.

Pinto-Meza, A., Caseras, X., Soler, J., Puigdemont, D., Perez, V., & Torrubia, R. (2006). Behavioural inhibition and behavioural activation systems in current and recovered major depression participants. *Personality and Individual Differences, 40*, 215–226.

Richell, R. A., Deakin, J. F. W., & Anderson, I. M. (2005). Effect of acute tryptophan depletion on the response to controllable and uncontrollable noise stress. *Biological Psychiatry, 57*, 295–300.

Risch, N., Herrell, R., Lehner, T., Liang, K.-Y., Eaves, L., Hoh, J., et al. (2009) Interaction between the serotonin transporter gene (5-HTTLPR), stressful life events, and risk of depression: A meta-analysis. *Journal of the American Medical Association, 301,* 2462–2471.

Rogers, R. D., Tunbridge, E. M., Bhagwagar, Z., Drevets, W. C., Sahakian, B. J., & Carter, C. S. (2003). Tryptophan depletion alters the decision-making of healthy volunteers through altered processing of reward cues. *Neuropsychopharmacology, 28,* 153–162.

Rothbart, M. K., Ahadi, S. A., & Evans, D. E. (2000). Temperament and personality: Origins and outcomes. *Journal of Personality and Social Psychology, 78*, 122–135.

Rothbart, M. K., Ahadi, S. A., Hershey, K., & Fisher, P. (2001). Investigations of temperament at three to seven years: The Children's Behavior Questionnaire. *Child Development, 72*, 1394–1408.

Rothbart, M. K., & Bates, J. E. (1998). Temperament. In W. Damon (Series Ed.) and N. Eisenberg (Vol. Ed.), *Handbook of child psychology: Vol 3. Social, emotional, and personality development* (5th ed., pp. 105–176). New York: Wiley.

Rothbart, M. K., Ellis, L. K., Rueda M. R., & Posner, M. I. (2003). Developing mechanisms of temperamental effortful control. *Journal of Personality, 71*, 1113–1143.

Rothbart, M. K., & Posner, M. (1985). Temperament and the development of self-regulation. In L. C. Hartlage & C. F. Telzrow (Eds.), *The neuropsychology of individual differences: A developmental perspective* (pp. 93–123). New York: Plenum Press.

Rudman, L. A., Phelan, J. E., & Heppen, J. B. (2007). Developmental sources of implicit attitudes. *Personality and Social Psychology Bulletin, 33*, 1700–1713.

Salamone, J. D., Correa, M., Farrar, A., & Mingote, S. M. (2007). Effort-related functions of nucleus accumbens dopamine and associated forebrain circuits. *Psychopharmacology, 191*, 461–482.

Salamone, J. D., Correa, M., Mingote, S. M., & Weber, S. M. (2005). Beyond the reward hypothesis: Alternative functions of nucleus accumbens dopamine. *Current Opinion in Pharmacology, 5*, 34–41.

Salamone, J. D., Correa, M., Mingote, S. M., Weber, S. M., & Farrar, A. M. (2006). Nucleus accumbens dopamine and the forebrain circuitry involved in behavioral activation and effort-related decision making: Implications for understanding anergia and psychomotor slowing in depression. *Current Psychiatry Reviews, 2*, 267–280.

Skinner, T. C., Hampson, S. E., & Fife-Schaw, C. (2002). Personality, personal model beliefs, and self-care in adolescents and young adults with Type 1 diabetes. *Health Psychology, 21*, 61–70.

Smith, G. T., Guller, L., & Zapolski, T. C. B. (2013). A comparison of two models of urgency: Urgency predicts both rash action and depression in youth. *Clinical Psychological Science, 1*, 266–275.

Sobin, C., & Sackeim, H. A. (1997). Psychomotor symptoms of depression. *American Journal of Psychiatry, 154*, 4–17.

Solanto, M. V., Abikoff, H., Sonuga-Barke, E., Schachar, R., Logan, G., D., Wigal, T., et al. (2001). The ecological validity of delay aversion and response inhibition as measures of impulsivity in AD/HD: A supplement to the NIMH multimodal treatment study of AD/HD. *Journal of Abnormal Child Psychology, 29*, 215–228.

Soubrié, P. (1986). Reconciling the role of central serotonin neurons in human and animal behavior. *Behavioral and Brain Sciences, 9*, 319–364.

Spoont, M. R. (1992). Modulatory role of serotonin in neural information processing: Implications for human psychopathology. *Psychological Bulletin, 112*, 330–350.

Stanford, M. S., & Barratt, E. S. (1992). Impulsivity and the multi-impulsive personality disorder. *Personality and Individual Differences, 13*, 831–834.

Strack, F., & Deutsch, R. (2004). Reflective and impulsive determinants of social behavior. *Personality and Social Psychology Review, 8*, 220–247.

Sutton, S. K., & Davidson, R. J. (1997). Prefrontal brain asymmetry: A biological substrate of the behavioral approach and inhibition systems. *Psychological Science, 8*, 204–210.

Tellegen, A. (1985). Structure of mood and personality and their relevance to assessing anxiety, with an emphasis on self-report. In A. H. Tuma & J. D. Maser (Eds.), *Anxiety and the anxiety disorders* (pp. 681–706). Hillsdale, NJ: Erlbaum.

Uher, R., & McGuffin, P. (2008). The moderation by the serotonin transporter gene of environmental adversity in the aetiology of mental illness: Review and methodological analysis. *Molecular Psychiatry, 13*, 131–146.

Uher, R., & McGuffin, P. (2010). The moderation by the serotonin transporter gene of environmental adversity in the aetiology of depression: 2009 update. *Molecular Psychiatry, 15*, 18–22.

Vohs, K. D., & Baumeister, R. F. (Eds.). (2011). *Handbook of self-regulation: Research, theory, and applications* (2nd ed.). New York: Guilford Press.

White, J. L., Moffitt, T. E., Caspi, A., Bartusch, D. J., Needles, D. J., & Stouthamer-Loeber, M. (1994). Measuring impulsivity and examining its relationship to delinquency. *Journal of Abnormal Psychology, 103*, 192–205.

Whiteside, S. P., & Lynam, D. R. (2001). The Five Factor Model and impulsivity: Using a structural model of personality to understand impulsivity. *Personality and Individual Differences*, *30*, 669–689.

Whiteside, S. P., & Lynam, D. R. (2003). Understanding the role of impulsivity and externalizing psychopathology in alcohol abuse: Application of the UPPS impulsive behavior scale. *Experimental and Clinical Psychopharmacology, 11*, 210–217.

Zapolski, T. C. B., Cyders, M. A., & Smith, G. T. (2009). Positive urgency predicts illegal drug use and risky sexual behavior. *Psychology of Addictive Behaviors, 23*, 348–354.

Zelenski, J. M., & Larsen, R. J. (1999). Susceptibility to affect: A comparison of three personality taxonomies. *Journal of Personality, 67*, 761–791.

Zuckerman, M. (2005). *Psychobiology of personality* (2nd ed.). New York: Cambridge University Press.

Name Index

A

B

C

D

E

U

V

W

Y

Z

Subject Index

A

B

F

G

H

I

L

M